Educator's LIFETIME ENCYCLOPEDIA *of Letters*

P. SUSAN MAMCHAK ◆ STEVEN R. MAMCHAK

**THE CENTER FOR APPLIED
RESEARCH IN EDUCATION**
West Nyack, New York 10994

Library of Congress Cataloging-in-Publication Data

Mamchak, P. Susan, 1944–
    Educator's lifetime encyclopedia of letters / P. Susan Mamchak and
Steven R. Mamchak.
      p. cm.
      ISBN 0–13–795436–0
      1. Schools—Records and correspondence. 2. Teachers—Handbooks,
manulas, etc. I. Mamchak, Steven R. II. Title.
    LB2845.7.M33   1998
    651.7′52′024372—dc21   98–9492
                                                       CIP

© 1998 *by* Parker Publishing Company

Acquisitions Editor: *Susan Kolwicz*
Production Editor: *Mariann Hutlak*
Interior Design/Formatting: *Dee Coroneos*

Printed in the United States of America

10 9 8 7 6 5 4 3 2

ISBN 0-13-795436-0

ATTENTION: CORPORATIONS AND SCHOOLS

Parker Publishing Company books are available at quantity discounts with bulk purchase for educational, business, or sales promotional use. For information, please write to: Prentice Hall Career & Personal Development Special Sales, 240 Frisch Court, Paramus, NJ 07652. Please supply: title of book, ISBN, quantity, how the book will be used, date needed.

PARKER PUBLISHING COMPANY
West Nyack, NY 10994

On the World Wide Web at http://www.phdirect.com

PRENTICE-HALL INTERNATIONAL (UK) LIMITED, *LONDON*
PRENTICE-HALL OF AUSTRALIA PTY. LIMITED, *SYDNEY*
PRENTICE-HALL CANADA INC., *TORONTO*
PRENTICE-HALL HISPANOAMERICANA, S.A., *MEXICO*
PRENTICE-HALL OF INDIA PRIVATE LIMITED, *NEW DELHI*
PRENTICE-HALL OF JAPAN, INC., *TOKYO*
PEARSON EDUCATION ASIA PTE. LTD., *SINGAPORE*
EDITORA PRENTICE-HALL DO BRASIL, LTDA., *RIO DE JANEIRO*

ACKNOWLEDGMENT

We gratefully acknowledge the contributions of those dedicated educators throughout the years who have written and crafted and revised and agonized over just the right word to get the idea across. The battle of effective communication was fought and won in your hands, and we are in your debt.

ABOUT THE AUTHORS

P. SUSAN MAMCHAK has held a variety of positions in public education, from classroom teacher to school disciplinarian. She is in demand as a lecturer, and conducts classes in teacher and parent effectiveness.

STEVEN R. MAMCHAK is a veteran of thirty-five years in the public schools. Recipient of a Governor's Award for Excellence in Education, he lectures extensively and conducts workshops for educators on all levels.

THE MAMCHAKS are a husband-and-wife team who have written over twenty books on various aspects of education, always stressing the need for proper communication as a basis for understanding. Together, they are a vital part of today's educational scene.

ABOUT THIS RESOURCE

As educators, we spend a great deal of our time on paper work. In itself, that is neither good nor bad, but it is a fact of academic life that every educator, from teacher's aide to superintendent of schools, knows only too well. Many educators speak about a "paper enemy"—that load of paper work which, if we do not find a way of conquering it, will most certainly end up mastering us.

Much of this paper work is mundane and pedestrian in nature. An inventory, or a schedule, or a list of assignments, or an attendance form may be annoying and time consuming, but it hardly poses an incredible challenge to our creative potential. Such things take time, but not a great deal of emotional or intellectual energy.

On the other hand, there are letters and other writing chores that do tax our abilities and eat up our time in the most trying of ways. These are the letters required for situations that do not fall into neat and comfortable compartments, but demand the greatest deliberation, the most diplomatic phrasing, and the choicest words. These are the letters that leave us staring at the paper, unsure even of how to begin

If we truly need examples of these writing chores, it is relatively easy to find them, for they are part and parcel of every educator's day. A student asks you to write a recommendation for a private secondary school or a college, and you have serious reservations about that student's ability. A student in your school develops a serious illness; a colleague is diagnosed with a terminal disease; a student's parent dies. You must write a note to alert parents to a student's behavior before it turns into a problem; you must inform a parent that a child's serious behavioral outburst is the last such incident the school will tolerate. A community protest group vehemently challenges a course you teach or a class in your school, and your response is expected. That scathing editorial in the local newspaper demands an answer. That order for which you waited for six months finally arrived, and it's missing the most essential elements. In short, there are enough difficult situations that require written response to keep us hard at work writing diligently for a significant part of each school day, and they present a significant problem to the busy, actively engaged, front-line educator. That problem is *time,* and it applies to everyone.

Every moment spent in planning, writing, editing, and revising these difficult school letters is a moment *not* spent in planning, researching, teaching, administrating, and being the educational leader that you, your school, and your community expect you to be.

While the existence of a problem does not automatically assure a solution, in this case, a solution is within the reach of every educator. *Educator's Lifetime Encyclopedia of Letters* is the answer that will allow you to dynamically and efficiently handle every school letter-writing task with sensitivity and dispatch, while freeing your time for those activities so essential to the outstanding professional educator.

Each and every letter, report, commentary, and article in this book has been crafted, shaped, and reshaped to handle the widest variety of school letters and personalize them to your particular needs.

In Section One, "Writing Effective Recommendations," you can find positive recommendations for a variety of occasions, as well as those that express professional reservation. With the strong and dynamic letters in Section Two, "Letters That Deal With Illness and Death," you'll learn how to handle those touchy and touching letters of sympathy and condolence. Look into Section Three, "Letters That Effectively Deal With Student Behavior," and you'll find the perfect correspondence to handle everything from a minor classroom infraction to the gravest of suspendable offenses. You may write that evaluation on all levels, from a student to a curriculum, with the models in Section Four. Section Five, "Writing for the Community," deals with everything from answering the claims of a community protest group to a directive opposing proposed community legislation. Section Six enables you to handle those devastating letters of complaint written to you, as well as those you may have to write yourself. In Section Seven, "A Guide to Letters Dealing With the Media," you will find everything from ground rules for dealing with the media in your school to a powerful response to a negative newspaper editorial. Section Eight contains a treasury of letters that apply to your job, as well as to the jobs of others. You'll be able to write some outstanding letters of thanks and appreciation with the letters you'll find waiting for you in Section Nine, while Section Ten offers some "unusual" letters to handle those "special" situations. Whatever your need may be, you'll find it addressed in the pages of this book.

The uses of *Educator's Lifetime Encyclopedia of Letters* are limited only by your needs, because these letters stand ready to serve you. Use them to find the *exact* words to match the *exact* feelings in the *exact* situation you wish to address. Use them as they are or, with the change of a word or phrase, you can handle those often difficult and troublesome situations by writing the letters and reports, notes and recommendations, evaluations and commentaries you require *without* spending hours of your valuable time searching for just the right words. The hard work has been done for you, and the letters in this book are here to meet your needs.

Educator's Lifetime Encyclopedia of Letters is a book you will want to keep readily available. You'll want it on your personal bookshelf—or among those books you keep on your desk. You'll want it within reach to efficiently and effectively help you handle those letter-writing situations that occur almost daily for the involved professional educator. You'll want it to save you valuable time, and to free you to be the dynamic and involved educator you want to be.

It is inevitable that a variety of situations—from the mundane to the extraordinary—will occur in our professional careers. Education, however, has always been a cooperative endeavor, and with the use of the models and sample letters in *Educator's Lifetime Encyclopedia of Letters*, there is not a single writing task that cannot be handled to the ultimate advantage of all involved—including yourself.

Those to whom you write will appreciate the thoughtful letters they receive, and you will appreciate having more time to be the educator you want to be.

P. Susan Mamchak
Steven R. Mamchak

CONTENTS

Section
One

WRITING EFFECTIVE RECOMMENDATIONS

Section
Two

LETTERS THAT DEAL WITH ILLNESS AND DEATH

Section
Three

LETTERS THAT EFFECTIVELY DEAL WITH STUDENT BEHAVIOR

Section
Four

COMPLETE GUIDE TO WRITING MEANINGFUL EVALUATIONS

Section
Five

WRITING FOR THE COMMUNITY

Section
Six

EFFICIENTLY HANDLING LETTERS OF COMPLAINT

Section Seven

A GUIDE TO LETTERS DEALING WITH THE MEDIA

Section
Eight

LETTERS THAT RELATE TO YOUR JOB

Section
Nine

WRITING EFFECTIVE LETTERS OF THANKS AND APPRECIATION

MODEL LETTERS OF APPRECIATION AND THANKS **187**

Section
Ten

WRITING SPECIAL LETTERS FOR EVERYDAY EVENTS

WRITING EFFECTIVE
RECOMMENDATIONS

*W*e know of very few educators, be they teachers or administrators, who have not been asked, at one time or another, to write a recommendation for a student. That recommendation may range from a simple letter, couched in general terms, all the way to a printed form to be completed by the educator and mailed to the institution in question, along with a very formal letter detailing the strengths and needs for improvement of the applicant. If you teach or are in education for any length of time, such a task will eventually fall to you.

The student in question obviously wants to be accepted in a new school, get that job, or become a part of that program. Your recommendation may well be at least one deciding factor in that process. Therein lies a very big problem. There are students whom we would gladly see in any school, on any job, in any program, because we know that they would give their all in any situation—she was the best student you ever had; he was an absolute model of positive cooperation. Not all our students, unfortunately, fit those standards. There are those students whose character is in question, whose academic standing is shaky at best, who have refused to engage in their own education. Any recommendation in these cases must be qualified. Above all, as educators, we must be honest.

The materials in this section represent recommendations and references that you are most likely to encounter as an educator. They represent both the positive, or unqualified, recommendation and the negative, or so-called recommendation with qualifications, for each area. There are even examples of letters for such unhappy times when you feel you must *not* recommend a student's acceptance, or must recommend against it.

EXAMINING THE STRUCTURE OF THE WRITTEN RECOMMENDATION

Before we get to actual examples of recommendations and references, let's talk for a moment about form. A recommendation, whatever it may be for, should be considered a formal document. As such, it should be presented by you in the best possible form. This is not something one jots on a sheet of loose-leaf paper, shoves in an envelope, and tosses in the mail. A student's future may be hanging on what you write, and your physical presentation of that written recommendation plays a strong part in the impression it will make upon its reader. Your recommendation should be error free, with all such facts as names, dates, and grades checked and double-checked, as well as grammar and spelling. It should be typed or printed (as with a word processor) on good stationery. It is preferable that the stationery have a printed letterhead, which may be your personal letterhead or that of the school or institution in which you serve. The envelope should be business size and carry a return address, either typed or printed. In short, the document will reflect you and your standing as an educator and should, therefore, project a sense of professionalism.

The basic internal structure of your recommendation should follow a pattern. The one we use is this:

1. Identify the student you are about to recommend.
2. Identify yourself and your qualifications for writing this.
3. State your recommendation (qualified or unqualified).
4. Leave yourself open to personal contact if necessary.

In the letters that follow, you will see this pattern repeating itself often.

Let's take a look at various examples of letters of recommendation, both positive and negative, that may just serve your purposes in a variety of situations regarding recommendations in which you find your letter-writing skills required.

MODEL RECOMMENDATIONS AND REFERENCES

1. Positive Recommendation to a Private School, I

Often, you will receive a request for a recommendation to a private school, academy, or boarding school. Frequently, the private school will send you a list of its criteria. Let us assume that this is such a case and that this is a best-of-all-possible-worlds scenario, in which you can give an unqualified recommendation.

Dear Dr. Coroneos,

It gives me great pleasure to write to you concerning Elizabeth Chang, a student who is seeking admittance to your school. As a teacher at the school Elizabeth is currently attending, I have known her for the past two years, and this year, I am happy to have her as a student in my language arts class. That course is part of our school's Gifted and Talented curriculum, and I have had several months in which to observe her academically as well as in the social interaction of the classroom.

With that understanding and knowledge, I am very happy to recommend Elizabeth Chang to you without hesitation and certainly without qualification. Indeed, in the twenty-seven years that I have been in education, rarely have I been privileged to teach a student of such academic ability, social awareness, and positive personality. Whether working out a complex problem in the classroom or serving on our school's student council or helping to organize a student activity, Elizabeth has the acceptance of her peers, the approval of her mentors, and the respect of all those who know her, including her teachers.

With your formal letter requesting this recommendation, you were kind enough to send the criteria for admittance to your institution. In that literature, you stress the term "Academics and Character" as going "hand in hand" to produce a student who will be prepared and eager for the challenges of higher education. Toward that laudable goal, you speak of such admirable traits as dedication, honesty, respect, responsibility, self-worth, integrity, and the like, along with a strong academic proficiency and an "unbridled desire to learn."

I respectfully suggest that those traits of character and academic accomplishment describe Elizabeth Chang. I recommend her for admittance to Hillcrest Academy without qualification and with only one regret—that she shall no longer be the active, vibrant, and challenging part of my class that I have looked forward to daily over the months she has been a part of my class.

Certainly, if I may be of any further service in this matter, I shall be most happy to assist in any way I can. Please feel free to contact me as the matter may warrant, and I hope that I have been able to bring this very special student to your attention.

She would be an asset to any school, and I know that she would shine brightly at Hillcrest Academy.

Yours sincerely,

NOTE: Observe how the very words of the school's criteria are used as a guideline to the recommendation itself, and also note how the basic internal structure outlined previously was used to advantage here.

This was a recommendation for a truly superior student. Not all the students you may wish to recommend are that outstanding, as we shall see in the next letter.

2. Positive Recommendation to a Private School, II

The previous recommendation was for a very special student. Many times, however, we are asked for recommendations for students who do not fall into that "superior student" category, but who are good and solid, nonetheless. They are not A+ students, but, to put it plainly, they are "good kids." Here is a recommendation for just such an individual.

Dear Admissions Officer:

I would like to bring to your attention a young man named Raymond Santiago, who has applied for admission to Lincoln Prep School in the fall of this year.

Currently, I have Raymond ("Ray," as he is commonly known) in my science class. I have therefore had almost nine months to get to know him both as a student and as an individual. I have come to know and like him, and it gives me pleasure to recommend him to you for admittance to Lincoln Prep.

Ray's academic record is a solid one. He has managed to receive solid *B*'s and *B*+'s in my subject, and he has always been on time with projects, reports, homework, and other academic necessities. Those times when he was absent due to illness, he always made an attempt to make up the work he had missed. I have found him quite adequate academically, and would classify him as a good student.

On a personal level, I know Ray to be a happy young man who smiles frequently and is always ready to "lend a hand." His brightness and cheeriness are infectious, and he truly does lighten my day. I have seen him perform countless acts of kindness for others—both his peers and the adults around the school. In my own mind, I think of him as a goodhearted child—one whom you cannot help but like.

You may reach me at the school at any time, if you feel that I may be of any further service to you. Please contact me if you feel that I may help you or Ray. It is a pleasure to help forward the growth and development of such a fine young man, and I stand ready to help.

I believe that Ray Santiago would make a fine school such as Lincoln Prep even better by his presence in it, and I recommend him for acceptance.

Very truly yours,

NOTE: Academically, you let the facts speak for themselves and concentrate on the lad's character, which is obviously his strong point. Here, you felt you could make an unqualified recommendation. There are times, such as with these next two letters, when you cannot—when your recommendation must be qualified.

3. Negative Recommendation to a Private School, I

In this and the next letter, you are going to recommend a student for a private school, but you are going to express your misgivings while doing so. In this first letter, your qualifications are on academic grounds. Notice how your misgivings are stated objectively, without the slightest bit of personal antagonism. Whatever your personal opinion may be, this is the better way to go. Let the facts speak for themselves; it will be better for you and for the student you are recommending.

Dear Mrs. Goodhand,

I write in regard to Carolyn Crosetti, a student in our school who has applied for admission to your institution at the start of the next semester.

As vice-principal of the school Carolyn currently attends, I have come to know her over the two years she has been in attendance. During that time, I have had an opportunity to get to know her on a personal basis as well as being able to review her academic record.

Personally, I find her a refreshingly vibrant young woman. I have never had to deal with her for disciplinary reasons over the time I have known her, and my personal association with her stems from Carolyn's involvement with the girls' soccer team, which I coach. In that activity, she is a definite asset, playing hard and making an individual contribution to the team as a very positive team player.

Academically, Carolyn maintains a cumulative C+ average for the current year. Records indicate that Carolyn and her parents have been into school for a number of conferences with individual and cluster teachers regarding her academic progress. A consensus seems to indicate that difficulty getting in homework and projects may contribute to the status of her grades. Her current teachers indicate that there has been some improvement in this matter, with occasional relapses. No teacher has indicated an attitude problem as a causative factor, and each teacher suggested that Carolyn has decided ability that needs challenging.

Your school, I believe, has a reputation for establishing just such a challenging learning environment. While it is understandable that no guarantees can be made, perhaps the environment that exists at Javonian Academy is just what Carolyn might need in order to pick up her academic standing. Your school may prove to be the right place for Carolyn to grow and prosper.

If I may be of any further service, or if you would like to discuss Carolyn's placement in greater detail, I am available at the school most days until 4:30 or 5:00 P.M., and I would be most happy to hear from you.

Sincerely,

NOTE: The negative of an average to low average academic record was presented here in a matter-of-fact manner, as was the concern about homework. Did you notice that no comment was made about them? Also notice that the writer's further comments were qualified but optimistic about Carolyn's academic growth. Such a letter would probably occasion a telephone call as suggested in the letter.

4. Negative Recommendation to a Private School, II

In this letter, let's deal with a student who is doing well academically but has some difficulties with peers and teachers in the realms of personality and behavior.

Dear Ms. Randowski,

Recently, I received a request from the parents of one of my students, Clemson Brown (known as "Clem"), for a recommendation for admittance to your institution, Santa Rosa Preparatory School, effective at the beginning of the next academic year.

I am the coach of our school's basketball team, and in that capacity, I have known him for two years. While I am not totally conversant with his academic record, I can tell you that the boys' records are reviewed every marking period, and any boy *not* carrying a *B* average in every academic subject is not allowed to continue on the team. I have never received an academic warning on Clem, nor have I ever had his name brought up by a teacher with a concern for his academic progress. I can only assume, therefore, that he is doing at least *B* work, if not better, and is in no academic difficulty at this time.

Behaviorally, I have observed Clem as part of our team for the two years he has been on it. I find him to be an aggressive player, to say the least. There have been three complaints from opposing coaches about unnecessary roughness on his part, and our team has suffered at least five field penalties over the past two years for that infraction due to actions on Clem's part. I have spoken to him on several occasions concerning this, and his reply has always been that when he is on the field, he "loses track" of himself because he is so absorbed in the game and doesn't realize what he is doing. Further, some of his fellow players have expressed concern that he is not a "team player," causing them to lose certain plays when he was not in his assigned position. I had spoken with him previously on this very subject when I personally observed that behavior.

On the other hand, he is the epitome of loyalty to the team, practices assiduously, and gives his all each and every time. I have also found him to be more than willing to help other players develop their skills.

Please call or write me at the school if I may be of any further service to you. I will gladly discuss Clem further if you deem that necessary. I am certain that Clem would benefit from a place like Santa Rosa Prep, and hope that Santa Rosa can benefit from Clem's skills.

Yours truly,

NOTE: This recommendation is qualified while still never interpreting the facts of the student's questionable behavior. The facts are stated and the way left open for further elucidation if the admitting officer so desires.

5. Positive Recommendation to a College or University, I

For the first recommendation to a public college or university, let's deal with the student who has truly impressed you—the one you wish to recommend without qualification.

Dear Dean Shannon,

I am overjoyed to receive your request for a recommendation for one of my students, Larry Po, who has applied for admission to _____ University. Larry is a student who has proven his abilities and worthiness time and again, to the point where it is not only a pleasure for me to recommend him for acceptance at your university but an honor to do so.

Time and again, Larry has shown his potential, his ability, his character, and his leadership abilities not only in my classroom but throughout our school itself, working in highly positive ways to better his school and help his classmates stretch their capabilities to the furthest.

Indeed, the only fault one can find in Larry is his unbounded enthusiasm, which is always at the fore and often keeps him running to the exclusion of anything like "free time." Well-placed suggestions by mentors and teachers, however, quickly channel that energy into positive avenues which benefit everyone, including Larry himself.

Over the years, I have met few students whom I would recommend without reservation. Larry Po is one of them, and I recommend him for admittance to your college wholeheartedly, and with complete confidence in his continued academic success.

Yours sincerely,

NOTE: This recommendation, obviously, is for a student about whom you can sincerely make the comments made herein. Not much is specifically detailed, but the letter glows with confidence in an outstanding student.

6. Positive Recommendation to a College or University, II

In the following recommendation, you go into a little more detail concerning the student.

Dear Dean Koslowski,

I received your letter requesting a recommendation for Maria Iscaldi, who is seeking admission to Harrison College in September of this year. Thank you for enclosing the "Character Criteria" list for Harrison as well; it was most informative.

I am happy to recommend Maria for matriculation at your college. She not only meets your high standards of character, but she is an outstanding student academically.

I have known Maria Iscaldi for the three years she has attended our high school. In that time, she has never been part of or experienced any behavioral difficulties in any classes or with any of the faculty and staff. Indeed, I may honestly say that she is highly regarded by the teachers, liked and appreciated by the staff of our school, and respected by her classmates. Her tenure as student council president in both her junior and senior years attests to that.

Academically, she has maintained a 3.8 average throughout her stay at our school. Certainly, that speaks to her mental acuity and overall academic talent. Although it is not yet general knowledge, she will most likely be the recipient of an award at graduation reserved for the highest academic achievement in her class.

Therefore, her academic abilities linked to her strength of character and genuine desire for learning allow me to recommend her to your attention in the most positive manner. She will most certainly be an asset to Harrison College, as she has been to our high school.

Yours sincerely,

NOTE: While there is considerable detailing in this recommendation, there is no need to include lists of grades, since the student will undoubtedly already have supplied a transcript to the college.

7. Negative Recommendation to a College or University, I

Now, let's look at a recommendation that is less positive and certainly less passionate. In this first negative recommendation, let's assume that you have only a few reservations—not enough not to recommend, but concerns you feel should be known by the institution.

Dear Dean Washington,

Thank you for your recent letter requesting a recommendation for Jason Bandersen, who has applied for admission to your college.

Academically, Jason is more than adequate to the task. I had Jason as a student in three classes over his high school stay, and my records confirm that he maintained a *B+* average in all of them. I found his mind sharp, his thought processes clear and logical, and his ability to grasp abstract concepts quite highly developed. No one can challenge his ability to learn and to apply that new knowledge to learn even more.

I would, however, be less than honest with myself and your fine institution if I did not mention a minor reservation I have concerning Jason. In all three of my classes that he attended, I noticed a marked tendency toward procrastination. Often, projects, papers, homework, and the like would be put off until the very last minute. Sometimes the projects were in on time, but often he was at my desk requesting an extension, promising to have the work in the next day or the next week. I would not have you think that this was an everyday occurrence, but it happened frequently enough that it concerned me and made me mention it here.

With that reservation, therefore, and the understanding that I most definitely feel that he would succeed in his college career, I can recommend Jason Bandersen to your attention.

Very truly yours,

NOTE: The reservation expressed here was mild, to say the least. It did not interfere with the recommendation to accept the student. However, what if your qualifications run a bit deeper?

8. Negative Recommendation to a College or University, II

In the following letter, the writer has reservations in both the academic and behavioral areas of the student under consideration. Here, the recommendation is one filled with concern.

Dear Dean Lee,

You have requested a recommendation for Brenda Kaufman, a student at our school who has sought admission to Merton University in the fall semester.

I am familiar with Brenda in two areas. She was in my classroom twice during her high school career, and I worked with her during a high school dramatic production in which I was the director and she an actress in the cast.

It concerns me deeply that I shall have to recommend Brenda with several reservations. In both classes of mine that she attended, she ended up with a *C+* average. While this is not a bad grade, it is far from indicative of what I felt she could have done. In my opinion, this was due to a lack of attention to what was happening in class—a general unconcern regarding homework or any nonclass work, often failing to hand it in or bringing it several days late, and, frequently, a lack of study for tests. This caused the grade which, had she applied herself, could easily have been a *B+* or an *A*.

During the process of the play production, I found her very often argumentative, both with myself and with other members of the cast. In one case, the enmity between her and another cast member grew so heated that I was forced to intervene for the good of the production. Three cast members saw me privately to request that I seriously speak to Brenda concerning the needed spirit of teamwork that she did not or could not exhibit at that time.

Therefore, I offer a highly qualified recommendation. Perhaps with maturity and the academic atmosphere for which your institution is noted, Brenda may find a place that will channel her energies into more positive academic and social pursuits. Certainly, I have seen this happen, and I would not wish to deny Brenda Kaufman the opportunity to grow in these areas.

Cordially yours,

NOTE: A less than wholehearted recommendation, certainly, but one that expresses the legitimate concerns of the educator writing the letter. You recounted what happened and what you personally experienced. This is always the best course to take when writing something negative.

9. Negative Recommendation to a College or University, III

The two previous recommendations expressed concern but fell short of actually not recommending the student to the college. The following is the strongest negative recommendation, leaving no doubt that the writer cannot recommend the student.

Dear Dean Alvarez,

I am in receipt of your letter asking for a recommendation for Howard Radczyk. Howard is currently a student of mine, and, in various academic capacities, I have known him for the past three years—as long as he has been a student at our school. I regret to inform you that I cannot, in all conscience, recommend Howard Radczyk for matriculation at your college.

Stated briefly, Howard's academic work has left a great deal to be desired, as a glance at his transcript will confirm. He has passed these high school years on a series of *D*'s and *C*'s, with an occasional *F*. While he will graduate, he will do so on a minimal basis. Moreover, while he was my student, I observed that he was frequently unprepared, handed in assigned work on an erratic basis, often paid no attention in class, and either failed outright or barely passed tests and quizzes. When I attempted to speak to him about this, he seemed unconcerned. His academic work did not improve.

Behaviorally, I have dealt with a number of student fights in which Howard took part. I have supplied work for him on at least five occasions while he was a part of our in-school suspension program (the work was not completed). I also offered to help him make up work after his return from three out-of-school suspensions, but he refused to attend. In class, I frequently had to watch closely that he did not disrupt others with his behavior.

I am sincerely sorry that I cannot offer a more positive report. However, I believe you will understand why, under these conditions, I regretfully cannot recommend Howard Radczyk for admission to your college. If you should wish any further clarification or have any questions, please do not hesitate to contact me.

Very truly yours,

NOTE: This negative recommendation is written with regret rather than passion. What is reported is what was observed, and not a personal commentary on it. Moreover, you have left it open that you are willing to elaborate should there be a further need.

10. Positive Recommendation for an Award

Schools constantly give awards to students, as do community groups, newspapers, service organizations, and a host of other people. Frequently, these awards are based upon the recommendations of individuals like you. Let's assume that you have received a request for a recommendation for such an award. This time, you fully agree with the choice.

Dear Mr. Gregovna,

I was delighted to receive your letter and learn that Lionella Fisher is in contention for the prestigious Megner Fellowship Award for outstanding academic and social achievement during her years at our school. I am doubly delighted that you have asked me to comment on Lionella and present a recommendation for her.

Lionella was a student of mine and also served on the student council for her three years at our school. As advisor to that group, I also had the chance to get to know her on a less formal but more personal level. Both in the classroom and in the hallways, I found her to be a highly motivated, highly intelligent, academically sound, personable, and gregarious young person filled with the joy of life, always ready to help others, and always spreading a degree of happiness wherever she went. Teachers and students appreciated, respected, and cared deeply for her.

Knowing the standards your group has set for the Megner Fellowship Award, I take pleasure in assuring you that you could find few examples of the integrity, academic prowess, and social aplomb representative of that award as clearly demonstrated as they are in the person of Lionella Fisher, a fine young woman and an outstanding student.

It is with great happiness that I recommend her to your attention without qualification.

Sincerely,

NOTE: Here again, no specific accomplishments are detailed, but you can include those if you wish. Your personal testimony as to your feelings about this student is effective by itself.

11. Negative Recommendation for an Award

What happens if you become aware that someone is being considered for an award who, in your opinion, does not deserve it? The following letter addresses just such a situation.

Dear Mrs. Halloran,

Recently, you sent me a letter asking for a recommendation of Jennifer Jasniak, a senior at our school, for the Denton Award offered annually at graduation. I am sorry to inform you that, in all conscience, I cannot recommend Ms. Jasniak for that honor.

The Denton Award has a reputation for being presented to that student who best represents those qualities of honor and forthrightness that we hope will be the hallmark of the leaders of tomorrow. As such, the recipient of it must be a person in whom those ideals strongly dwell.

On six or seven occasions, I have personally watched Jennifer Jasniak reduce another student to tears by criticizing the other student's looks or manner of dress. In two of those cases, the student who was being criticized literally fled from the room, much to the apparent delight and laughter of Ms. Jasniak and several of her companions. On one occasion, there was a "letter-writing" campaign against a young woman that almost caused that young woman's breakdown. We were able to stop it just in time, and we found Ms. Jasniak and her group at the middle of it.

Personally, I do not feel that this behavior is representative of the recipient of the Denton Award. Certainly, I find no "honor" in it. Therefore, I do not feel able to recommend Jennifer Jasniak for this award.

Sincerely yours,

NOTE: If you have stated your case succinctly and mentioned only incidents that you personally have observed, it can never come back to haunt you. The rule for all recommendations should be: "Be thorough, but be objective." Speak from your heart rather than your temper, and all should be fine.

12. Positive Recommendation to a Special Academic Program

Virtually every school presents a program of a special academic nature at some time. Be they advanced training for students gifted in art or music or an academic enhancement group, these special academic programs generally take their students on a number of criteria, from standardized test results to teacher recommendation. Here is one such recommendation.

Dear Dr. Liang,

Thank you for your recent letter asking my opinion concerning the entrance of Stephen Moreno, a sixth-grade student at our school, into your "Exceptional Learners" program. I am aware of the nature of your program and have become well acquainted with Stephen over the past several years. I feel qualified, therefore, to recommend Stephen to your special academic program. Indeed, I would go so far as to state that Stephen is most likely the exact type of student for whom your program was conceptualized in the first place.

Rarely have I seen a boy with Stephen's potential who has fallen as far behind. Most certainly, attempts to get him to live up to that potential have been made time and again by a host of very dedicated faculty and guidance personnel, all to little avail.

I am extremely happy, therefore, that Stephen may have a chance in your special program. I have read with interest the statistics on the success rate of "Exceptional Learners," and I have every hope that Stephen will add to their impressive stature. Stephen Moreno is the particular type of student who would benefit from your special academic program, and I recommend him for placement as soon as possible.

If I may be of any assistance, please feel free to call upon me.

Yours sincerely,

NOTE: The recommendation here is simple. You know the program; you know the student; you feel professionally that they would be suited to each other; you therefore recommend the student. Despite its brevity, it is effective, and, as you will note, leaves lines open for further communication.

13. Negative Recommendation to a Special Academic Program, I

Let's start with a scenario where you have some minor reservations—enough that you cannot give your wholehearted approval.

Dear Ms. Longelk,

Thank you for your recent request for my opinion regarding the placement of a student, Patricia Orandel, in your Special and Talented Education Program (S.T.E.P.). I assure you that I have given the matter some thought. I appreciate the fine work you do, and I want only the best for Patricia as well.

Therefore, I feel that I shall have to recommend her to you with some reservation, which I would like to explain. While her academic average is indicative of a high degree of intellectual prowess, and her résumé is reflective of a high degree of involvement, it is in the day-to-day functioning of the classroom that I find cause for concern.

During the time she was in my class, I noticed a tendency in her toward intolerance of other students who could not grasp a concept or perform an academic task as quickly or with as much dispatch as she. This expressed itself for the most part with heavy sighs and rolled-up eyeballs when an incorrect answer was given and, upon occasion, with some remark or other—generally about the brightness of the student involved. A few times, these remarks hit home with such a rapier quality that the object of her words ended up in tears.

I have personally spoken to Patricia about this, but I came away with the impression that I had not made the point sufficiently relevant to her to have her stop the behavior.

Again, I must stress that this has nothing to do with her academic progress nor with her work for the good of the student body through her position on the student council. It is, however, something that concerns me, and something which, I felt, should be noted in my letter.

I wish continued success to the S.T.E.P. program, and I stand ready to help in any way that I am able.

Most sincerely yours,

NOTE: While this letter concerned a minor character defect, it was enough that this educator felt it had to be addressed. Notice that it is couched objectively, retelling what the writer personally witnessed, and it is also put into perspective. Nonetheless, the writer's reservation is duly noted.

14. Negative Recommendation to a Special Academic Program, II

The previous negative recommendation was an example of what to write when your concerns are nominal. In this letter, let's look at a case where you sincerely feel that the child should not be a part of that special academic program.

Dear Dr. Ramier,

Yesterday, I received from you a request for the recommendation of one of our students, Kelly Buntain, to your advanced placement program at Yost College.

Dr. Ramier, we here at Rock Township High School are not only aware of the fine work you are doing at Yost College in the field of secondary education; we have seen and marveled at the results of your advanced placement program in the lives of several of the students whom we have previously recommended to you. We are further aware of the high standards, both personal and academic, that are required of students engaged in your program. Indeed, we applaud your efforts.

That is why, with regret, I must decline to recommend Kelly Buntain to your attention. After a good deal of reflection and consideration, I must tell you that in my professional opinion, Kelly is *not* suited to your specific requirements at this time.

While Kelly began her high school career with outstanding grades in her sophomore year, the first semester of her current junior year has shown a marked decline in academic status, and her teachers have been unanimous in asking Guidance to investigate this downturn. Moreover, there have been a number of reports of incidents involving Kelly's behavior that is a marked change from that which we have previously witnessed. Fighting, inappropriate language, defacing school property, and the like are not activities we had come to expect from Kelly, and we are anxious to understand these changes while we still may be of help.

As I am certain you will understand, the behaviors I have outlined above are indicative, to us at least, of a child with a problem. Of course, we intend to investigate and get to the source of that problem; certainly, we intend to give whatever help is necessary to provide remedies for her difficulty; obviously, our concern is for Kelly and her continued positive development. Given the nature of her status both behaviorally and academically at the present time, however, I feel that we have little alternative but to recommend against her placement in your program.

When circumstances change, or should new light be shed on this situation, I assure you that we will not hesitate to contact you concerning our reappraisal of the situation and Kelly's academic and personal progress.

Again, I thank you for your concern and your understanding. If you should wish any further clarification, we would be most happy to have you contact us. In the meantime, congratulations on the success of your special academic program as it continues to meet the needs of young people throughout our community. Please count us among your supporters, and please call upon us whenever we may be of service.

Yours truly,

NOTE: Here was a case where you could not equivocate, even a little. A direct turndown such as this should always be objectively documented and written with regret, and open an avenue of help for the student—all of which is done in the letter above.

15. Positive Recommendation to a Community Program

When you recommend a student to a community-based program, remember that the community will be judging your school by the performance of the individual you recommend. This may not be fair, but it is almost always the case. Great care must be taken, therefore, when you write a recommendation for such a student. This first letter is for a student you feel confident will make a good representative of the school.

Dear Mrs. Gelschatz,

What a joy it was to hear of your community action program, "Speaking Up For Our Schools." The idea of selecting a student from each school in our township and having him or her speak at various community clubs and organizations is a fine one, in my opinion, and it should certainly allow the public to gain an inside look at our schools—something which we are most eager to have happen.

Now, of course, you task me with a monumental labor—to recommend a student from my school for participation in your group. Believe me, that has given me cause for deep reflection.

After more than a little agonizing, I have come up with a ninth-grade student whom I witnessed speaking in a debate recently. While only a freshman, she has so gained the confidence of the forensic coach that he has placed her in his front line of speakers, and she has already been responsible for one club victory. When I heard her speak in the recent debate, I was personally impressed by her seemingly natural abilities to persuade in the smoothest possible manner through the proper choice of words and a clarity of delivery that went far beyond her years.

Her name is Calisha Henderson, but most people call her "Cally." She currently maintains a B+ average, and every teacher to whom I have spoken has only positive things to say about her. It seems that she is personable and likable as well as a talented speaker. In short, Calisha Henderson seems just the person for your program.

I have spoken with Cally and have explained your program to her. She was most receptive to the idea, as were her parents, with whom I also spoke. I have no reservations, therefore, in providing you with her name, address, and telephone number (enclosed). I have advised her that you may be calling her soon, and I am assured that she will be receptive to your proposal.

It gives me great pleasure to recommend this outstanding student to your attention, and I look forward to hearing about your group in the near future. Please don't forget our very active PTA when formulating your plans.

If I or the school may be of any further assistance, please feel free to call upon us at any time.

Sincerely yours,

NOTE: You were asked to perform a task for this community group; you researched them and their needs, and you have come up with a student whom you can truly recommend as well as one who will, in all likelihood, reflect well upon the school; you have involved the child and her parents and set up some very positive lines of communication between the community group and the school. We'd call that a good day's work!

16. Negative Recommendation to a Community Program

You cannot, for the reasons detailed earlier, recommend just anyone to a community program. Indeed, if you truly feel that the individual who is up for recommendation will be detrimental to your school's reputation, then you have a responsibility to give a negative recommendation. Such a situation is assumed in the following letter.

Dear Ms. Clements,

I am in receipt of your letter requesting a recommendation for Ralph Boyd, a student at our school, for participation in your community service program of playground volunteers. We are, of course, familiar with your fine program and the work and dedication you put into it, so we take the recommendation of one of our students to that program to be a very serious matter.

I sincerely regret, therefore, that I do not find it possible to recommend this student for participation in your program. Indeed, we are somewhat amazed that Ralph placed his name in contention for your organization.

This is Ralph Boyd's third year in Tanshire Middle School, and as his guidance counselor, I have been involved with him for his entire tenure. While some students literally breeze through school with little or no difficulty, others find hardship at virtually every turn. Unfortunately, the latter description best fits Ralph Boyd.

Over his middle school career, Ralph has been suspended a total of seventeen times, ten of those occasions for extorting money by physical threat from smaller children. The other instances involve fighting, intimidation, destruction of property, and other violence-related activities. I have spoken to Ralph in my office on numerous occasions when the classroom teacher felt his presence could no longer be tolerated. In all those instances, I have never seen Ralph regret anything other than the fact that he had "gotten caught." Attempts to reach the home have met with noncooperation, and Ralph's situation at our school has not changed significantly over his stay.

You have done a fine job with your community program of playground volunteers over the years, and if you should wish to have Ralph Boyd as a part of that program, that is certainly your decision to make. As a representative of Tanshire Middle School, however, I deeply regret that we shall not be able to recommend him to that position, with or without qualification.

I am sorry that I could not have had a better report for you. We think your program has great merit, and if we may be of any service in the future, please accord us the privilege of helping.

Very truly yours,

NOTE: Here is an example of an individual who verges on the hard core and, if recommended, might cause a great deal of damage to the program—and very possibly to you and your school's reputation. Please note, however, that even though it seems rather clear that this fictional student wants to join the program in order to have new victims to extort and terrorize, the letter writer stops short of saying that (since that would be opinion) and lets the facts speak for themselves, allowing the program director to draw his or her own conclusions.

17. Positive Recommendation for a Job Outside School

The request for a recommendation for a job can come in two forms. First, the request may come from a fairly large company that has its own personnel department, making the request rather formal in nature; second, the request may come from a smaller, local business, such as a local deli, a small gift shop, or a corner grocery, and be given on a much less formal basis. This first, positive recommendation, assumes the student has applied to a large company and you have been sent a formal request for a recommendation.

Dear Mr. Scarpelli,

I have received your request for a recommendation for Tasha Greene, a student in our school who has applied to your company for a position as mailroom clerk for the months of July and August of this current year.

It gives me great pleasure to recommend Tasha to you for this position. I have known this student professionally for almost three years, and I am aware of her academic record and her character both in class and in those social situations afforded by the school. I find it a pleasure to be acquainted with such a fine young woman.

In Tasha, you will be getting a worker who is a quick learner, eager to perfect every skill she acquires; you will be employing someone who takes pride in all that she does, which is reflected in an outstanding job in whatever area she may be assigned; you will have an employee who is personable without being familiar, cheerful in the face of adversity, and unflustered under stress. Those are qualities one finds in few employees nowadays, but they are attributes that Tasha carries with her as a matter of course.

Certainly, I could supply a transcript of Tasha's outstanding grades as well as testimony after testimony from faculty and administrators as to her character and abilities. One day on the job, however, will be enough for you to appreciate them for yourselves. I think that, as she enters college in September, she will look back on her association with you with great satisfaction, and I believe that is the way you will feel about her.

It gives me extreme joy to be able to recommend her for the noted position with your company, and to do so without reservation.

Please feel free to contact me if I may be of any further service to you.

Sincerely,

NOTE: Although this letter was filled with superlatives for a superlative student, it remains a formal reply to a formal request for recommendation. It is always pleasant to be able to say positive things about an outstanding student. Look upon that as one of the side benefits of the job.

18. Negative Recommendation for a Job Outside School

In this example, let's assume two things: first, that the request comes from a small local business, and second, that you have some reservations about the student who has applied for the job. You try to keep the tone informal but still objective.

Dear Mr. Kim,

Thanks for your letter asking me for a recommendation for Kenny Zenotis. According to your letter, Kenny has asked you for a job as a stock clerk and all-around cleanup person in your market, and you would like to hear from us about it.

First of all, Mr. Kim, I know your market and have shopped there quite a few times. May I wish you continued success with your business.

Next, I know Kenny, having dealt with him in school over the past two years. Kenny is doing moderately well in his studies and seems to have average to above-average abilities that carry him through school happily, without any great troubles or difficulties. Moreover, although he does not participate in any extracurricular activities, he is well known and generally liked by his classmates, and his teachers have some positive things to say about him. He has a good personality, and throughout his years with us, I have never had to deal with him for a disciplinary or behavioral problem.

The one minor difficulty that has been observed and reported by his teachers and others who have dealt with him is that he does not initiate action. By that, I mean that it is reported that he almost always waits to be told what to do next. He does not finish one task and then look around at what has to be done next and go to it. Rather, he finishes one job and waits for the teacher or whoever is in charge to direct him into what he should be doing next.

Please do not mistake me. He finishes what you give him to do, but he still requires strong direction beyond that. He is not a "self-starter." I'm certain you can appreciate that phrase. Kenny is, however, honest, happy, and a pleasant young man who works well at what is assigned.

The final decision as to whether or not to hire Kenny is, of course, yours. I can recommend him to your attention with the single qualification that is noted above. I wish you continued prosperity with your market, and I invite you to call me any time if I may be of service.

Sincerely yours,

NOTE: This might be termed a qualified recommendation, in that the one attribute of the candidate that might affect his performance on the job is explained, along with emphasis on "Kenny's" good points. Note also that the writer explained the term "self-starter" before ever using it. Suit your terminology to your audience.

19. Recommendation of a Colleague

Inevitably, the time will come when you are asked to write a recommendation for a colleague. When this happens, it is again advisable to keep the recommendation fairly objective, even if the colleague is a personal friend. A professional recommendation filled with glowing rhetoric may enter the zone of overkill for the reader, while one that allows positive facts to speak for themselves has a much more beneficial result and reinforces the worth of the candidate.

Dear Dr. Mantree,

I am extremely happy to recommend to your attention Mrs. Miriam Ortiz, who currently serves as seventh-grade guidance counselor at Tenshire Middle School. As a counselor at the same school, I have had the opportunity to work closely with Mrs. Ortiz for the past five years and have become familiar with her personally as well as in a professional capacity.

As head counselor, I can testify to the fact that Mrs. Ortiz is extremely efficient in all her record-keeping tasks. In the five years I have known her, never once has she been late with a report; never once have her files been missing any information regarding a student. Indeed, if we need to find something in the office, it is generally assumed that Miriam will know where to find it.

Next, I have personally seen her go beyond the call and nature of her assignment to help the children she serves. I have seen her work many long hours on cases that others might well have labeled hopeless, and I have seen some astounding results because of her refusal to quit working for the good of her children. Moreover, she is always willing to help others, and stands available and approachable to members of the faculty as well as students, many of whom seek out her understanding and discreet counseling.

Perhaps most impressive is her dedication to the students of the school. Not only does she serve as guidance counselor, but she voluntarily became the advisor to the school's student council and has raised the level of that organization to one of the most respected activities in the school. She also formed and mentored a special Saturday morning tutoring session for students with academic difficulties, making and supervising all the arrangements personally, obtaining permission for building use, and getting volunteers. This program alone has proven such a success that the school is considering expanding the concept to other schools in the system.

One could not, however, assess Mrs. Ortiz's career without mentioning the one factor that, while intangible, is the hallmark of her success in counseling—her love and concern for her students. In the halls, I have seen students vie with each other to be near her. She is greeted respectfully and affectionately throughout the school, and I have never seen a student reluctant to enter her office.

Because I work so closely with her, I am in a position to observe my colleague in her work. I have found her always concerned, always ready to help her students and her fellow educators, always willing to go that extra distance to make certain that everything is handled, and handled well and efficiently—to the ultimate benefit of the student or teacher involved.

Add to this the accuracy, professionalism, dispatch, and effectiveness with which she performs her assigned tasks, and you have someone especially worthy of your consideration. It does give me great pleasure to wholeheartedly recommend to your attention and consideration a very fine guidance counselor—someone I am personally happy to call my colleague—Mrs. Miriam Ortiz.

Please call me if you feel that I may be of any further help or should you wish elaboration on any particular detail.

Very truly yours,

NOTE: While it is obvious that you like the person you are recommending, it is also obvious that you are recounting facts that either you have personally witnessed or that are verifiable objectively. As such, it is a strong recommendation. Of course, you could have gone into longer descriptions of the programs she started, but it is just as strong as it is, and perhaps even more so for its relative brevity.

20. Recommendation for a Teacher

In the final letter of this section, let us present a standard letter of recommendation for a teacher who, we will assume, has taught in your school. While you know this person, it is on a professional basis only. You may consider yourselves acquaintances but not friends. The teacher has sent out his résumé, and you are asked for a recommendation.

Dear Dr. Schallert,

This letter is in reply to your request for a written recommendation for Mr. Preston Sternfeld, who has applied to your school system for employment as a certified classroom teacher.

Currently, Mr. Sternfeld is serving as an eleventh-grade science teacher at Rock Township High School. He carries five academic classes, one of them an honors biology class. He also manages a homeroom, has one period of library supervision, and supervises and serves as advisor for our high school's science club. According to our records, this is Mr. Sternfeld's seventh year at Rock Township and his twelfth year in teaching.

A review of teacher evaluations for the past several years indicates that Mr. Sternfeld continues to do a good job, and that his teaching is often "innovative" (I quote from past evaluations) with a "marked concern for the individual learner" and "outstanding classroom management techniques." He is also noted and commended in these evaluations for his "efficiency in record keeping" and his "cooperation within his department."

While I do not know Mr. Sternfeld well, other than in our professional relationship, I have always found him pleasant, professional, and efficient when we were working toward a common goal for school or community.

I feel justified, therefore, on the basis of my review of his past evaluations and his general record here at Rock Township High School, to recommend him without reservation. I am sure that he would make a fine addition to your school system and be a benefit to the school in which he was placed, as his record here clearly indicates. Indeed, I am certain that students and faculty will miss him.

You may call upon me at your convenience if I may be of any further service to you in this or any other matter.

Sincerely,

NOTE: Here, you have seen a complete recommendation reconstructed from a review of documents (in this case, evaluations). Notice that no attempt was made to try to convey an intimate knowledge of or friendship with the subject, but the evaluations and the facts of record were allowed to speak for themselves. Even so, when the facts are good, so is the recommendation.

LETTERS THAT DEAL WITH
ILLNESS AND DEATH

$\mathcal{F}$ew tasks are more difficult to accomplish than the writing of a letter of sympathy to someone who has just lost a loved one. That statement is true universally, whatever the profession or job in which you may be engaged, but it strikes home with particular vehemence when the place is the school and the one who has died is a student filled with life, who brought a daily smile to your lips—or a beloved teacher, someone who has touched the lives of so many others. At times like these, the task is Herculean.

Nor is it only death that occasions the writing of these letters. At times, an illness may threaten the stability of a family, and if that family is the family of a member of the faculty or of a student at your school, there is a feeling of obligation to say something about it or write some message that will be of hope and encouragement.

While such letters may be difficult to write, they serve a definite purpose and often accomplish things we do not realize. One woman, who has a letter of sympathy from her deceased husband's principal, says that she considers it a treasure and a very fond reminder of her teacher-husband. Periodically, she will take it out and read it and find comfort in its words.

Of course, not all letters of sympathy will achieve that status, but every sincere and heartfelt letter is appreciated, if not at the time, then certainly afterward. Saying what is in your heart and then polishing that statement with some of the insights and models that follow will go a long way toward a tailor-made letter of sympathy from you that will be both appreciated and remembered.

Keep in mind as you write that *sincerity* is the key word here. Some letters are more difficult than others to write, because you do not have the same feelings about every teacher or student who is ill or has died. You may have to reach a little to say positive things in some cases. They do exist, however; find them and say them with sincerity.

UNDERSTANDING THE BASIC LETTER OF SYMPATHY

A good letter of sympathy is one written with the heart rather than the pen. While this is excellent advice in general, remember that even the most spontaneous and heartfelt of documents can stand a little polishing. Remember, too, that in the emotional heat of the moment, you may say something that may not express what you mean in the best possible manner. It is therefore a very good practice to have someone you know and respect go over the letter before you send it. This simple expedient could save much discomfort later on.

There are certain things that a sensitive individual never places in a letter of sympathy. They are clichés, true, but to an individual in emotional torment, they become "killer clichés," to be avoided at all costs. While they may be well-meaning, these phrases are, at best, abrasive to the mourning individual.

Killer Clichés to Be Avoided

"You'll get over it."	"Time heals all wounds."
"It's all for the best."	"In time you'll forget."
"He/she certainly did suffer."	"He'd/she'd want you to be strong."
"You'll find someone else."	"I'm sure you'll miss him/her."
"It happened to me, and I survived."	"You must think of yourself now."

If you are going to recall something about the deceased individual, make certain that it is appropriate to the time and place of your letter. For example, you may think that the time the two of you had "one too many" was hilarious, but the person's spouse may not consider that incident appropriate or one that he or she would wish to share. Be circumspect; relate only those incidents that place the deceased in the best possible light and that may be shared with the intimate family as well as the general public.

Be genuine rather than flowery. The mourner does not need poetry as much as understanding, sympathy, and support. Going on about "crossing the bar" or "the great beyond" may or may not be the stuff of poetry, but it is definitely not the substance of the letter of sympathy.

Now, if you are a person of faith, and you wish to share that faith and whatever comfort it may bring, that is appropriate and often deeply appreciated, but your feeling must be genuine, and you should keep an eye to the faith of the person to whom you are sending the letter, in order that there be no unintentional embarrassment.

As for the rest, let your heart dictate. In the following section, you will find examples of letters of sympathy for everything from the nonthreatening illness of a student to the unexpected death of a superintendent of schools. Use them as examples or adapt them to your specific needs with the change of a name or circumstance.

Say what you feel in your heart and use the letters that follow as your guides, and you will be writing an effective and appropriate letter of sympathy that will truly be a blessing to the one who receives it.

MODEL LETTERS OF SYMPATHY AND UNDERSTANDING

21. Nonserious Illness of a Student

A good general policy, if a student is out for more than three days, is to call the home, or send a letter. The illness may be an extended cold or flu, or something with which the school can help. Keep this initial contact light. If it is something serious, the home most definitely will let you know.

Dear Mr. and Mrs. Tantanian,

We miss Benny! It's been three days now that he hasn't been in our classrooms and halls, and we are hoping that everything is all right. We are also wondering if there is anything that we can do. We can't give him that tender, loving care that you can while he is ill, but we can and do offer homework assignments, textbooks sent home, and even a student aide, if necessary, to keep Benny on track and to keep him from feeling lost or "left behind" when he does return to regular classes, which we sincerely hope will be soon.

Could you let us know how Benny is progressing? We'll spread the news to his teachers, and should you like us to do so, we'll get the assignments Benny needs to keep current with his class while he is in the business of getting better.

While it is our every hope that Benny's illness is soon over, should he require longer than a week at home, please contact us and let us know. I assure you that the school stands ready to help however it may in Benny's recovery.

Let's hope that Benny feels like his old self very quickly, and that we see him at the school really soon. We miss him, and we want him back. Believe me, he'll be most welcome!

Yours truly,

NOTE: Parents have told us that receiving a letter of this sort showed them that the school really cared, and that their son or daughter was more than a number or statistic. It also provides you with a written record of your attempt to follow up on the absence, should anything such as truancy or abduction due to parental dispute be involved. In all, it is a nice, human touch for the school to provide.

22. Nonserious Illness of a Teacher

There are some real differences between this and the previous letter. With a teacher, you will generally know if the illness is serious or temporary, since an educator who will be out for an extended stay has to be covered. Therefore, you know that it is something troublesome but not serious, such as a cold or flu. This is the situation here, and the writer understands that the teacher is well on the road to recovery.

Dear Norma,

I think you have inspired me. I am going to write a book, which I will entitle *100 Illnesses America Loves*. At the top of the list, I will place the common cold, or whatever variation of it you may have at the present moment. I will tell of how that ailment allows the victim the opportunity to lie in bed, sip hot tea with lemon, catch up on reading, and even watch disreputable daytime TV shows with impunity! All this, of course, while the rest of her associates (that's us, in case you didn't know) slave away in the halls of this educational institution to bring light into darkness and keep Little Leslie from smearing bubble gum into Little Evan's hair!

Seriously, Norma, we are sorry you are ill and delighted to hear that you are now on a definite road to recovery. Colds can be nasty, but you had our best wishes and prayers with you all the way. How we look forward to your return! We have allowed all your work to pile up, and you should be able to get through the back-log by staying until 8:00 P.M. for the next month or two!

Actually, all you really have to do to make us all happy is get back here. We all miss you—your kids perhaps the most of all. We all need your smile and those happy words you spread about so frequently and so well. We need your sunlight, and your kids need that excellent, dedicated, and caring teacher they have come to love.

Take your time getting well, because we want you well and rested when you return. Most of all, we want *you*. Come back to us as soon as you are physically able; you know how welcome you will be!

Best wishes,

NOTE: Obviously, writer and recipient are very good friends, at least on a professional level. The tone of the letter is light and breezy, with humor pervading. Underlying that is a genuineness of feeling that cannot help but cheer the indisposed teacher. One word of caution, however: Use humor only in a nonserious situation and only where you consider yourself a friend of the one to whom you are writing. In any other situation, you stand a chance of being misunderstood.

23. Nonserious Illness of an Administrator

This letter could be from one administrator to another or from a faculty member to an administrator who was temporarily indisposed through illness. Either way, note that the tone has become a bit more formal, and it is not quite as light as the previous two letters. A teacher representative might write a letter like this to an ailing principal or vice-principal on behalf of the faculty.

Dear Mr. Golubinski,

On behalf of the entire faculty of Rock Township High School, may I say how sorry we were to hear of your bout with the flu. We are all aware of just how nasty and physically enervating that can be. Indeed, in the not-so-distant past, you have had a number of occasions on which to write to individual faculty members concerning their similar situations.

We understand that you are over the worst and well on your way to recovering your strength and characteristic good health. We are thankful for that, and the entire faculty wishes you the speediest of recoveries. It is our hope that you will take your time and get some well-deserved rest and then return to us, fully refreshed and ready to resume your duties as vice-principal.

We look forward to your return, and if there is anything that we may do to aid you in the meantime, either in or out of school, please understand that you may call upon us at any time.

For the faculty and staff of Rock Township High School, I am

Very truly yours,

NOTE: This letter of concern or sympathy is short and formal. Here, the writer, who is acting as a representative for the faculty, is writing a formal letter of sympathy to an ailing administrator. As such, the writing is a bit more restrained, and personal anecdotes or reflections are not appropriate. Nonetheless, the letter is friendly and concerned, and affirms good wishes throughout.

24. Serious Illness of a Student

The sympathy letter for the serious illness, be it of a student, teacher, or administrator, requires an entirely different approach from that of the previous letter for an illness that was not considered life-threatening. In these letters, there should be a real tone of concern, and if an offer to help is made, it should be genuine.

Dear Mrs. Constable,

I know that I speak for everyone at Tanshire Middle School when I tell you how shocked and sorry we were to hear that Teckeish has been diagnosed with meningitis. Of course, we are familiar with this particular illness, having dealt with a number of cases in our student body over the years, but it is never easy to hear of it, particularly when it affects someone as upbeat, positive, and well liked as Teckeish.

If it gives you any comfort, in every past case of meningitis in our school, the student involved has always made a full recovery and returned to school a happy and functioning student. By that, I do not mean to minimize the seriousness of Teckeish's illness nor discount the amount of time necessary for her full recovery, but I *do* intend to place that "candle at the end of the tunnel" for all to see.

During her process of rest and recovery, you can be assured that the school will make every effort to keep Teckeish on a par with her classmates, keep her current, and have her feel a part of this school—*her* school. We will be in contact with you to arrange for that in about a week.

Moreover, we will not forget Teckeish in class. You can expect cards and letters from Teckeish's classmates while she is in the hospital, and weekly messages thereafter. We have done this for other students, and hope that Teckeish will enjoy it, and that it will help her feel connected with us.

The entire faculty stands with me in assuring you that our thoughts, prayers, and best wishes are with you during this time, and we are quite sincere in offering you whatever help we may be capable of giving. We ask you to try us in this; you'll find that we are more than ready to help.

Please keep us advised of Teckeish's progress, and we'll take it from there. We know this is a difficult time, and we wish to make it as easy as possible as far as your relation to our school is concerned.

With every hope for Teckeish's swift and complete recovery, I am

Very truly yours,

NOTE: Just one insight: Most parents who have a child with a serious illness are concerned, next to the child's welfare, with the child's relationship to the school and how the illness will affect the child's school career. Notice how this letter addresses that problem and invites the parents to ask for help.

25. Serious Illness of a Student's Parent

The serious illness of the parent of a student can have serious repercussions in the life of that student. There may be marked behavioral changes as well as changes in schoolwork and student productivity, particularly as the illness progresses. Often, the school—if it has an active guidance department—can help the student get through this trying time, especially if the appropriate people are informed early on in the process. The following letter is a reply to one such notification.

Dear Mr. Tau,

We were extremely saddened by your recent letter informing us of Mrs. Tau's illness and her subsequent need for both surgery and a prolonged hospital stay. Most assuredly, you have our sympathies as well as our support and prayers.

Your letter expressed concern for the progress of your son and daughter, Peter and Leslie, both students at our school, during the period of your wife's illness and protracted recovery. We appreciate your concerns, and we stand ready to address them and perhaps remove some of that burden from you.

I can personally assure you that Peter and Leslie will receive whatever special care they require during this trying time. Your children's teachers have successfully dealt with children in similar situations, and their insight, kindness, and expertise are Peter's and Leslie's without asking. Moreover, our highly trained guidance personnel will be made aware of the situation immediately. Your children will be the focus of discreet attention—not singling them out—but providing them with all the support they will need at this time.

We are more than happy to supply these services, and you may rest assured that we look upon these efforts for Peter and Leslie with a concern second only to yours.

Again, you have our deepest sympathies on your wife's illness. We shall write to her separately and extend out best wishes for her recovery. In the meantime, please be assured that we know, we understand, and we care. We will work, as we know you will, toward the very best for your children during this difficult time.

If we may be of any further service, please do call. We want to help.

Yours sincerely,

NOTE: Sometimes, when dealing with the serious illness of a student's parent, the other parent needs support and assurance as well. That was the case in this letter. The knowledge that a caring school is watching out for their children can go a long way toward helping a family get through a serious illness such as this.

26. Serious Illness of a Teacher

When a teacher—especially a well-liked or well-respected teacher—becomes seriously ill, it can affect the entire school. The following letter was written to the ailing teacher, and then posted for the entire school to see, as well as being read over the public address system. Note its simple and direct language.

Dear Mr. Nulty,

We heard about your illness, and we are very sorry. If we could, we would make it go away and have you back with us right now. We can't do that, of course, but we can tell you that we miss you, and we are all looking forward to the time when you will be well and will be able to come back to us to once more be our teacher and our friend.

We all want you to get better, so please do what your doctor tells you and take a nice, long rest. We want you back here, but we want you healthy. While you get better, you should know that you have all our prayers, good thoughts, and best wishes helping you.

Your classes have something special that they are going to send you, but we just wanted you to know that we really care for you as you have cared for us over these many years.

Please get well soon and come back to us.

Very truly yours,

The students, teachers, and staff
of Colbert-Brett Elementary School

NOTE: The objective of this letter was not only to express sympathy to a well-liked teacher but to involve the entire elementary school in the process—to make each child feel that he or she had a part in expressing care and concern. Did it achieve its goal? You can be the judge of that, but note the simplicity and the straightforward way in which it is presented. It is plain enough for each child to understand, and forceful enough to touch the heart of the teacher involved.

27. Serious Illness of an Administrator

One key to writing a letter on serious illness is to be genuine. Flowery prose is not what is needed. The ailing person needs to know that he or she is acknowledged—validated, if you will. Toward that end, an expression of the positive expectation of his or her return is not out of place.

Dear Margaret,

How sad we were to hear of your recent diagnosis. There is no one here at the school who does not wish you continued health and prosperity, so it came as a shock to hear that you would be hospitalized for an extended period and then face a long recovery. I'm certain it came as quite a surprise to you as well.

Margaret, by now you should know how highly we value you at this school—as the vice-principal and personally, as a dear friend, colleague, and confidant. I am so sorry to hear of this illness, and I want you to know that when I offer you any assistance possible during this time, I am not merely writing words; I am totally serious. You have done so much for this school and for me personally, that it will be a privilege to be able to help. Please call upon me!

In all of this, I will admit that I am being somewhat selfish. You see, you are extremely valuable to us on a professional basis; I want you back at your job and the school needs you back. All of us will be looking forward to the time when you resume your duties and this school breathes a collective sigh of relief that you are back where you belong.

We want you well. You have our prayers and every good wish available. Take whatever time you need; get whatever rest you have to; come back to us.

You are of extreme value as an administrator and a friend. We'll miss you here, but we will not lose touch with you, and we'll all look forward to the day when you return.

Best always,

NOTE: This letter would pass between people who were friends as well as colleagues. Although certainly it could be adapted to other situations, this letter aims at assuring the ailing administrator of the need for her return and the extent to which she is genuinely missed—both personally and professionally. That's not a bad combination.

28. Terminal Illness of a Student, I

The very words "terminal illness" carry a negative impact. Being informed that someone has a "terminal illness" means that, barring something miraculous, the person is going to die. In a letter to this individual, you do not mention "getting better," because that is not a choice, and generally, the individual knows or feels it to be so. This type of letter is very delicate. First, let's look at a letter to the student's parents.

Dear Mr. and Mrs. Connors,

Are words adequate to express the inexpressible—to place on paper that which may only be experienced within the human heart? I feel they are not, yet that is the only way we have of even attempting to communicate those feelings which we hold so deeply.

Nothing I can say will express the shock, the deep sorrow, and the sense of devastation we all felt when we heard of Lateshia's illness. We remember her smiling face, her inquisitive mind, her winning personality. Whether as a student, a classmate or a friend, Lateshia is someone we have come to know, to admire, to respect, to call our friend—a special and wonderful person. Perhaps this is why our shock and sorrow go so deep.

This is also why we assure you that we are sincere in offering any help that we can at this time and in the future as you may have need. Please, we invite you to allow us the privilege of helping. It would, indeed, be our honor.

Please accept our deepest sympathies and know that you have our prayers and our deepest concern. Call upon us soon.

Sincerely,

NOTE: This letter is written to and for the parents of the terminally ill student. Delicacy is the hallmark here. The words "death," "suffering," "pain," or any words of this type should never be included, whatever your sentiments may be.

29. Terminal Illness of a Student, II

The letter written to the terminally ill child's parents is hard enough to craft. Even more taxing is the letter to the terminally ill child. Understand, as you read the following letter, that whatever you end up writing should be geared to the child's level of understanding. Forget your vocabulary and speak from your heart.

Dear Shanie,

I'm very sorry that you are not feeling well. All of us at Maranisu Elementary School wish it could be better, and all of us are sorry.

Your mom and dad tell us that a group from your church comes by every day and spends some time with you. Well, we want you to know that there are people here who are praying for you, too. Everybody knows you and cares for you, and our thoughts are always with you.

Maybe I shouldn't tell you this, but your class is preparing a surprise for you that will be delivered to your house in a short time. Now, I can't tell you what it is, or it would spoil the surprise, but your class has worked on it, and I know you will like it. Look for it in a few days.

If you want to talk to your teacher or me or anyone here, have your mom give us a call and we'll see to it.

We all hope and pray that you will feel better. We love you, you know.

Your friend,

NOTE: One very practical thing that you can do is reflected in this letter. You can arrange for the terminally ill child to speak to any person he or she wishes at the school. Have a parent be the contact, to be sure; it is a small thing that can brighten the life of such a child. Keep the letter simple, appropriate to the child's level, and—above all—sincere.

30. Terminal Illness of a Student's Parent

The effects of terminal illness on the family are fairly well known, and the school—when it is a parent who is so affected — can play a significant part in helping students get through a difficult time. The following letter of sympathy is to the spouse of the terminally ill parent, and its goal, besides consolation, is reassurance that the children will receive special attention from the school.

Dear Mrs. Spinaldi,

It is needless to say that we at Hawthorne High school were deeply and grievously wounded by the news concerning Mr. Spinaldi's condition. We know how powerfully it affected us, and we can only guess at how devastating it must be for you and your family.

Mr. Spinaldi has been and remains a friend of this school, and we remember with pride his continuing efforts and involvement with our PTA for the betterment of this place for students and teachers alike. We have come to know him, like him, and respect him deeply. It is with the sincerest regret, therefore, that we learned of his current circumstances.

I want you to be assured of two things: First, we stand ready to help in any way possible. We are extremely sincere in offering whatever help we may be able to provide, and we invite you to allow us the privilege of doing so. Second, we assure you that your children, Lisa and Cosette, will be afforded every resource of this school to help them get through this most serious and trying time. We both know that they cannot help but be affected, but we also know that care, individuals willing to talk, and a concerned staff can go a long way toward aiding them on this difficult journey. That help will be theirs.

You have our thoughts and our prayers, and you also have our hands and our resources, should they be of use to you.

Please, do not hesitate to ask.

Most sincerely,

NOTE: In these letters on terminal illness, the offers to help must be genuine, and should the individual take you up on the offer, you and the school must follow through. Knowledge that you will do so would be of comfort to the terminally ill person, as well as his or her spouse and children.

31. Terminal Illness of a Teacher, I

In the case of terminal illness of a teacher in a school, faculty and students want to respond in some way. The following letter is written by the school's administrator and tries to be representative of everyone's feelings. This first letter is to the ailing teacher's spouse; the second is to the teacher personally.

Dear Mr. Havanakis,

When we heard of your wife's condition, there was not one of us who was not deeply affected by the news. Not a teacher, administrator, secretary, maintenance worker, or cafeteria person failed to see me personally or in some other way express their great sorrow. Several asked if I would convey those feelings to you on their behalf.

That alone is a wonderful tribute to Mrs. Havanakis and the type of teacher she is. Her life has touched so many people, and in each case, the individuals so affected have come to appreciate her beauty of spirit as well as her expertise as a teacher of great power and a human being of equally great warmth and affection.

That makes the news so much harder to take in. We offer you our deepest sympathies, and we would like you to know that the prayers, good wishes, and best hopes of the entire school are with you and your wife.

Please contact us and allow us to help during this very trying time. That would be our privilege and our honor. Keep us informed, and know that we are here for you.

Yours sincerely,

NOTE: Although this letter is somewhat general in nature, it definitely ties the ill teacher to the school and even praises her as an outstanding educator. There is a limit to how much one can say in a letter like this, but kind words about the person's spouse may be remembered long after the conclusion of the affair. Indeed, letters like the ones in this section are often kept for decades after the passing of the terminally ill individual.

32. Terminal Illness of a Teacher, II

Now let's examine a letter to the teacher himself or herself. Here, the tone should be somewhat more informal, since you had an acquaintance with the individual. The same cautions still apply, but try to be more personal. If, for instance, you called this person by his or her first name in the school setting, then by all means do so here as well.

Dear Marcia,

Since you are a very valuable part of this faculty, you know only too well how difficult it is to get them to agree on anything! We all, however—and that's ALL — agreed that we want you to know the high regard in which we hold you; we want you to know the special place you have earned in our hearts; we want you to know the wonders that you accomplish.

What wonders are we talking about? We speak now of the hundreds and hundreds of children who are fortunate enough to have sat in your classroom, to have listened as you opened their minds, to have received that spark of learning that turns into a glowing flame over and over again, because you fan it into blazing light.

We want you to know that you make us happy, every day. We want you to know that we learn from you, just as your children did. We want you to know that we remember; we remember and are proud that we count you as one of us. We are here for you, and we would count it a privilege to be asked to help.

I speak for everyone in this school when I tell you that you are truly loved.

God bless you,

NOTE: The terminally ill person is never relegated to the past tense in this letter. Put yourself in that person's position; you wouldn't want to read anything that spoke of the way you "used to" do something or how things were "before all this happened." Keep it present and you'll keep it personal.

33. Terminal Illness of an Administrator

The school administrator holds a unique position because of the highly visible nature of his or her job. Consequently, whatever happens is swiftly known throughout the school and often the district as well. Here, a fellow administrator addresses the situation.

Dear Harry,

You and I have sat on many a committee together, and we are both well aware of how many words were generated by those sessions in terms of policy and curriculum, press statements, and the like. If I had them all to use and several million more besides, I do not think they would be adequate to express my feelings at this point.

We've known each other for a long time, Harry, and we have grown to like each other—and I, personally, have come to respect you deeply. As we worked together, I learned of your sense of humor, your gentleness, your incredible strength, and yes, let me say it—your nobility of character. Nothing has changed in that regard.

I came to know a man who meets all challenges, who gives all he has to fight for what is good and proper, who inspires others by setting a standard—his personal standard—to which all others aspire. I assure you, nothing has changed in that regard.

Now, as many challenges come your way, I make so bold as to ask you for a favor. Please, my colleague and my friend, let me help. Indeed, those you touch so deeply are standing with me, and we would consider it an honor and privilege to be able to lend whatever support is necessary.

Please, use us, and also know that we are here for Alicia and Jennifer and Megan as well.

The school system you serve so well stands behind you; the thousands of children you touch stand behind you; we who love you stand behind you. I know that nothing has changed in that respect. Please contact us very soon and let us know how we may serve you.

Always,

NOTE: The present tense is used, as we discussed earlier. Also, this type of letter must be written by someone who can genuinely mean all that is being said. The seriously ill—and in this case, terminally ill—are quick to pick up the slightest trace of falseness. Be genuine; be sincere.

34. Death of a Student, I

When a student dies, it is a trauma for the entire school. You've heard this before, but old people are supposed to die—not children. Everyone is affected in one way or another. This first letter is directed to the parents of the deceased child.

Dear Mr. and Mrs. Eldridge,

I could search the dictionaries of the world for the right and proper words, and I know that I would never find them. No mere words can adequately express that weight in our hearts that is the focus of our deepest sorrow and concern.

The years that Tommy spent with us were happy ones. His teachers remember a bright and happy child, always eager to learn, alert, and inquisitive—a gentle spirit who often went out of his way to help other children and be their friend. The children of this school have, I know, already written to you, and their concern speaks for the friendliness and personality that Tommy always exhibited. I recall with fondness the young man who worked with me on a number of schoolwide projects and who always had time for a cheery hello in the halls of this school.

We wish to honor your son with a special plaque presented at a schoolwide assembly in the near future. Now is not the time to discuss it, and I will be contacting you in the near future, but I want you to know that we remember Tommy, and we will make every effort to see to it that our school never forgets.

Again, our deepest sympathies, prayers, and gentle thoughts go out to you during this most trying time. Please let us know if there is anything at all that we can do for you. You need only ask.

Yours sincerely,

NOTE: The death of a child is the singular most traumatic event a parent can go through. Keep that in mind, whatever you write. We have found that good, positive, solid, and warm memories of the child are always appreciated by the parents. Just make certain that you say them from your heart. Never address what "might have been," but make an effort to show parents the child as he or she was, in the most positive of perspectives.

35. Death of a Student, II

Now, let's look at a slightly unusual letter of sympathy for a student who died. This letter is addressed to the students of the school the child attended, in this case an elementary school. This letter was read over the public address system to the entire school and then was posted prominently for all to see.

To the Students of Round Ridge Elementary:

Just a little while ago, a very sad thing happened to all of us here at Round Ridge School. One of our students died. Her name was Lanea Wilson, and she was a fourth-grade student in Mrs. Onman's class.

As you probably know, she became very ill, so ill that in spite of everything that was done for her, and in spite of all that we hoped, she did not recover. Lanea died. That means that she will not be coming back to us; we will not be seeing her again. It is all right if we feel sad about that, because we will miss Lanea, and we will be sorry that she is not with us to share what we are doing, which she was such a real part of in the past.

What we will do for Lanea now is remember her with love. We will see her, not in person, but in our minds and memories on the playground where we ran and played and laughed together; we will see her in our minds and hearts in the halls and classrooms where she learned and grew and was such an important part of us.

We will keep that memory of Lanea alive in our hearts and minds; we will keep our love of her ever fresh, ever new; we will continue to see her with the eyes of memory, and we will cherish that memory as something very special—something very special indeed.

In loving memory,

NOTE: This may sound simple, but we think it is also very effective. It addresses death in a way that children can understand, yet it expresses very positive emotions and an outlook for students to consider without complicated philosophies. Written with taste and consideration for the age level, it can be very effective.

36. Death of a Student's Parent

Every school we were ever a part of made particular efforts to give special attention to a student who was returning after the death of a parent. Sometimes, this took the form of a visit to the guidance office or a special talk with the teacher or even the principal. Here, a letter of sympathy is also offered. It is understood that this letter will undoubtedly be seen by the child's remaining parent as well.

Dear Geraldo,

We are glad that you are back with us at Bernard Middle School. We want you to know that we are very sorry about your father. We wish that it had not happened, and our hearts go out to you during this sad time. If you want to talk, about that or anything at all, we are ready to talk with you. Mrs. Schulte, our guidance counselor, has asked me to invite you to come in and visit whenever you feel like it. She is an easy person to talk to, and she enjoys talking with you.

We welcome you back, Geraldo, and we want you to know that we will do everything we can to get you back on track with your classmates and in all your classes. Your teachers will see to that, and if there is anything you don't understand, please ask, and we will see that you get an answer. We are certain that you will be back on course in no time at all.

If there is anything that we in the main office can do for you, we want you to come in anytime. ANYTIME!

This is your school, and we want you to feel an important part of it. Let us help.

Yours truly,

NOTE: The offer, of course, is genuine, and should the student take you up on it, it must immediately be put into practice. This offer of positive support at a time of crisis is something that is often remembered for years afterward.

37. Death of a Teacher, I

Two letters of sympathy on the death of a teacher are presented here. For this first one, we will assume a letter from an administrator who knew the deceased educator both personally and professionally. Here, genuine feeling and positive memories are the hallmark of the writing.

Dear Lee,

There are no words, no verbal expressions that can do justice to the anguish of the heart at times such as these. Bill's passing has touched us all so deeply, and our sympathies and condolences are yours.

As you know, I was acquainted with Bill for almost twenty years, from the time I first came to this school system. Over those years, we became friends—people who genuinely liked and cared for each other, and who shared much of the good times and the bad.

I remember so much about him, but most of all, I recall the selfless way in which he gave of his time, talent, and considerable educational expertise to all who touched him, as well as to the many he touched. His students actively vied for his attention; his colleagues respected him and sought out his company. He was a happy, personable educator who helped me on so many occasions—someone who always had time to talk, time to share, time to be a friend. Your husband was an outstanding teacher, a fine human being, and a good friend.

Please call upon us in the days to come to help you with anything you wish; you will find us grateful to be of service.

Sincerely,

NOTE: A letter of sympathy that recalls positive memories or, as in this case, recounts the personal values that you knew in the individual is always proper. Just make certain that all the memories shared are good ones; keep the memories positive.

38. Death of a Teacher, II

This second letter is much less personal, and would be sent by an administrator who had no personal contact with the teacher other than as principal to teacher, if that applies. Consequently, the letter is more formal.

Dear Mr. Sierra,

As principal of Rock Township High School, it was my privilege to know your wife, Andrea Sierra, as a valued member of the faculty of this school. Indeed, as part of my duties, I had the opportunity to observe her teaching skills and interaction with the students. Watching her teach was an enjoyable activity; it was obviously something she loved, and she did it extremely well.

Our sorrow at her passing goes beyond words. She shall be missed by everyone who knew her—administration, faculty and staff, and student body. Our hearts go out to you and your family at this most difficult of times.

The student council of our school, with the full approval of the administration, has expressed a desire for a memorial to your wife. I will contact you at a later date to provide more details, but I thought you would like to know that the entire school joins me in expressing our personal grief at the loss of a fine person and outstanding teacher.

We extend our deepest sympathy and condolences to you and your family. If there is anything you may need from us, please do not hesitate to ask.

Most sincerely,

NOTE: This letter is almost universal in scope; it could be used in almost any situation. The previous one was far more specific, personal, and warm. Also note that if any memorial is planned, now is not the time to discuss it. A mention of the intention, however, could well add to whatever comfort a letter of this type might afford.

39. Death of an Administrator, I

Without doubt, an administrator touches everyone in the school. Therefore, when an administrator dies, letters of sympathy might come in from all quarters. In this first letter, let's look at something a representative of the faculty might write, and later we'll view a letter from a colleague.

Dear Mrs. Canenas,

On behalf of the entire faculty of Red Elk Middle School, I wish to express to you our very deep sense of personal loss and our profound sympathies on the death of your husband, Dr. Alfred Canenas, who served as the principal of our school.

All of us knew Dr. Canenas on a personal basis; it was impossible not to. Often, we would see him beckoning to us at our classroom doors, only to find he had come to ask after a child who was ill at home or how the paperwork was going on that new house we were purchasing. Somehow, he seemed to know about us, and very obviously, to care about us as individuals.

In his duties as an administrator, we can tell you firsthand that his evaluations were fair and impartial; that he demanded no more perfection from others than he was willing to work for himself; that even if you disagreed with him, never once did you doubt his sincerity, his respect for you and your opinion, and his deep concern for the welfare of the students of this school. He was a tireless worker for the education and personal growth of all about him, and no one could help but be impressed by his intelligence, expertise, and genuine warmth of spirit.

The faculty of Red Elk Middle School have lost a principal and a friend. Please believe that we share in your sorrow. We offer our very deepest sympathies and stand ready to help in any way for which you may care to call upon us.

Sincerely,

NOTE: This letter, from a faculty representative, attempts to reflect the feelings of the group as a whole; recounting some of the fonder personal memories of his interaction with the teaching staff is a good way of conveying those feelings. Also, if there was any major conflict between the two sides, it should definitely not be mentioned in this letter.

40. Death of an Administrator, II

Now, let's take the same person we are calling Dr. Canenas, and assume the same circumstances relative to his passing. This time, however, the letter of sympathy will be written by a fellow administrator. Note the differences.

Dear Sylvia,

There is not an administrator anywhere in this township who is not shocked, grieved, and overcome with sorrow at Alfred's passing. Upon hearing the news, I just felt that I had to write and express to you my very profound sympathies on the loss of your husband, and my colleague and friend.

Sylvia, I could tell you that Alfred Canenas was a great man, but that would be akin to informing you that the tide comes in twice a day—nothing more than a statement of the very obvious. He spent a good part of his life working for the children of this township, engaged in the betterment of education for their benefit, fighting for the best "his kids" could get. He was a man of dedication and honor, and I, for one, am very glad that I was given the opportunity of working with him and calling him my friend.

Do you remember that vacation the four of us took together? As we stood overlooking the Grand Canyon, do you recall that Al looked back at us and whispered, "How would you like to supervise playground patrol in THAT?" That was so much like Al, school constantly on his mind, the kids he loved a part of what he lived and breathed, and always on the lookout for bigger and better ways to improve their education and that of the children of the entire community.

You know that Mary and I will be with you throughout this time, but I want you to know that our prayers are with you now and will continue to be. We won't offer you help, Sylvia; we'll just be there.

His love and his care will live on; we'll all see to that.

With our love,

NOTE: Of course, the difference here lies in what was remembered and the much warmer and very familiar tone of the letter—not only from a colleague but from a friend as well.

Please understand something about the use of first names in a letter of this sort. You use the first name of a spouse only if you would do so on a social basis. In the letter above, it is natural, since they were obviously friends before Dr. Canenas's death. In the letter from the faculty representative, however, calling her "Sylvia," when it seems obvious that the only contact they might have had would have been a faculty dinner, would sound condescending and paternalistic at the very least. A formal address, especially in letters of sympathy, will never go amiss. If the addressed individual later asks you to call him or her by a first name, that is fine. Once the individual gets the impression that you are being condescending, however, even if it is not true, it will be a long, long time being remedied.

41. Death of a Community Leader

There are individuals in every community who, while not directly connected with the schools, nonetheless have a decided influence on and in the schools—a mayor, police chief, head of emergency services, local judge, and the like. A mayor who supports education can do a great deal of good for the school; we all know this to be true. Therefore, when a community leader of this stature dies, it is fitting and proper for the school to respond. Here is an example of such a response.

Dear Mr. Gennois,

All of us at Rock Township High School were so deeply saddened to hear of Mayor Gennois's passing. While there is no one in this township who is not affected by your wife's death, we at the high school feel a particular sense of loss, since we have come to know her not only as mayor of this township but as a friend of education and a frequent and very welcome visitor at our school.

We realize how difficult it is to find comfort and consolation at a time such as this, but if those qualities may be found at all, they are part and parcel of the legacy of honor left behind by Mayor Jennifer Gennois. We at Rock Township High School are well aware of the time she gave so freely as both speaker and guest lecturer in certain social studies classes and symposiums, providing invaluable insights into our democratic system of government. Moreover, there was not a single graduation in the five years of her office when she was not an invaluable part of our graduation ceremonies, something that was anticipated with enthusiasm by each graduating class. She gave so freely of her time and personal effort.

We are aware, too, of her efforts with the township committee on behalf of funding for our school. Her work in that regard may not be widely known, but those of us who do know are so very appreciative of her tireless work for the children of Rock Township.

More than all of these examples, Mayor Gennois was also a friend who often dropped by the school "just to chat," frequently ending her stay with such phrases as, "If I can do anything for the kids, make sure you let me know."

In short, Jennifer Gennois was a woman of stature, a dedicated and forceful public servant, and a true friend of education and the children of our community.

You have our deepest sympathy, and we join you in mourning the passing of a truly outstanding individual.

With deep sorrow,

NOTE: Let's speak a moment about honesty in the letter of sympathy. A letter such as this one will be effective if—and only if—the writer can be sincere in what he or she states. We will assume that in this case, the mayor truly was a "friend" to the schools. We all know that this is not always the case, and to say so when it obviously is not true would be to denigrate yourself as well as the reputation of your school. It has been said that you can find some good in anyone if you look hard enough. Let that be your key. Say only those things that you can really mean.

42. Death of a School Board Official

The school board or board of education in a town can be the source of much contention. Indeed, we read almost weekly of conflict between a local board and some local civic group, parents' group, or teachers' organization. Moreover, even administrators can become involved in arguments over curriculum, funding, personnel, hiring practices, and more. The field of battle, quite often, is the board offices, especially during the "open" part of the meeting. The battle can get quite heated.

In this example, we will assume the death of a member of the school board. Here, the letter of sympathy attempts to express condolences, even though there may have been disagreements in the past.

Dear Mrs. Kwan,

It was just today that we learned of the passing of your husband, Lee Kwan, who currently served as the president of the Rock Township Board of Education. We extend to you and your family our deepest sympathies at this most trying time.

Since Mr. Kwan served on the board for well over ten years, we at Rock Township High School got to know him, not only in the offices of the board, but as a visitor to our school as well. He took his position very seriously, and was always willing to work unceasingly for what he believed to be the ultimate welfare of the children of this township. All who knew him found this an admirable and honorable trait in him. One could only admire his drive and vigor.

While being on a board of education virtually assures one that he or she will meet with opposition, Mr. Kwan was never one to allow his feelings to be swayed once he had come to what he believed was an equitable solution—a solution that bettered the system for the sake of the children of the township. Indeed, while it was, perhaps, inevitable that we sat on the opposite side of some issues, never once was there a doubt in my mind about your husband's sincerity, strength of resolve, or commitment to the good of our children, whom we are all sworn to serve.

We shall miss him. Our sympathies go out to you and your family, and the entire educational system of our school stands ready to help in any way you should require.

May we all find comfort in the memory of one who truly sought the good of our children. That is an epitaph worthy of a worthy man.

Sincerely,

NOTE: Did you understand that the principal writing this letter and the deceased school board member did not get along? Nowhere were their differences stated, except as a base to express regard for the individual's strength of belief. A sympathy letter is no place for argument, justifying your positions, or attacking the stance of the deceased, no matter how much you may have contended in real life.

Section
Three

LETTERS THAT EFFECTIVELY DEAL WITH STUDENT BEHAVIOR

*E*very educator understands that a student's behavior plays a very large and significant part in that student's education. Of course, every student misbehaves at one time or another, but that misbehavior is usually minor, is easily handled by the teacher at the time of the infraction, and if it is repeated, is repeated infrequently. Plainly put, a student is not likely to destroy his or her education because he or she talked during class or passed a note to a classmate once in a while.

Unfortunately, as we can all attest, not all student behavior is that innocent; some student behaviors need attention right now. If left unchallenged and ignored, some behaviors will harm not only the offending student but his or her classmates and the progress of their education as well.

EXAMINING STUDENT BEHAVIOR AND THE HOME-SCHOOL CONNECTION

Certainly, everyone realizes the need to "do something" about the behavior of the offending student. The difficulty often arises when we begin to consider just what to do. Such punishments as detentions and the like may serve an immediate purpose and stop the unwanted behavior for the time being, but they do little to alter the child inside and alleviate the unwanted behavior through a change of heart or attitude on the part of the offender. Punishments alone simply do not work.

While exactly what to do will undoubtedly be debated long into the future, one thing does get results. The behavior of a student changes significantly when a solid home-school connection is established and maintained. When the home and the school are both informed as to what is happening with the child in the school environment, and when both are working together to see to the child's education, the child finds the two greatest forces for change in his or her young life—the home and the school—working together. In that situation, behavior *does* improve and everybody wins—especially the student, whether he or she appreciates it or not.

This home-school connection can be established, in most cases, through good home-school communications, and most often that means letters from the school. If there is a secret to establishing that connection, it is this: *Don't wait until the child misbehaves to contact the home!* If the only time parents receive a note or letter from school is when the school is telling them what a naughty child they have raised, what do you think will happen to subsequent letters from school? On the other hand, if they have received notes telling of the positive behaviors or projects or activities of their son or daughter, then if a problem does arise, they are far better disposed to cooperate with the school in dealing effectively with the child's behavior.

Of course, this tactic is not going to work in all situations nor with all parents, but it is a start, and it has worked with extremely positive results time after time. Try sending home some notes on "good" behavior, and see if the home is not there and supportive when the "other kind" of behavior needs attention. There is no need to "divide and conquer" when you can "connect and win"!

In the pages that follow, you will find some examples of letters that compliment a student's good or even outstanding behavior. In the other letters that deal with behavior, from the improper all the way to the criminal, you will still detect the tone of a desire for change within the student for the betterment of that student as well as the others involved. Bridges, so to speak, are never burned, and there is always a way left open to deal in a positive manner with the offense and bring the offending student back to the right path for his or her sake.

Let's see how this works in practice.

MODEL LETTERS THAT DEAL WITH STUDENT BEHAVIOR

43. Teacher Note on Good Student Behavior

This is an example of the type of note that a teacher or an administrator would send home as part of the "good news" from school, a very effective program. See how it helps to positively reinforce the "home-school connection."

Dear Mr. and Mrs. Palandrina,

I just wanted to tell you about the wonderful thing Teddy did in class today. Another child tripped and dropped her books and drawing supplies so that they scattered all over the room. While some of the other children stood by and laughed at the unfortunate child's accident, Teddy went out of his way to pick up all the spilled items and return them, even enlisting the aid of some of the other children who were just standing by.

I will let Teddy explain the exact details to you, but I want you to know how proud I am of him and how happy I am to have him in my class this year. I'm certain we will all have a great year, and if I may be of any service, please feel free to contact me at any time.

Give Teddy a great big hug for me!

Health and Happiness,

NOTE: Positive and happy in tone and intent, this is the type of letter that many parents will keep, post on the refrigerator, and share with relatives. For building confidence in the school, it cannot be beaten.

44. Teacher Note on Poor Student Behavior, I

This first letter on poor student behavior assumes that you have already built a good home-school connection. The attempt here is to remedy a situation before it becomes troublesome.

Dear Mrs. Hwang,

I have contacted you several times before about some of the very good work that Jenny has done in class; that is why I feel confident about informing you of something that has the potential of becoming troublesome. Let me quickly add that with the ability to work together that has been the hallmark of our relationship, it need hardly turn into a problem at all.

You see, Jenny has always been prompt with her homework, so when she missed an occasional assignment, I did not count it as significant, since she always made up what she had missed. About two weeks ago, I noticed that she had not made up one of her missed assignments, and when I spoke to her, she seemed rather uncommunicative, giving neither an explanation nor an offer to do it. Later in that same week, another assignment was missing, again without an explanation or attempt at making it up. Last week, three assignments were not turned in, and when this morning came and there was yet another missed assignment, I knew it was time to contact the expert—you.

If something is wrong, I assure you that I will understand and do everything I can to help Jenny back to the happy, productive student I have known her to be and would like to see again. If it is merely that she is "being frisky," as my mother used to say of me, then I know that proper urging from her home and from the school will see her back on the road to good, solid learning in no time at all.

Please let me know how we can work together to get Jenny's homework back to its normal level of excellence. You may write me or, if you wish, contact me at the school, and I will most certainly call you, so we can talk it over.

I look forward to hearing from you on this. Jenny is one of my favorite students, and I know that, working together, we can get this problem behind us as quickly as possible.

Best wishes,

NOTE: Here, the problem was minor and home-school cooperation was expected to solve it. Of course, not all problems are so simple, nor is cooperation from the home automatically forthcoming.

45. Teacher Note on Poor Student Behavior, II

Let's look now at another note from the teacher about a more serious behavioral difficulty, again enlisting home cooperation in the problem's solution. Note a difference in tone and in approach in this letter; the offense is considerably more serious, as is any incident involving violence from one student toward another.

Dear Mr. and Mrs. Tallfeather,

I've written to you in the past on a number of occasions, both those in which Adam excelled and those in which improvement was needed. Unfortunately, this is one of those latter instances.

This afternoon, I observed Adam push and shove another student and then knock the books and papers from her desk so that they spilled all over the floor. I happened to be in a position where I witnessed the entire incident, and there is no question as to what took place. I immediately questioned Adam as to what happened, and all I got was a confused story punctuated with phrases such as "She deserved it!" and "She's a geek!" Upon dealing with the girl involved, I ascertained that Adam wanted to take her notebook to copy something from it, she refused, and he retaliated. When I confronted Adam with this, he did not deny the story.

That's why I am turning to you. Certainly, I must deal with what happens in my class, and I do not think that a single incident such as this warrants taking it before the school administration, but something must be done to convince Adam of the seriousness of physically striking out at someone else's person or property.

I have reported this incident to the vice-principal, and I have assigned Adam detention with me on Thursday. At that time, I intend to speak seriously with him about this incident in the hope that any behavior of this type will end right here. I am informing you because I know that you will wish to speak to Adam about this incident as well. If Adam can be made to understand that what he did was wrong and that such behavior is not acceptable anywhere in society, neither at home nor in school, then I think we stand a good chance that Adam will not be repeating that behavior in the future.

Working together, we can make a meaningful difference in Adam's life. Thank you so much for the wonderful and heartfelt cooperation I have come to expect from you.

Please contact me if I may be of any further service.

Very truly yours,

NOTE: Here, the cooperation from home is not just requested, it is expected. Moreover, the incident is handled much more sternly than in the first note, and the parents are informed that this is a serious matter. The tone of the letter remains one of cooperation and working it out together, but it is much more serious than the first, and the reader cannot help but recognize that. Also, you may want to involve administration, since this incident involved violence. That would be your call.

46. Letter on Serious Classroom Infraction, I

When dealing with the really serious classroom behavioral problem, it is best to tell what happened exactly as you saw it and in an objective manner. It is also well to state what actions you have previously taken in the matter and their effectiveness or lack of effectiveness. Note that the word "cheating" is never used anywhere in this letter, although the behavioral infraction is clear to all. Note also how this first letter ends on a hopeful note, while also letting it be known that disciplinary actions will escalate if nothing is changed in the future.

Dear Mr. and Mrs. Haranian,

Today, the students in my class took a test covering the unit of work we have been doing over the past several weeks. After the test papers were passed out and students had gotten down to business, I began the process of monitoring the exam, something I have done since I started teaching. I began to walk around the room, observing the students as they wrote answers on their papers.

It was then that my attention was drawn to Cassie. Usually, she sits erect at her desk and appears relaxed and comfortable, but today she was hunched over, reading her paper and writing as her left arm covered the process while she kept glancing right and left. As I approached her desk, she turned and saw me, and she began to make rather hurried movements. As I came abreast of her desk, she turned once more, and a small stack of index cards fell to the floor.

I bent over and picked them up. As I did so, I glanced at the topmost card and there read the material that would answer one of the questions on the test. A quick study of the other cards revealed that each one contained information we had studied, on which this test was based. I chose to do nothing to embarrass Cassie, so I merely took the cards to my desk and allowed the test to continue.

At the end of the class, I asked Cassie to remain, and I corrected her test in her presence. The first three questions were answered perfectly, while all subsequent questions were completely inaccurate. I then asked about the index cards that had dropped from her desk, and at first she said she was just holding them for a friend and then claimed that they were hers, but she didn't know that she couldn't use notes during the test.

As you are aware, since we have involved you in all past actions, this is not the first time that Cassie has been involved in something of this nature. Twice before, she has attempted to use information during a test or quiz that was not allowed; twice before she has either claimed that the illicit material wasn't hers or that she didn't know she wasn't supposed to have it or—in one case—that a boy put it on her desk before the test.

I think you will agree that it is time to put an end to this once and for all. It is Cassie who suffers the most from cultivating a habit that will only lead to more and more trouble for her, both in school and in life. I am aware of how deeply you care for your daughter, and I know that we both wish to work together for Cassie's ultimate good.

I have scheduled a conference for Tuesday morning at 10:30 A.M. I shall be there, along with Mrs. Clark, the guidance counselor; the vice-principal, Ms. Loganu; you; and Cassie. If you cannot make it, please contact me at once and we will set up another conference at the very earliest opportunity. We need you, and we shall most certainly accommodate your schedule.

We want what's best for Cassie, and we know that you want the same thing. Working together, I have no doubt that we can remedy this situation—that we can help Cassie to leave these unfortunate incidents behind her and become the kind of student all of us know she is capable of being.

I look forward to working together with you for Cassie's ultimate good.

Yours sincerely,

NOTE: The tone of this is stronger; past actions are detailed; definite steps have been formulated to help deal with the problem. Not many people would agree that this letter could be misunderstood.

47. Letter on Serious Classroom Infraction, II

Now, let's look at a situation where the problem involves a student's acting out. Here, it is not a character violation, such as cheating or lying, but an outright behavior that is considered not only undesirable but hostile and dangerous.

Dear Mrs. Enseoux,

I had a most unpleasant task to perform this afternoon. I had to take a child to the nurse after he had struck his head on a desk when he fell. The boy was bleeding, frightened, and in a highly upset emotional state. I tell you of this incident because the boy would not have fallen and injured himself if your son, Alan, had not stuck the window pole into the aisle and tripped the boy.

I was across the room at the time, but I was turned toward the place where the incident occurred, and I saw Alan take the window pole from its place on the wall, stick the pole between the feet of the boy walking down the row, and then pull back on the pole—causing the other boy to trip, fall forward, and strike his head sharply on the edge of a student desk. When I went to assist the fallen boy, I observed Alan in one corner of the room, pointing to his fallen classmate and laughing heartily.

After the injured child had been cared for, I got coverage for my class, took Alan to the main office, and confronted him with what I had personally observed. Alan denied doing it at first, but after I confirmed that I had been watching directly, he shrugged his shoulders. I asked why he had done it, and his exact answer, which I recorded at the time, was, " 'Cause it was so much fun!"

As you are aware, we are very concerned about Alan, as we are certain you are. We were serious when we offered help on all those previous occasions, and we are serious in offering help now. Such behavior cannot and will not continue, as it poses a distinct threat both to Alan and to his classmates.

For Alan's sake, we must meet, and a conference will be arranged within the next few days. You will receive a separate notice that Alan has been suspended at least until the time of our meeting, which he must attend as well.

The time when we must address Alan's behavior has come, and I am hopeful, for Alan's sake, that he can get the help he needs to remedy this very grave situation.

Sincerely,

NOTE: Alan, the student in this incident, is headed for serious trouble, if he is not there already. This letter is not in place of discipline, but in addition to the suspension he has already received. Nor is this letter a plea for help from the home, it is virtually a demand for assistance. Indeed, when it gets to the point described here, something has to be done fast, and this letter informs the home of that in no uncertain terms.

48. Letter on Serious School Infraction, I

The previous letters were on infractions in the classroom. Now, let's look at a letter that might be sent home for something that happened under the jurisdiction of the school rather than the teacher. This first one is on something very common to almost every school.

Dear Mrs. Remirez,

Sometimes we do things without thinking. We don't mean for the results to turn out badly, but many times they do anyhow, in spite of our wishes. Sometimes, a moment of thoughtless action can result in difficulty with which we then must live. Such, I believe, is the case involving your son, Marco.

Earlier this afternoon, another boy was brought to the nurse's office with a bloody nose. The situation was handled without great difficulty, and the boy returned to class. There did not seem to be any complication, although, as in all injuries, we advised the boy's parents to take him to their own physician, if they so chose.

The boy had received the injury as he stood by his locker during the change of class. Another student came running down the hall, rounded the corner, and ran into the boy, sending him directly into the locker door, causing the injury. The incident was observed by two teachers who administered first aid and took the runner to the main office. Do I have to tell you that the runner was Marco?

Now, even a quick look at your son's school records is enough to see that Marco does well academically and has the trust and approval of his teachers. We understand, as well, that this is a middle school, and these things happen. There is, however, a rule about running in the halls (for just such occasions as this, I may add) which is strictly enforced, and about which Marco had been well informed. To his credit, Marco admitted to the infraction, seemed genuinely sorry, and inquired many times about the condition of the injured boy.

I am assigning Marco to central detention for a period of one week, beginning Monday. During that time, he will learn about safety and running in the halls. If you, at home, enforce that same message, then this incident will be over quickly, he will have learned a valuable lesson, and he won't be running in the halls of the school again.

Very truly yours,

NOTE: Incidents like this happen, particularly at the middle school level. Compare this letter, however, to one that states, "Your son ran in the halls, causing injury to another student. Five days detention." Which letter better builds that home-school connection?

49. Letter on Serious School Infraction, II

This letter deals with an infraction by a "difficult" student. Previous attempts to help are detailed, and the reporting is objective, in the event that this letter might be used in a later legal action.

Dear Mr. and Mrs. Weltner,

This afternoon, I dealt with a situation that ended in my watching a young man being taken away by ambulance to the emergency room. Believe me, it was not a pleasant experience.

The young man being taken away turned out to have a broken nose, received from your son, Gregory Weltner. There were a number of witnesses to this altercation which took place in the food line of the cafeteria. A teacher on duty there also heard and saw the last few seconds before the conflict. Later, Greg freely admitted the incident, confirming what I had received from the teacher and student witnesses.

On the line, Greg had told the other boy to give him (Greg) two dollars. The boy responded that he didn't have that much to give. Greg responded, "Give me the _____ money!" That was when the teacher's attention was drawn to him. The other boy said, "But, I don't . . ." At this point, Gregory punched the boy in the face, knocking him to the floor, and then jumped on the prone student and began kicking him. He stopped only when restrained by the teacher and several other students. Greg was not injured other than an abrasion on the knuckles of his right hand, which was treated by our school nurse. The other boy was treated for a broken nose at the emergency room of St. Anselm's Hospital and released to his parents.

The boy's parents have been advised of what happened, and it is now up to them as to what legal remedies, if any, they intend to pursue.

As you know, we have spent a great deal of time and effort trying to deal with the needs of your son Gregory. We have held conferences where all of us have been present, we have tried the alternate school program, we have obtained special counseling for Greg. We have even tried highly specialized one-on-one programs—all, it seems, to no avail. This recent incident is merely the culmination of a number of more minor but equally upsetting incidents involving his negative reaction to school and his classmates. Indeed, I have documented much that I wanted to share with you, and would have written you within days, had this latest incident not occasioned this letter.

Under separate cover, you will receive Gregory's letter of suspension. Before that suspension expires and Greg returns to school, I must see all of you in my office. Greg's behavior is rapidly approaching the point where, for the good of the students and the school, we must seek more serious solutions, perhaps in the courts, perhaps before the board of education.

In any event, we will formalize a solution to this problem. Please call the main office when you receive this and make an appointment within the time frame of the suspension when we may all meet. We are eager to find an answer.

Yours sincerely,

NOTE: It is important, especially when considering serious consequences, that you show in your letter a desire to help the student overcome the problem. Make certain you detail the actions taken previously. Other than that, a strong disciplinary situation needs a strong response, both in person and in letter form.

50. Letter Complimenting Outstanding Behavior

As a respite from letters steeped in trouble and difficulty, here's a letter that would be a joy to write. This letter to parents tells when a child has done something outstanding for the school or classmates—something above and beyond what is expected. Here's a student who did something right—very right!

Dear Mr. and Mrs. Kaserian,

I cherish the time I spend writing a letter like this one. So much of the time, I am required to compose letters dealing with the negative—fights, violations of rules, violent behavior—that any opportunity I have to write concerning truly outstanding behavior on the part of a truly outstanding student makes my day brighter, indeed. I speak, of course, of your daughter Doris.

This morning, as the children were getting off the school buses, two smaller children were "fooling around." The teacher on duty told them to get inside the building, but—still playful—they darted around the end of one school bus, as if to run across the length of the driveway, unaware that another school bus had just arrived and was pulling up at an angle that neither child could see and toward which they were headed. The teacher who saw this at a distance was yelling for them to stop, but they kept on going, into what surely might have been a very serious accident.

Just at that moment, Doris became aware of the danger, sized up the incident, and acted swiftly and decisively. Without hesitating, she ran to the two students, grabbed one by the collar and the other by his arm, and pulled them back, just as the school bus passed by—missing them by what seemed like inches.

The two children have been reprimanded for their recklessness, their parents have been notified, and I had the opportunity to congratulate Doris on her bravery and presence of mind. I also told her that I would be letting you know of her good deed, her outstanding behavior. To her credit, Doris told me that she did not think that what she had done was "so great." The two boys' parents and I think otherwise.

Doris has our admiration and is to be congratulated on her selfless act.

Yours truly,

NOTE: Never let the opportunity of writing a positive letter home go by. Not only does it go so very far toward building the home-school relationship; it helps to reinforce good behavior, and that's a real plus.

51. Letter on Infraction Involving Police, I

Most of the disciplinary infractions about which you will write will involve only the people within the school. Occasionally, the offense becomes so bad that outside authority must be brought in. Here are some examples of letters concerning these incidents. The first involves a student without a background of previous offenses.

Dear Mr. and Mrs. Mosandi,

This afternoon, one of our female teachers on routine hall duty entered the girls' room, as she is required to do by school policy in the performance of her assigned duty. There, she found your daughter Makeish and another student. The teacher observed a cloud of smoke surrounding the two girls and personally observed Makeish blowing smoke from her mouth and holding the cigarette. Again, according to school policy, the two girls were brought to the main office, along with the cigarette.

Upon examination and full testing by a qualified expert, the cigarette was found to be marijuana. At first, Makeish told me that she was "only holding it" for the other girl, but upon being faced with the eyewitness account of the teacher, Makeish admitted that she and the other student were "sharing" it.

As you may be aware, since it has been highly publicized, Rock Township School System has adopted a "zero tolerance" attitude toward all illicit drugs. Part of that policy, as stated in School Policy 765.32, states that "possession or use of any controlled dangerous substance shall immediately be reported to Township Police."

The police have been notified, and you will be hearing from them shortly pursuant to this matter. Under separate cover, you will receive notice of Makeish's suspension from Rock Township High School for a period of five days, effective immediately.

Makeish's record is clear up until this instance. Her academic record shows well-defined progress and a firm academic footing. Several of her teachers expressed surprise at this infraction and characterized her behavior as highly acceptable in class. It appears that this is a first offense.

I would appreciate it, therefore, if you could call my office as soon as possible. I would like to get together with you and Makeish. If this is the type of error that can be handled and not repeated, you will find that the school is ready to offer all the aid and assistance it is capable of providing. If this is a single error of judgment, let us all work together to see that it becomes something from which Makeish may learn.

I'll look forward to hearing from you very soon.

Sincerely yours,

NOTE: The matter-of-fact statement of what happened, and even the reference to school policy under which the reporting teacher and the administration acted, is most important here. Something like this precludes a charge of favoritism or vindictive action. The offer to help at the end would be the school's decision, but it is seemingly justifiable with this student's apparent error in judgment rather than criminal intent.

52. Letter on Infraction Involving Police, II

This next letter involves a student with a long background of antisocial behavior. Note the references to what has been tried in the past, and note the much stronger tone of this letter over the last one.

Dear Mr. and Mrs. Johnson,

Earlier this afternoon, Rock Township Police were notified that your son, Paul, was found selling certain substances to two other students here at Rock Township High School. The incident was discovered and reported by two teachers who had gone to the school storage area to look for some textbooks. They observed Paul take money from the other two students and pass them glassine envelopes containing a white, powdery substance that, upon later police analysis, turned out to be cocaine.

The two purchasers were brought to the main office, but Paul turned and ran. We could not locate him anywhere in the school and could only assume that he had left school property.

I know that you are aware of our township's "zero tolerance" policy on drug possession and use in the schools. Indeed, I remember going over that policy with you and Paul on the three previous times that this has happened. You will understand, then, why the police were notified at once. They came to the school, took the cocaine with them, and, as this is written, are searching for Paul.

The last time that this occurred, I was specific in detailing our policy and exactly what would happen should this take place a fourth time. Under separate cover, therefore, I am sending you a notice of Paul's suspension from school until such time as a hearing may be arranged with the superintendent of schools and her staff. Again under separate cover, you will receive notice of times, dates, and your full legal rights regarding this hearing, such as your right to legal council, access to records, and the like.

I hope you understand that I take this action with sincere regret. In the past, the school has worked vigorously in Paul's behalf, offering counseling, alternate school programs, and specialized programs for his improvement. Indeed, you were a part of all these efforts, and we have involved you from the very onset of Paul's difficulties. It seems that this has been to no avail.

Consequently, it is hoped that the severity of this final action of the school will impress upon Paul the necessity of changing his behavior or being removed from our school system.

Let us hope for the best for Paul and for all concerned.

Yours sincerely,

NOTE: Here's a case where you've done all that the school can offer. In this letter, the "hard line" is evident. Read it again, and see if you could possibly misinterpret the school's statement that it will not tolerate the behavior anymore.

53. Letter on Behavior Warning of Serious Consequences, I

Although several of the previous letters, including the last one, warn of consequences should the behavior continue, let's look at an incident on an elementary level and then on a middle school level, where the intent of the school is to keep something that has started badly from becoming worse and possibly leading to the necessity of writing a letter like the one above.

Dear Dr. and Mrs. Dinkins,

Your daughter Danielle, a fifth-grade student at Kellog Elementary, is being assigned three nights of office detention beginning Monday, October 4. The reason for the detention is the subject of this letter.

This afternoon, the gym teacher noticed a group of students gathered together at one corner of the athletic field. When she approached these students, several of them ran, but Danielle and a few others stood there when confronted by the teacher. Danielle had one arm behind her back, when one other student said, "It's not mine; Danielle brought it in; it's hers. "

When asked what was behind her back, Danielle surrendered it without any further hesitation. The item was a small bottle of liquor, like those used on airlines. Its label indicated that it contained gin, and the school nurse later confirmed that the liquid was certainly high in alcohol content. The bottle was approximately one-half full when found.

None of the children involved showed any signs of use of the substance, and Danielle admitted taking it from your cabinet at home. She said that she just wanted to "show it around" and had not taken any of it.

Since our policy on all drugs—and that includes alcohol—is widely known and reinforced with our students periodically, Danielle knew that it was not acceptable to bring this item to school. I have advised her that with our policy of "zero tolerance," any event such as this is taken most seriously. Now, at this first offense, the detention, with some private counseling, is all that is required, but you should know, as does Danielle, that a repetition of this act will result in sterner measures.

Let us assume, however, that this is but a childish mistake that, now remedied, will not be happening again. If this is the case, then Danielle will have learned a valuable lesson, and it will all be forgotten very soon. If you will reinforce what we have insisted upon in school, we are sure that will be an end to the situation.

Yours most sincerely,

NOTE: Undoubtedly, if a pattern of negative behavior can be stopped before it begins, everyone benefits, including the child. Indeed, it has been noted that the worst thing that could possibly happen to a child who misbehaves is that he or she get away with it. The warning is clear, and it is apparent that the school will work toward what is best for the child.

54. Letter on Behavior Warning of Serious Consequences, II

Now, let's go to the middle school and make the misbehavior somewhat more serious. This is an example of a "no nonsense" approach that definitely goes along with the "zero tolerance" point of view.

Dear Mr. and Mrs. Nonenburg,

This is not an easy letter to write, but neither was it easy for me to wait in the emergency room of Parker Memorial while one of our students was tended to by a team of emergency personnel. The student was being treated for a severe laceration of the scalp and a possible fractured skull, both suffered when your son Eric tripped the student in the hall, jumped on him, and proceeded to grab him by the hair and bang his head into the hard terrazzo floor repeatedly—until two teachers could finally pull him off the other boy. By that time, Eric had managed to inflict the injuries detailed here.

The parents of the other child have been informed, and whatever legal recourse they may wish to take is, of course, up to them. Here at the school, however, we have a very clear course of action.

You will receive a formal letter of Eric's suspension from school. That letter will also request a conference involving Eric and you before his return to school. I wish to make extremely clear that the school has no tolerance whatsoever for this type of behavior, and we will not have it in our schools. It matters little who said what or did what; we will not have disputes settled in the blood of our students. This is an incident that will not happen again.

Now, we remove Eric from the school for a period of time in order that this message may be impressed upon him. Before his return, I will make it clear to him, as I hope I am making it clear to you, that a repetition of today's incident will result in more concentrated efforts by the school, which may include contacting the police or even beginning procedures for Eric's permanent removal from school.

We are always hopeful that every situation may be remedied happily. In fact, we want that to be the case. We are, however, just as ready to protect the majority of our students in any manner that is necessary.

Please feel free to contact me at any time.

Sincerely,

NOTE: One caution should be made clear about a "warning" letter: Never imply anything you can't do. In this letter, the administrator could, given the incident described, request the start of expulsion procedures or call the police. Were this an elementary school, and had the offending student just pushed the other boy, there is no way that expulsion could even be considered. Therefore, make certain you can deliver before you promise.

55. Letter of Suspension, I

Here starts a series of four letters of suspension, informing parents that a child has been suspended from school. This first letter is a short and very formal one—one that you might almost consider a form letter.

Dear Mr. and Mrs. Heselakis,

This is to inform you that your child, Helena Heselakis, has been suspended from Fairlawn Middle School for three days, February 14, 15, 18, _____. She may return to school on Tuesday, February 19, _____.

Your child was suspended for violation of the board of education rule against smoking on school property, which carries with it an automatic three-day suspension. Before your child returns to school, we require that you contact this office and attend a conference concerning this incident. Please call the Guidance office at 555-1234 to arrange for this meeting.

Please feel free to contact us should you have any questions.

Yours sincerely,

NOTE: You can see how cut and dried this letter is, and that may suit your purposes, if all you wish is notification. Certainly, it details all that is required of such a notification, and might even be turned into a form in which the only changes made each time are the names and the specific violation.

56. Letter of Suspension, II

Let's subtitle this one "Letter of Suspension With Concern." While still fairly formal, this letter more personally expresses a desire to help the offender change and an expectation of cooperation from the home.

Dear Mr. Montoya,

This is to inform you that your daughter, Marissa Montoya, a sophomore at Monterey High School, has been suspended for a period of three days, effective immediately, and may return to school on Wednesday, April 12, _____. This action was taken because Marissa violated board of education rules by throwing food in the cafeteria and injuring another student.

We are most anxious that an incident of this nature does not occur again. We are deeply concerned about Marissa's future, as we are certain that you are. We are, therefore, eager to cooperate with you for Marissa's ultimate benefit.

Consequently, we invite you to contact the school and arrange for a conference with Marissa's guidance counselor and me. We do not intend to dwell on the past, but we hope to formulate, with your aid and cooperation, a program of positive growth and improvement in Marissa's school career.

Please contact us soon, and let us see if we can work together for the good of your daughter.

Very truly yours,

NOTE: This letter, while informing the home of a suspension, is still quite conciliatory in tone, concerned about the child involved, seeking parental cooperation in the most positive of ways. This letter might be used with a first offender, in order to make certain that it remains a one-time-only infraction.

57. Letter of Suspension, III

Now, we'll look at a letter of suspension for someone who has a history of misbehavior, as well as previous suspensions. Note the change in tone, and also note that the request for a parental conference is made in the mode of "an offer you can't refuse."

Dear Mr. and Mrs. Hickman,

Please be informed that, while we regret the action, your son Daryl is suspended from attending this school for a period of two weeks, in accordance with the policy of Landsend Township School Board. This suspension is for Daryl's selling of controlled dangerous substances, to wit, marijuana and cocaine, to fellow students here on school property.

I know that you are aware of our school board's "zero tolerance" program concerning drugs in the school. I know that you are also aware that this is not the first time we have had difficulty concerning your son and drugs. Three times over the last two years, Daryl has been referred to this office for what turned out to be drug use. At those times, we contacted you, asked for conferences, involved guidance, provided for special guidance and programs for Daryl, and tried to keep a close home-school contact for Daryl's ultimate good.

Now, we have this most recent incident. This is most serious of all, since we must consider whether it is in the best interest of the school to remove Daryl on a permanent basis.

On Thursday morning, October 17, _____, at 10:00 A.M., a meeting will be held in my office. I will be attending this meeting, as will the assistant superintendent of schools, the board's attorney, and a board representative. You are most earnestly asked to attend, as a disposition on your son's case will be made at that time. You have many legal rights in this regard, and a statement of those legal rights has been enclosed for your information.

I look forward to seeing you on October 17. In the meantime, should you have any questions, please do not hesitate to call.

Most sincerely,

NOTE: This letter lays it out in no uncertain terms. It also all but commands the parent to attend that meeting. If such meetings involve legalities within your system, make certain the parent is well aware of any and all legal rights that apply to the situation.

58. Letter of Suspension, IV

In this fourth letter of suspension—the strongest yet—a major disciplinary infraction has occurred with a student who has been a chronic behavioral problem. Here, there is no request for cooperation, for circumstances have gone beyond that point.

Dear Mr. and Mrs. Sagassi,

Please be informed by this letter that your son Frank, a junior in Rock Township High School, is herewith suspended from attending school for an indefinite period of time. His presence on school property during this time shall be considered trespassing, and police authorities will be contacted to facilitate his removal. He will not be allowed to return to this building until such time as a determination on how to proceed with Frank's case is made by the Rock Township Board of Education.

This morning, Frank was caught by a teacher as he was going through her handbag, which was in a drawer in her desk. When she returned from having spoken to another student in the hallway, Frank had removed a purse from the handbag and had the money in his hand. When the teacher questioned him, Frank took a wooden yardstick from the blackboard ledge and proceeded to break it over the teacher, striking her in the head and face. He then left the room, shouting that if the teacher said anything, he would hurt her even worse.

Of course, the incident was reported, and the teacher is currently being treated for head and facial injuries as well as shock at Patterson/Overlook Medical Center.

Whether that teacher presses individual charges of assault is her decision. It will be up to the board to decide on legal pursuit of this matter, following a hearing involving personnel from the board. You will be advised under separate cover of the time, place, and your legal rights involving this matter.

This is a most serious incident, and it seems to be the culmination of a number of incidents involving violence since Frank entered our school. We have told him and you in the past that this behavior will not be tolerated, and we are now prepared to act upon that.

Please impress upon Frank the utter seriousness of this matter.

Yours most sincerely,

NOTE: This is an extremely serious infraction, and one worthy of the kind of stern action that is outlined here. The letter advising of legal rights, mentioned as being sent under separate cover, is given on p. 65.

59. Letter of Suspension to Alternate School Program

The alternate school program seems an ideal solution to suspension of first offenders or those who exhibit genuine remorse for what they have done. Here is a letter to parents of such a suspension, and the particulars related to it. This program is also frequently referred to as in-school suspension.

Dear Ms. Whitedeer,

Please be advised that your daughter Shana has been suspended for a period of three days, from November 15 through November 17, _____. During that time she will be placed in our school's alternate school program. This action was taken because Shana was found smoking in the second floor girls' lavatory.

Shana has been suspended from the regular school program and will report to the alternate school program room at 8:05 A.M. each morning of those three days with her homework, necessary books, and materials. She will remain in the A.S.P. room for the full day. Luncheon orders will be taken and delivered from the cafeteria, or she may bring her own food and drink from home. These days will be used for intensive work. Students are expected to cooperate fully with the teacher. If this fails to occur, the time in the program may be extended or the student may be suspended out of school.

Your daughter will be under the supervision of Mrs. K. Kelley, who has had experience with alternate school programs for many years and will do all in her power to make Shana's stay a profitable experience.

You are strongly urged to discuss this with Shana in order that this action may be for her ultimate benefit.

If you have any questions, please feel free to contact me at 555-2345.

Yours sincerely,

NOTE: An in-school suspension, or alternate school program, can be an excellent learning situation, if it is administered with conviction. Note that even here, parental involvement is requested and expected.

60. Open Letter to Parents on Suspension Policy

If rules are to be effective, everyone must be aware of them. The following open letter is sent to all parents of the students of a school, and in it, the behavioral policies of the school are made clear. In those infrequent but troublesome moments when a parent may argue that he, she, or the child "didn't know," a record of a letter like this is most helpful.

Dear Parents:

In answer to many inquiries concerning the behavioral policies on suspension from Staggerford Middle School, perhaps the following statement, adopted by the school board as of September 18, _____, may be of interest to you:

The Staggerford School Board has the authority to make reasonable and necessary rules governing the behavior of students in school. These rules apply to all students going to, attending, and returning from school and those on school-sponsored activities. In addition, we hold that teachers have a right to maintain a suitable environment for learning, and administrators have the right and responsibility to maintain and facilitate the educational programs.

Moreover, the principal is authorized by state statute to suspend students for cause. Rules and regulations will be published and reviewed with students at the opening of each school year and will be posted in a prominent location within the school. Copies will be made available to students and parents upon request.

At present, the following incidents will result in immediate referral to the principal and are to be considered grounds for suspension:

1. Smoking anywhere on school property.
2. Fighting (beyond a push or shove; supervisor's discretion).
3. Profanity and/or obscenity to any teacher or supervisor.
4. Vandalism to school property or the property of any other person on school grounds.
5. Threatening violence or actual violence against any teacher or student.
6. Possession of or being under the influence of a controlled dangerous substance. (In addition to suspension, the board has determined that the police will be informed.)
7. Stealing.
8. Throwing food or causing potential harm to anyone in the cafeteria.

These rules are delineated here in order to provide students with a definition of limits of acceptable behavior and to equip school administrators for their disciplinary responsibilities.

It is to be understood that the principal may suspend a student for reasons other than those stated, if done for good cause. The Staggerford Township School Board retains the right to study each case, and the board's decision is the final authority.

We hope this statement will answer many questions. If you should desire any further clarification, please feel free to call me at 555-2345.

Sincerely,

NOTE: This would certainly lay out reasons for suspension, and it seems fairly comprehensive. You would, of course, include anything particular to your system.

61. Open Letter to Students on Behavior and Suspension

The last letter was to parents. This one would be written to students in a school, possibly as part of the materials they receive at the start of the school year.

To All Students:

In any school it is necessary that rules and regulation be established for the safety and well-being of all. As a student of this school, you should recognize that the school's authority extends from within the school itself to all areas surrounding the school, to the playgrounds and play areas, and to the buses and bus stops.

Here are some of the more common rules of the school:

1. Students are always required to follow the instructions of the classroom teacher.

2. Smoking, profanity and/or obscenity to a teacher, and fighting are forbidden and will result in immediate suspension.

3. Students will not engage in any action that may be potentially harmful to any other student (e.g. / throwing objects, running in the halls, pushing someone).

4. Students will not deliberately damage any school property.

5. Students will not bring to school any of the following: radios/CD players; toy pistols, water guns, or anything considered a weapon; cigarettes, tobacco, firecrackers, matches, and the like; sharp or pointed instruments; any other dangerous object or substance; drugs of any kind (possession of any controlled dangerous substance means automatic suspension and notification of authorities).

6. Misbehavior on school buses may result in suspension from bus privileges and/or suspension from school.

7. Students will not leave a classroom without permission, nor are students to cut classes or be absent from school without excuse.

If these rules are understood and followed, there is no reason why your time at Staggerford Middle School will not be happy and productive. The vast majority of students get through the school with little or no trouble with the behavioral code. Suspension is a last resort, and we use it only in extreme cases for extreme misbehavior.

If we all understand that we are here to learn, and if we all cooperate in that process, these years will be happy ones for everyone.

Sincerely,

NOTE: Here again, everything is spelled out, and there is no student who can use the old cry of "I didn't know!" These rules seem reasonable and fit virtually all infractions we can think of, but study your own policies and make such a letter fit your school system.

62. Statement of Rights in Expulsion Procedures

Here come the really tough letters. You do not expel a second-grade student for calling a classmate a "bad name." Expulsion is a tacit admission that the school has failed, can no longer help or deal with this student, and that—for the good of all others—the student must be removed. It is a step taken carefully and only after much reflection. In several letters before, we have referred to a statement of rights during the expulsion procedures. The following is an example of such a statement.

Dear Mr. and Mrs. Potter,

As you have been informed, your son Walter has been scheduled for a hearing before the board of education to determine if he should be expelled from the Madison Township School System. You have been informed of the time and place of that hearing, and the following information is provided as an explanation of your legal rights during this procedure.

In case of an expulsion proceeding, your child and you have the right to the following elements of due process:

1. A written statement of the charges against your child and the grounds justifying the sanction to be imposed.
2. A hearing.
3. A means of effective appeal.

Toward that end, you and your child have the following additional rights:

1. The hearing must be held within a reasonable time (generally 21 days) of the initial infraction.

2. You and your child may be represented by a lawyer.

3. The hearing may be held by the board of education or by a hearing examiner appointed by the board.

4. You are entitled to a translator where necessary.

5. You are entitled to the rudiments of an adversary proceeding. Courts have held that these rudiments may include the right to be presented with the names of witnesses against you and copies of statements and affidavits of those witnesses, the right to demand that any such witnesses appear in person to answer questions, and the right to testify and produce witnesses on your own behalf. The precise nature of the hearing depends upon the circumstances of the particular case, such as the sanctions to be imposed or at what level the hearing is heard.

6. A record must be kept of the hearing procedure. You are entitled, at your own expense, to a copy of that transcript.

7. The proceeding must be held with all reasonable speed.

8. If your child is found innocent, you may request that any written entry referring to the incident be expunged from your child's school record.

9. RIGHT OF APPEAL: You may appeal a decision made by school officials to the superintendent and the board of education. If that is unsuccessful, there are two more possible channels of appeal—first, to the commissioner of education, and then (within 30 days after the commissioner has made a decision) to the state board of education. You may appeal your case in court, without going through the administrative procedures outlined above, but the court may require you to exhaust those channels within the local and state school systems first. Your local board of education also has the right of appeal.

We hope this list of your rights has been of value to you. If you have any questions, please call the board offices at 555-9876.

Most sincerely yours,

NOTE: While this letter is fairly comprehensive, if you are ever in the position to write something of this sort, be sure to have the board attorney look it over before it is sent out.

63. Letter of Expulsion

This is the end of the line. The hearing has taken place and the student stands suspended. The final entry in this unit is the letter you must write to the parents of the expelled ex-student.

Dear Mr. and Mrs. Potter,

During the regular meeting of the Staggerford Township Board of Education, held on Monday evening, December 8, _____, the results of the hearing held concerning your son, Walter Potter, were considered. You were duly informed of the hearing, and you actively participated in it. The board voted unanimously to expel your son from the public schools of this township for his continued violations concerning the possession, use, and selling of illegal drugs on school property.

I sincerely regret to inform you that this action terminates any connection between the schools and your son. He may not attend any public school within the township; his presence on the campus of any of our schools will be treated as trespassing, and the proper authorities will be notified. The board will prosecute any attempt to disrupt or interfere with the smooth running of the educational system.

While we regret the necessity of this action, our primary goal is the continuing education of all of the students in our township, and we will not tolerate the use or sale of drugs of any kind on our school campuses.

Certainly, you may contact me if you have any further questions.

Respectfully,

NOTE: In this, as in all the letters regarding behavior, suspension, and even expulsion, the key has been objectivity. Particularly when describing an outrageous act of a student, let the facts speak for themselves. Do not enhance them with words that convey your attitude, such as "disreputable" or "despicable" or "cowardly." In short, never get angry in such a letter. Keep it calm, factual, and as short and to the point as the material covered will allow. If there is to be any offer of help or requirement of a conference, present that objectively as well. Make certain that the parent is kept well informed at all times, remain as objective as possible, and your discipline will stand.

COMPLETE GUIDE TO WRITING MEANINGFUL EVALUATIONS

*S*chool is a place of almost constant evaluation. Administrators and supervisors evaluate teachers and aides, teachers evaluate students, central administration evaluates administrators, parents evaluate the school, the school board evaluates the curriculum, the media evaluate all of the above, and everybody evaluates the food served in the cafeteria on a daily basis!

The humor aside, evaluation is a very real part of every educator's duties. If the evaluation consists merely of adding up a column of figures and dividing the answer by another figure, then it is a fairly simple task, but honestly, have you ever known it to be that cut and dried? No matter who is doing the evaluation or who is being evaluated, evaluation involves so many human factors that it is never easy. Perhaps that is the reason that so many evaluators depend upon those check-off lists of criteria.

You won't find those here. We're going to talk about written evaluations of all kinds and in a variety of situations, both positive and negative.

TAKING THE STING OUT OF WRITTEN EVALUATIONS

Unless we see a flagrant disregard for what is right and a devastating lack of good teaching or administration or just plain humanity, we are often loath to write evaluations that might be considered critical or point out something that, in our opinion, might need some improvement, major or minor. Many people simply cannot put down on paper anything negative, even when the situation merits it. Moreover, the individual getting the evaluation might well take exception if the only things mentioned are those that are considered unsatisfactory or that are of the "needs improvement" type.

Fortunately, in most cases, there is a way to write a meaningful evaluation that says what you want it to say without falling so heavily upon the subject that there is a sense of attack. There is a way to write an evaluation that takes the sting out of the negative and is very likely to be taken to heart, with an effort made toward improvement by the subject. How does one go about that? Simple, make a sandwich!

Here's what it looks like:

COMPLIMENT
CRITICISM
COMPLIMENT

Call it "criticism" or "needs improvement" or "area to be developed" or whatever else you may please, but it will be better received and noted if it comes "sandwiched in" between compliments.

Suppose a colleague asks you to listen to a speech she is going to give and to give her your "honest opinion" about it. Let's further suppose that this person is extremely enthusiastic about the topic and has obviously done considerable research. Your problem comes from the fact that you can't hear her beyond the second row.

Now, note the "sandwich" criticism:

> Your enthusiasm for your subject is obvious and an audience cannot help but catch fire from you. Because your speech is so important, make certain you keep your voice up, even with a microphone, so that everyone will hear every word. It is apparent that you have put in a great amount of tireless research, and I know your audience will want to hear every word.

Do you see the formula at work? Did you notice the compliment, followed by the criticism, followed and ended by a strong compliment? This type of evaluation may take a few seconds longer, but the dividends are tremendous.

See if you can find this technique at work in some of the following evaluations. Be aware, however, that not every positive evaluation has an accompanying negative—or that the challenge to sandwich overwhelming negatives between even two positives may be impossible for even the most positive of evaluators to meet. If you can do it, the evaluation—and the person being evaluated—will surely benefit.

MODEL EVALUATIONS FOR A VARIETY OF SCHOOL OCCASIONS

64. Informal Evaluation of Student Progress

Teachers and administrators are constantly being asked to evaluate the students who come within their purview. This may be done informally, as when you are asked if you think a student could handle a certain task or position on a club or team, or formally, as on a progress report or a formal request by a child study team. It might also be as simple as a note from a parent asking, "How is my child doing?" Let's start with one of those, and let's make it a happy occasion for a good student and likable child.

Dear Mrs. Fanworth,

Thank you for your note requesting the status of Bob's progress in class so far this marking period. Your concern is duly noted and appreciated.

I am very happy to report that this new marking period has brought with it a burst of positive behaviors on Bob's part. He is much more attentive in class, asks questions that reflect that he has been listening closely, and volunteers answers during questioning and review periods.

While the quantity and regularity of Bob's homework has improved markedly, the quality of it could stand some applied effort on Bob's part. Bob's homework many times shows that he has not checked it over once he has finished with it. Consequently, tiny errors tend to mar the whole effort. If you could work with Bob on this at home, I am certain that this aspect of his work would improve as well.

Finally, I am overjoyed to report that Bob has become much more accepted by his classmates. He is now being asked to play on teams, has become an asset in the classroom as a "tutor" to other students, and has made several new friends with whom he eats lunch—and they seem to be getting on well.

Again, I thank you for your interest. Rest assured that I will keep you apprised of Bob's progress. I like Bob, and I am sure that he will continue to do well.

Yours sincerely,

NOTE: Here, the "compliment sandwich" is in actual use, and you can surely see the impact that it would have on a parent—certainly better than merely writing that a son or daughter needs to improve homework. Also, since everything in education is interrelated, you should notice the steps toward establishing that "home-school connection" mentioned in Section Three.

65. Formal Evaluation of Student Progress, I

While you will certainly have requests for informal evaluations like the last letter, there are also times when the evaluation must be a bit more formal. Here, we are assuming a request for a student evaluation that comes from a child study team. Note the differences between this and the first, informal, evaluation.

Dear Dr. Olanger,

I am in receipt of your letter of April 23, _____, requesting my evaluation of the progress of Noreen Bornani, a student in my class. As of this date, three of the school year's four marking periods have passed, and I have had three quarters of the school year to observe Noreen's progress.

Noreen's grades have been consistent throughout the period. She has received a C+ each of the three marking periods. Her major academic difficulty seems to be studying for tests or quizzes, since my records indicate that low marks or failure on major tests keep her marking period grades at their current level. She is attentive most of the time in class, and has most of the answers when called upon.

I would emphasize, however, that the answers come only when called upon, for I have never seen Noreen volunteer to answer a question. Even though I have shared this with the home and tried personal encouragement on many occasions, Noreen still does not take an aggressive or active part in this particular process.

Moreover, Noreen tends to be a "loner" socially. I have often seen her sit by herself and read or play a solitary game rather than join in with the other children, even when the other children have asked her to join them. I have seen her rebuff a number of children who wanted her to join them in some activity. This continues to the present time.

I would emphasize that she has always been pleasant, and I have never seen her get angry or "act out" in any way. By the same token, I have never seen her instigate anything. She waits to be called upon, never volunteers for anything, does not join other children in play by her own choice, and does the work necessary to pass the class and very little else.

I certainly hope that this information will be of use to the child study team. I truly feel that she needs help in social adjustment, before her introversion reaches a point where it may become detrimental to her continued progress.

Please feel free to contact me again if I may be of any further service.

Most sincerely,

NOTE: In the case above, you are answering a specific request for an evaluation. The ideal rule for evaluation requests such as these is this: Answer the question! This is not a place to go roaming or putting in extra details. For that kind of evaluation, consider the next entry.

66. Formal Evaluation of Student Progress, II

Now, let's look at the kind of evaluation of a student that might be placed in the child's permanent record folder. If your school requires such an evaluation, you must be careful what you write—for the student's sake and for yours. See the NOTE below.

Evaluation of Manuel Assante:

Manuel Rivera Assante was a student in my Freshman English 101 class during the school year _____-_____.

During that time he earned a *C*+ for the first two marking periods, a *B*+ for the third period, and a *B* for the final marking period. His midterm exam grade was *B* and his final exam grade was *C*+. His yearly average was *B*.

Throughout the year, Manuel often volunteered for chores around the classroom and did most of the assigned tasks well. There was occasional need for direction, but once told explicitly what to do, he did the task, worked at it tirelessly, and always completed the assignment. His social adjustment with his peers was standard for his age, and he seemed to have no trouble fitting in with the other children in the class.

Manuel does not seem to deal well with overt criticism. When it is given by a teacher, his head lowers, and he does not speak. Should the criticism come from a classmate, he is quick to react, both verbally and physically. He seems to need some work on controlling that area.

On the whole, however, Manuel appears to me to be a normal, healthy, well-adjusted child for his age and grade. Generally, I have enjoyed having him in class this past school year. I feel he should do well in the future.

Respectfully submitted,

NOTE: When writing an evaluation for a student's permanent record, remember the same rule we established in those letters on behavioral problems. Let the facts speak for themselves. Never write something like "This boy is dishonest" or "This girl is a bully and a cheat." That is letting yourself in for trouble, as it may be brought out that you are branding that child for life. Just tell what happened and let that be your testimony. Of course, if your evaluation is good, no one is going to object if you end it on a positive note, as was done here.

67. Positive Evaluation of a Teacher

Evaluation of the teachers in a school is a part of the work of administration. Whether that evaluation comes many times a year or as infrequently as once a year, it is a point of contention in many situations. Many evaluators prefer preprinted forms for evaluation for just this reason. Here, they need only check off a column next to an attribute observed. Inevitably, the administrator or supervisor is going to have to write a formal statement of evaluation, so here are two—the first for an outstanding teacher, and the next for a teacher who needs improvement.

Re: Observation of Daniella Landers, Teacher

As part of my administrative duties, I observed Mrs. Landers during her third period math class on Tuesday, October 21, _____. I was present for the entire period.

The opening of the class involved a short review that led in to today's work. The review went well and the children seemed interested. At the conclusion of the short exercise, the teacher placed on the board what the class was going to learn that day. Mrs. Landers then taught the lesson, using visual aids, humor, great insight, patience with those who required further explanation, and a genuine enthusiasm for her subject that was contagious. The teaching was followed by small-group work that reinforced the concepts taught. The children were brought back to full class just prior to the end of class and the homework was assigned and placed on the board, where it was further explained by the teacher. The class ended with the children smiling as they exited the room, cheerfully bidding good bye to a teacher they truly appeared to like and respect.

Classroom activities were clearly related to instructional objectives that teacher and students understood. Mrs. Landers exhibited outstanding classroom management techniques and maintained discipline with a soft word and, at times, a mere look. While no students were singled out, there was definite attention paid to differences in learning styles and rates. In many innovative and creative ways, Mrs. Landers saw to the needs of each individual child in that class.

Mrs. Landers is a member of a number of educators' professional groups, is currently working toward a master's degree in early childhood education, serves as treasurer of our PTA, and serves on a number of community-related activities involving children.

I feel that Mrs. Landers is an outstanding example of a professional educator, and we are most fortunate to have her at our school.

Respectfully submitted,

NOTE: If you have one of those observation check-off sheets available, apply it to the letter of evaluation you have just read. We'd expect that virtually all areas on that list are covered in this letter. Here is an excellent evaluation for an excellent teacher. Now let's take a look at an evaluation where the conditions are not so ideal.

68. Negative Evaluation of a Teacher

Be realistic; there can be good and bad in anything—from politicians to police, from preachers to teachers. That does not lessen the great value of the good ones, but is merely stating a fact with which we must deal. Not everyone is a born teacher, and not everyone should be in a classroom. If it becomes necessary to write a negative evaluation of a teacher, you might consider the letter that follows.

Re: Evaluation of Jennifer Norcross, Teacher

As part of my administrative duties, I observed Mrs. Norcross during her period six social studies class on Thursday, April 16, _____. I was present for the entire period.

Mrs. Norcross arrived two minutes late for class. Although I tried not to interfere, I had to separate two children who had gotten into a fight.

When Mrs. Norcross appeared, she yelled at the children several times before relative quiet was restored. She then required the children to open their books and proceeded to read three pages of text to them. One child interrupted, "May I read?" Mrs. Norcross said, "No," and continued reading. When she had finished, she told students to take out paper and pencil and answer the questions at the end of the unit in the book. The remainder of class time was spent doing this. When the bell rang, Mrs. Norcross began to write a homework assignment on the blackboard. By that time, more than half the class was out the door.

At one point during the class assignment, one boy raised his hand and held it up for over a minute without being recognized. He finally called out, and told the teacher that he did not understand a particular question. Mrs. Norcross said, "Well, show it to Martine; she knows everything!" and indicated another child in the room. During the time the children worked at their individual desks, Mrs. Norcross first walked up and down the aisles and then returned to her desk, where she apparently corrected papers for the rest of the time. There was much talking and physical interaction between the children, and several children were working on subjects and projects other than social studies. Mrs. Norcross did not seem to notice, or did not interfere if she did.

In my professional opinion, Mrs. Norcross needs a great deal of improvement in order to continue as a professional educator. Her objectives for the class were unclear and did not match those in her lesson plan book. She exhibited a weak control of the class, showed poor classroom management skills, and made no effort that I could see to accommodate differences in learning styles in her students. Indeed, I am not convinced that anything of positive value was learned that day in that class.

It should be noted that Mrs. Norcross has served on the Faculty Benevolence Committee for the past three years. She seems to get along well with other members of the faculty, and there have been no altercations of which I am aware. She has never been late to school, and she provides extra help one afternoon each week.

In all, I can only evaluate Mrs. Norcross as a teacher in great need of improvement. While certainly it is the hope of us all that she will take advantage of the help that will be forthcoming, at the present time we could issue no recommendation for her as an educator.

Respectfully submitted,

NOTE: Make certain, whatever evaluation you write, that you check the policy of your school district regarding this process. If there is anything specific to your system, such as meeting within three days of the observation or writing a statement of how the system hopes to have the teacher improve, include that as required.

69. Positive Evaluation of an Administrator

Within any given school system, it is not only the teachers and students who are evaluated, but someone has to evaluate the evaluators, so to speak. Consequently, here is a letter evaluating an administrator who has obviously done a good job.

To: Superintendent and Board of Education of Wiley Township
Re: Evaluation of Dr. Amos R. Washburn, Principal of Wiley High School

In my capacity as assistant superintendent for the Wiley Township School System, I have prepared the following evaluation of Amos R. Washburn, Ph.D., currently serving as principal of Wiley High School.

One of the first things you will notice on a trip to Wiley High School is that the students and the faculty seem to genuinely like Dr. Washburn. He is greeted in the halls frequently and in a friendly manner by any number of students, teachers, and school workers, and he acknowledges each one of them in a positive manner. The atmosphere is that of people who are glad to be there—glad to be doing what they do.

This friendliness, this positive interaction, this unspoken enthusiasm marks Dr. Washburn's tenure as principal. He leads by example, maintains a happy and safe atmosphere where students can learn and teachers can teach, is a strict disciplinarian yet cares deeply about the development of the students under his charge, is always available for dialogue, and encourages development on all levels of the school and the education it offers.

Through observation and effective departmental meetings, Dr. Washburn has ensured that the curriculum is implemented and that all teachers have what they need to teach it. In the past, he has been personally responsible for the removal or transfer of some eight teachers, and has been assiduous in replacing them. The faculty, therefore, feel themselves engaged in meaningful educational activity, and one would be hard pressed to find a negative comment about Dr. Washburn among them. He, in turn, speaks quite highly of the faculty, and exhibits a sense of pride in them.

Dr. Washburn's "Your Pride Shows" program for students has reduced the vandalism budget considerably and has resulted in renewed interest within the community in those events, both of a sports and artistic nature, involving the schools. Revenues and attendance at sporting events, as well as at plays and concerts, have risen significantly. Students, teachers, workers, and fellow administrators feel a pride in their school that has brought new life to the area.

Dr. Amos Washburn's physical administration of Wiley High School, his competent work with the school budget, his work on the township's curriculum committee, and his continued openness to the entire community have made him an administrator of note and distinction, and one whom I may unqualifiedly recommend to your attention.

We are indeed fortunate to have Dr. Washburn in his current position. He is a credit to himself and a definite asset to Wiley Township School System.

Respectfully submitted,

NOTE: Well, this was certainly a principal under whom most educators would fight to work! As with teachers, however, not all administrators are perfect for the job. Some may need improvement—some quite a bit. Let's take a look at one of these in the next evaluation of an administrator.

70. Negative Evaluation of an Administrator

The administrator can make or break the school. When the former happens, it's a joy; when the latter occurs, something has to be done, and done quickly. The process could well start with a negative evaluation like the one that follows. Notice that those persistent facts keep speaking for themselves without a great deal of comment.

To: Superintendent and School Board of Ralston Incorporated School District
Re: Evaluation of Loren Featherstone, Principal of Gundersen High School

As part of my duties as assistant superintendent of personnel, I submit this following evaluation of Loren Featherstone, currently serving as principal of Gundersen High School.

Mr. Featherstone has been principal of the high school for just under two years, having assumed the position upon the retirement of the former administrator. As of September, Mr. Featherstone will be entering his tenure year in the office.

To any long-term employee of the district (and I place myself in that category), it is obvious that things have changed at Gundersen High School. The school that once had twenty-three extracurricular activities—exclusive of sports—now has only six. That will be reduced to five when the school newspaper closes in September due to lack of interest and the inability to find a faculty sponsor.

The school, which has run without incident for the past ten years, last year spawned some twenty-six teacher grievances—eighteen of them unresolved at this time and awaiting contractual adjudication.

The faculty, through its bargaining agent, has expressed a vote of "no confidence" in Mr. Featherstone. Among the grievances is the assertion that the curriculum is not being taught, because of lack of guidance and direction from the administration of the school—as well as a lack of teaching materials, despite a sufficient budgetary allotment to ensure that such a situation did not occur.

The records available (and not all requested records were available) indicated a 27 percent rise in truancy, a 17 percent rise in reported disciplinary infractions, and a 38 percent rise in the vandalism budget over the past two years.

Moreover, teacher dissatisfaction seems to be at an all-time high, as indicated by teacher absences and several letters of complaint received by the board. This is paralleled by several movements in the community concerning the current condition of the school.

During frequent visits to the school, I always found Mr. Featherstone in his office, where, I was repeatedly told, he spends the majority of the school day.

It is with the deepest regret, therefore, that I must accord Mr. Featherstone an evaluation of *Unsatisfactory.*

Respectfully submitted,

NOTE: As with the teacher's evaluation, be sure to check your individual board policy for the proper form or content in your individual case, but this gives you a general idea of its composition. Notice that there is not one personal comment, except for the words, "with the deepest regret," in the entire evaluation. Let those facts speak.

71. Special Evaluation of a School Employee

There are times when we might wish to place a special letter in an employee's folder that has to do with the job he or she performs. While not, strictly speaking, an evaluation, it is nonetheless a commentary on performance and, therefore, in the manner of an evaluation. Here's an example of one in a very positive vein.

Re: Special Commentary on Performance of Harold Andrews

Harold Andrews has served as a custodian in Garrett High School for the past seven years. Past evaluations show that he has always performed his assigned duties in a satisfactory manner.

Recently, on the afternoon of our drama club's spring production, the teacher in charge of getting the auditorium ready for the audience of parents and friends who would attend the evening presentation became very ill. She was so ill, in fact, that she had to be taken to the emergency room of Mainland General Hospital.

Because of the lateness of the hour, this left a group of students unsupervised, and an auditorium uncleaned and with no chairs set up.

Mr. Andrews was not responsible for that task; it was not required for his position. Nevertheless, Mr. Andrews called the vice-principal to arrange for someone to come to the school to supervise, and then he took over personally. He supervised the students until the vice-principal arrived, and then organized the students, cleaned the auditorium, and saw to it that the chairs were properly set up.

I wish to emphasize that Mr. Andrews was not required contractually to do any of the above, but he did so voluntarily and changed a potentially difficult scenario into a well-ordered and functioning operation. Needless to say, the students were very grateful to Mr. Andrews and highly complimentary of his efforts.

I personally wish to thank Mr. Andrews for his sensitivity to the needs of our students, and for a job very well done indeed.

Sincerely,

NOTE: This "evaluatory" (to coin a word) letter is one to place in an employee's file for that service "above and beyond the call." Not only is it a nice gesture, but it is appreciated by the employee as well.

72. Positive Evaluation of a School Employee

The teacher's aide, custodian, lunch room assistant, and other staff members play a very important part in the functioning of the modern school. As with all school employees, their performance is evaluated in a variety of ways, and is often dependent upon contractual obligations. Here is one example of a positive evaluation.

Re: Mrs. Kelna Fisher, Teacher's Aide

Mrs. Fisher serves as a teacher's aide on the fourth-grade level. She has been employed by the township in this capacity for the past six years; the last three of those years she has worked in this school. This is my second evaluation of Mrs. Fisher for the current school year.

Mrs. Fisher most satisfactorily fulfills the requirements of a teacher's aide. Indeed, based upon my personal observation and the written commentaries of the teacher(s) involved, there is nothing within the job description that Mrs. Fisher does not do—and do well. She is well liked by faculty and students alike, and she seems to genuinely enjoy both her job and the people with whom she works.

Her work with the children is exemplary. She is friendly and warm toward them while still maintaining the discipline that is needed for good teaching. Her patience is well noted by both teachers and this observer, and this serves her well in working with children who need several alternate learning methods to grasp certain concepts. Indeed, the school has received several letters from parents thanking Mrs. Fisher for the work she has done with their children. These letters are enclosed for your perusal.

Because Mrs. Fisher meets every single one of her job requirements with ability and dispatch; because she is respected and sought after by faculty and students; because parents, students, and faculty have voiced support for her continued good work, I would rate Mrs. Fisher's performance as *Outstanding* for this time period.

Respectfully submitted,

NOTE: As with any other school employee, you should first check to see if there are certain methods of presentation or even a required objective sheet that must be made out according to the negotiated contract, where that is pertinent. Of course, not many people are going to object to something as positive as the one above.

73. Negative Evaluation of a School Employee

A negative evaluation for a school employee is serious business, as it can mean the termination of that individual. Usually, that drastic an action comes at the end of a long process of negative evaluations and only after help and encouragement have been offered to enable the person to perform the job adequately. In the following letter, this is pointed out in detail.

Re: Mrs. Tess Jassic, Custodian

This is my fourth evaluation of Mrs. Jassic this school year.

In September of this current school year, I received a number of complaints from faculty and staff that certain rooms were either not being cleaned or were so poorly cleaned as to be virtually as dirty as before. This was not a schoolwide problem, and, upon investigation, I found that these were the rooms assigned to Mrs. Jassic. At that time, I spoke to her immediate supervisor, who then contacted her. At that time, an "Evaluation of Services" form was filed with the central office as required by contract.

In October, I again met with Mrs. Jassic's supervisor and informed him that there had seemingly been no improvement, since complaints were still coming in as to uncleaned rooms, and I personally witnessed incidents such as piles of dirt swept into the middle of the room and simply left there. I was assured by Mrs. Jassic's supervisor that there would be improvement.

In Novermer, the situation had not been remedied, and teacher complaints were still coming in on a regular basis. Adhering to the policy stated in the contract, I now met with Mrs. Jassic in the presence of her supervisor, Mr. Andrews; Mrs. Caulfield, a representative of the Maintenance Workers Union; and Mr. Pierce, a representative of the board of education. At that meeting, I asked directly about the state of the rooms. Mrs. Jassic's answer was that if I or the teachers didn't like it, they could do it themselves—a remark for which she later apologized at the urging of Mrs. Caulfield. Other than that, she had no answer and sat silent through the rest of the meeting. Finally, at the insistence of Mrs. Caulfield and Mr. Andrews, it was decided to give Mrs. Jassic another chance to do her job in a proper manner, and she was given a new area to clean.

As of this date, I have received eighteen complaints concerning the condition of the rooms to which Mrs. Jassic had been reassigned. Indeed, upon personal inspection by Mr. Andrews and me, several rooms appear not to have been touched at all.

Therefore, in accordance with contractual procedures, I am filing an evaluation with a rating of *Highly Unsatisfactory*, with a recommendation that Mrs. Jassic be removed from her duties, with all due process, as soon as possible.

Respectfully submitted,

NOTE: Look at two things in this document: First, see the references to "contractual procedures," indicating that these were followed to the letter. Second, note the chronological order stated along with the precise steps taken. That's a strong document.

74. Positive Evaluation of a Special School Event

Many times, teachers and students work long and hard to put on special programs for the school. These may range from a presentation just to entertain, to those programs that educate and inform, such as a holiday program or a program on drug abuse. A positive evaluation of such a program is deeply appreciated by all involved, particularly if it can be as positive as this one.

Dear Mr. Tallchief,

What a delight it was to watch that highly informative and entertaining assembly program that you and your class presented for the school this morning! It was abundantly evident that some monumental effort went into it. The result was a performance that both faculty and students enjoyed and benefited from. That, of course, is no small task, and you and your class accomplished it beautifully.

Your use of the school facilities is to be complimented, as is your obvious understanding of children. The pace was excellent and moved in such a manner that it was virtually impossible for any student to lose interest. Indeed, the interest of the assembled school was evident.

The content of your program was especially sensitive and geared to touch an age-appropriate response in each student. It was simple enough for the youngest to understand and powerful enough for the most sophisticated student to appreciate.

In short, I think your special program was just that—very special!

I shall make time to drop in later this week and tell the children personally how much I appreciate their efforts. In the meantime, please tell them how much I enjoyed it. Also, please know how much I appreciate your efforts on behalf of your students and this entire school.

Most sincerely,

NOTE: This is the type of letter that, while not a formal evaluation, a teacher or supervisor or whoever was in charge might well want placed in his or her permanent record. Not all special programs turn out so well, however, as we'll see shortly.

75. Negative Evaluation of a Special School Event

They can't all be winners. Over many years in the public schools, we have seen some school "special" programs that left us wondering how something of that nature ever got into the school in the first place. If you want to say something about that type of event, consider the following.

Dear Sir or Madam:

When our parent council was looking for a special event for our students on the last day of school before the winter break, a number of programs were offered for consideration. One of the deciding factors in choosing you was your brochure, describing your program and its contents. Since this was to be a special event for our students, and since your brochure seemed to indicate a program of special merit, we contracted with you for that particular day.

I would bring to your attention several facts about the special event that you provided:

1. Your brochure states, "a troop of lively performers." One gentleman arrived, and he was over 45 minutes late, necessitating an emergency change in scheduling for the entire school.

2. Your brochure states, "clowns pour from the stage while trained acrobats perform feats of daring and skill." *One* clown does not a plural make, nor does the fact that he did one handstand later in the program constitute fulfillment of the promise of your literature.

3. Your brochure states, "timely, relevant material that instructs and entertains." I have asked several teachers and parents present, and we are still in doubt as to what message was being presented. Indeed, several children had to be removed from the auditorium during the performance when long pauses occurred as the performer checked to see what was next, leaving the audience of children wondering what they were doing there.

Given the circumstances, this school and the parent council would be more than justified in withholding the remainder of the fee for which we contracted. We are not going to do that, however, and your check is enclosed. Upon consultation with the others involved, I want you to know that this is the last check your organization will ever receive from us, and you may be assured that we will advise our sister schools in this township as well.

Sincerely,

NOTE: If you are not satisfied with that special event, it is a reasonable thing to tell the providing company about it. We've found that when ordering an outside program, it is wise to talk to someone who has seen it already. Any company should provide you with references for this purpose.

76. Positive Evaluation of a School Program

There are any number of special school programs being run in the schools of this nation. These range from special help in math or English to programs for "latchkey kids," as they are called. Some are wonderful, and some could stand improvement. Let's evaluate one of the good ones first.

Dear Ms. Tong,

It has now been approximately six months since you began your special school program, "You're in Charge!" Since our community consists of many families where both parents (or a single parent) must work, a great many of our children come home after school to an empty house—a house that will remain empty until a parent returns from work later in the day. The program you sponsored aimed to meet that need by providing the children so affected with a place where they could learn how to be alone in the afternoon and how to deal with the simple household problems that have a way of occurring.

That is exactly what your program has accomplished! We have had letter after letter from very satisfied parents, who have seen a marked improvement in their children's self-confidence and efficiency in handling that part of the day when parents are not present. In one case, a potential mishap was totally avoided when a youngster encountered a defective outlet in the home and proceeded according to safety guidelines you had taught her, thereby averting serious trouble.

That you have established and run this program after regular school hours, and without any additional compensation, only adds to the respect that parents, students, and your fellow educators feel for you.

Again, I congratulate you on the success of your fine program, and I invite you to see me at your convenience so that we may determine if there is any way in which this school can help you as you continue.

Yours sincerely,

NOTE: Some school programs are excellent, some need improvement, and some should not go on. This particular program worked—and worked well—and the evaluator says so. Again, this could be placed in the teacher's file.

77. Negative Evaluation of a School Program, I

The evaluation of a program that is not essentially bad but needs some improvement to continue should be treated the same way as a regular evaluation of anything where improvement is needed. Note the change in tenor in this first negative evaluation.

Dear Mr. Olinski,

This is the third year in which your "After-School Math Club" has been in existence. In that time, literally hundreds of children have attended these sessions, and profited from what they have found there, being helped to cope with the curriculum of the school's various math classes. For this alone, you are to be commended for your dedication and insight.

Recently, a new class has been approved by the school board and added to our curriculum. This course in computer math began this school year and will continue as a major part of the math curriculum. The teachers of this course have remarked that their students seem to need extra help in this subject, and even those attending your "After- School Math Club" are seemingly having trouble.

I wonder if I may set up a conference with you and the teachers of computer math. Perhaps we can bring out the specifics of what the students need to effectively handle this new subject, and how your special group can be of greatest help.

Again, I have every confidence that students will soon be gaining support and enrichment from your outstanding school program in this math class as well. Please let me know when that meeting can be arranged.

Thank you so much for your dedication and support.

Yours most sincerely,

NOTE: That evaluation was fairly mild, merely wishing for an already competent program administrator to learn some new materials. The "compliment sandwich," mentioned earlier, worked nicely here.

78. Negative Evaluation of a School Program, II

Now, let's look at a school program that, however well intentioned it may be, simply does not work. While still objective in nature, this evaluation leaves no doubt about the evaluator's opinion of the program.

Dear Miss Kellog,

When you started your "Easy English Program" about a year ago, you were certain that it would meet a need of the students in this school. Indeed, in the first few months, more than twenty students came after school to have you help them with their English skills. I am certain that they are grateful for your efforts, as is this school.

After that primary response, however, the participation in your program dropped to about five students. It is my understanding that three of them improved their grades while the other two maintained the status quo in their grades.

We are now two months into the new school year, and I understand that no new students have shown up for the program, and that previous participants still in the school did not return.

While that grieves me personally, it does raise a question or two. Given these circumstances, do you think the program should continue? If so, then how do we increase the use of the program?

Frankly, at present, it seems that discontinuing the program would be the logical thing to do. We cannot force students to attend, and there seems to be no great or crying need for the program.

You are to be commended for your efforts and concern, but it would certainly be no reflection on you if the program were to shut down until there was a future need for it.

Please let me know your wishes as soon as possible.

Sincerely,

NOTE: Programs often run their course, so to speak. What may once have been a highly successful program may simply not be relevant any longer. The evaluation above seems gentle enough while making the point that the program may no longer be needed.

79. Positive Evaluation of Text or Learning Material

When textbooks are to be chosen, it is inevitable that there will be debate as to the content and presentation of the work. Concern over the "moral content" of the textbook will be handled in Section Five. Here, we are talking only about the readability and suitability of a text to fit the curriculum.

To: Textbook Selection Committee

Re: *Imagination* (Silver Edition), Seventh Grade

The publisher suggests this anthology of literature for seventh-grade English, language arts, or reading.

The first thing that attracts the potential reader is the extremely colorful cover. This is not a promise unfulfilled, as the full-color illustrations used throughout the text are of the same quality, extremely attractive to children, and reflective of the various stories and poems presented.

The writing is age appropriate and at the proper grade level. Interest for seventh graders should run high, as the poems, essays, short stories, and plays reflect a wide variety of subjects of interest to that grade level. A number of contemporary entries make this book fairly universal, covering topics from life on the streets of the city to living on a modern-day ranch.

Even a short perusal will assure the reader that the book is gender sensitive, presenting males and females in a variety of roles. Moreover, the races are treated evenly and with understanding. There is a veritable treasure chest of activities as part of each literary form exemplified, and the book contains a progressive reading program that the reading teacher should really appreciate.

In short, I would most definitely recommend this textbook for adoption, as I feel that it meets the needs of the current curriculum and would be highly motivational and enjoyable for the seventh-grade student.

Respectfully submitted,

NOTE: This type of evaluation is seen all the time on any textbook selection committee. In fact, some committees have eliminated this form of evaluation and provided check-off sheets instead. You would, of course, adopt the procedures of your particular organization.

80. Negative Evaluation of Text or Learning Material

It is not only textbooks that require evaluation. Sometimes, learning materials, particularly those that have been around for quite some time, can stand a closer look. It is amazing how some things have changed, and those learning materials as well as the texts should be kept current.

Dear Mr. Strickland,

Recently, I was looking through a particular set of learning materials that were meant to increase reading comprehension. The materials consisted of a number of large cards, each containing a very short story or factual information, that the child would read, followed by questions to be answered and checked by the teacher. There are several sets of these materials, and I found sets still in use in three reading classrooms.

The copyright date is _____. That is amazing in itself, that they have survived so long and have been in use so long, but what is even more eye opening is that they reflect the culture of that day in a way that we no longer find acceptable.

I refer to the stories. Some are gender-hostile, while others are, in my opinion, downright sexist. Certain members of minority groups appear only in domestic or subservient roles, and stereotyped sex roles predominate. In short, while that may have been culturally tolerated at the time of its publishing, it certainly has no place in today's society with today's understanding.

It is my suggestion that these learning materials be removed at once, for I fear that others besides myself may find them offensive.

I am at your disposal in this matter; please let me know your decision.

Very truly yours,

NOTE: Reasons for the negative evaluation must always be given. A statement such as "This is terrible; get rid of it" simply will not do. The evaluation above says virtually the same thing, but properly . . . properly!

81. Positive Evaluation of a Curriculum

The need for a curriculum is evident. It is, however, a guide and not a master. Indeed, the first working year of any curriculum should be one of adaptation and even experimentation. Here is a letter of evaluation of a curriculum reflecting that philosophy.

To: Superintendent Dr. David Lear
Re: Curriculum for Seventh-Grade Science (Middle School Level)

It has now been one year since the implementation of the seventh-grade science curriculum at Fair Oaks Middle School. In that time, faculty and administration have had the opportunity to interact with the curriculum and come to a familiarity with and understanding of it.

There was, undoubtedly, an express need for a new science curriculum; the old one was at least a decade old, and failed to reflect the newest advances in science. This curriculum is up-to-date and contains such self-monitoring as to incorporate in the curriculum any contemporary major scientific findings.

The texts chosen, as well as the lab program that the curriculum implements, are both exciting and informative. Indeed, it has been a hallmark of this curriculum that students are actually eager to get to their lab projects.

Teachers find the new guidelines and teacher aids to be most helpful, and if there is a single criticism, it is that there is too much material to get through in a single school year.

The students have also responded well to the curriculum. In general, the grade averages have risen one whole grade over the last year of the old curriculum, and this year's standardized test revealed a 17 percent overall rise in the area of science.

It seems that teachers, students, and the school as a whole are benefiting from the implementation of this new curriculum, which should give us all a great deal of satisfaction.

Respectfully submitted,

NOTE: This curriculum worked. Here, again, the facts were allowed to speak for themselves, resulting in a positive evaluation of a newly installed curriculum.

82. Negative Evaluation of a Curriculum, I

Suppose a curriculum doesn't work; this would have to be set down in an evaluation as well. Again, in this negative evaluation, we are going to allow facts to speak rather than personal opinions.

To: Superintendent Dr. David Lear

Re: Curriculum for Seventh-Grade Science (Middle School Level)

It has now been one year since the implementation of the seventh-grade science curriculum at Fair Oaks Middle School. In that time, faculty and administration have had the opportunity to interact with the curriculum and come to a familiarity and understanding of it.

There was, undoubtedly, an express need for a new science curriculum; the old one was at least a decade old, and it failed to reflect the newest advances in science. Unfortunately, this new curriculum concentrates on the basics of science, which is desirable, but neglects to tie in those basics with any of the scientific breakthroughs and advances that are taking place all around us.

The text chosen, as well as the lab program, has its drawbacks. The text, while scientifically accurate, is of such a nature that it is above the comprehension of most seventh-grade students. Indeed, a recent readability study showed it to be written on a 10.6 level. The lab program, while interesting, is implemented once every three weeks, and seventh graders quickly lose interest in things for which they must wait and wait.

Teachers complain that there is a perceived lack of direction with the text and materials; many are out searching for materials to supplement the current curriculum.

Student response to the new curriculum has been unremarkable. While there has been no drop in classwide grade averages nor on standardized test results, there has been no improvement either. One teacher went so far as to comment, "It looks as if we have replaced nothing with more nothing!"

While no one has been harmed through this new curriculum, the consensus seems to be that the new curriculum, if it continues to remain in effect, will require a great deal of work to become the shining example of science and education we all hoped it would be.

Respectfully submitted,

NOTE: This, in effect, is the same letter that was used for the positive evaluation. Only the facts were changed to reflect the purpose of the evaluation.

83. Negative Evaluation of a Curriculum, II

In this letter, we shall show an evaluation of one aspect of a curriculum, when the curriculum as a whole is fine. While this letter is certainly an evaluation, it is presented as a personal viewpoint with the objective of adding to the value of the curriculum and improving a potential trouble spot.

Dear Dr. Perez,

I would like to bring to your attention an aspect of the new science curriculum for the seventh grade. It is something that, for me, stands out as a potential trouble spot in an otherwise outstanding curriculum. If I feel that way, perhaps others do as well. If that is the case, it is best dealt with now.

As you are aware, a strong component of the new curriculum involves its lab research program. This biweekly lab session is proving to be a great favorite with the students. Not only is it interesting to them, but it is a gratifying part of teaching science as well. Certainly, the materials for teachers are abundant, and very clear and helpful. That is why I would not like to see the program come under attack.

Looking down the line, I see that in approximately two months, the lab program will deal with animal anatomy. One particular lab involves the dissection of an animal (either a cat or a fetal pig). Quite frankly, I have no objection to this lab, and I think it is a wonderful way to learn. Not everyone feels that way, however.

You may or may not be aware that no less than eleven students in the seventh grade are children of community members who belong to a very active antivivisectionist group. The group has been a part of organized protests against local companies that use animals for research. You may recall the pictures in the paper last year of the leader of the group being dragged away in handcuffs. That person is a member of our PTA.

Now, it may be that they have no objections to dissecting laboratory samples from a biological supply house, but then again, they might.

No curriculum exists on its own, but each must be measured as far as its impact on the community and school is concerned. Therefore, it might be wise to begin discreet inquiries into their philosophy before implementing a part of the curriculum that, although it is of undoubted worth, might bring unwanted turmoil to our gates.

If I may be of any service, please do not hesitate to ask.

Yours sincerely,

NOTE: The entire curriculum was not challenged, and the writer even compliments it as a whole. One potential trouble spot is delineated, however, and solid reasons given as to why this might be a trouble spot. Personally, we'd rather get a letter like this than find the press on our doorstep. Wouldn't you?

84. Negative Evaluation of a School or School System

The last two letters of evaluation in this section are not formal evaluations, because, with the exception of such groups as the Middle States Evaluating Committee, schools do not get formally evaluated. They are, however, under evaluation each and every day. Members of the public, whether they publish it or not, constantly evaluate the schools their children attend. Here is one such negative evaluation. We'll save the positive one for last to end our section on an up note.

To Whom It May Concern:

What is a school? Should you ask that question of a stranger on the street, the words might vary, but I believe the content would be the same. A school is a place where teachers teach and children learn and grow.

Indeed, is this not the essence of education as we know it? Competent, knowledgeable, dedicated teachers engaged in a process of guiding young minds—passing on knowledge and training students to handle that knowledge, helping students to grow not only mentally but physically and socially as well, developing the type of citizen who will enter the community and enrich it by his or her presence—this is what a school is all about.

There was a time when I believed that Rock Township High School was just such a place. I truly believed that, until I took a closer look.

What I found astonished me. I have found teachers in classes for which they were not certified. I have found teachers who are perennially late for their assignments and whose lack of reports holds back the entire administrative process. I have found good and dedicated teachers who are frustrated by a lack of the most basic supplies. I have found administrators who let all this continue—administrators content with the status quo.

And that's not all. If school is to be a place where children grow and learn, then I must ask myself what they are growing into and what they are learning at Rock Township High. This year, absenteeism is at an all-time high. The vandalism budget at the school shows a 15 percent increase over that of last year. Where once there were as many as twenty extracurricular activities, this year we see only five, and it is my understanding that even these are in danger of disbanding.

To me, this paints a picture of a school that is desperately in need of help, and a school system that is either unwilling or unable to provide that desperately needed care. In short, we have evaluated our school, and it has failed to measure up to what this community wants, needs, and should have—not for the sake of appearances, but for the future of our children.

With deep sincerity,

NOTE: This is an example of something that might be used effectively if drastic changes were needed in a school or school system. One could run for the school board on the basis of such a letter. At the very least, it would stir controversy and debate. Let's hope, however, that the need for a letter like this one is rare.

85. Positive Evaluation of a School or School System

Let's again use the letter we just wrote. The form is a good one, with the positive or negative aspect relegated to the content. Now, let's end this section with a letter voicing a very positive evaluation of the school.

To Whom It May Concern:

What is a school? Should you ask that question of a stranger on the street, the words might vary, but I believe the content would be the same. A school is a place where teachers teach and children learn and grow.

Indeed, is this not the essence of education as we know it? Competent, knowledgeable, dedicated teachers engaged in a process of guiding young minds—passing on knowledge and training students to handle that knowledge, helping students to grow not only mentally but physically and socially as well, developing the type of citizen who will enter the community and enrich it by his or her presence—this is what a school is all about.

I have always believed that Rock Township High School was just such a place. Now that I have taken a closer look, I no longer just believe that, I know it to be true.

What I found enriched and edified me. I found a faculty whose credentials were impeccable, including many with master's degrees, and virtually all involved in continual personal academic growth. I have found them enlightening the lives of their students—backed up by an administration that supports them, sees to it that they have the materials and supplies they need, and provides an environment where teachers can teach and students learn to the best of their abilities. I found an administration that was determined to keep the highest educational level for the students of Rock Township High.

And that's not all. If school is to be a place where children grow and learn, then I firmly believe that we are sending them to the right place to do just that. The facts speak for themselves. This year, absenteeism has declined to an all-time low. The vandalism budget at the school shows a 20 percent decrease over that of last year. Where once there were as few as six extracurricular activities, this year there are twenty-six being offered, with proposals for new organizations coming very frequently from a faculty that cares, an administration that supports, and students who are interested, enthusiastic, and vitally involved in their education.

To me, this paints a picture of a school that is doing something very, very right, and a school system that is continually striving to provide the very best possible education for the children of this community.

Indeed, we have evaluated our school, and it has more than measured up to what our community wants, needs, and should have, not for the sake of appearances, but for something far more precious—the future of our children.

Sincerely,

NOTE: Isn't it amazing how the change of a word or phrase, or the particular arrangement of written words, can change the entire mood, tenor, and even the understood purpose of a written piece? Of these last two letters, one might be used to start a reform movement, and the other could well be sent by a board of education member to the editor of the local newspaper, or be part of a brochure advertising the desirability of the school.

If there is a moral, let it be this: In every evaluation you write, informal or formal, from a letter on an assembly program to a formal evaluation of a principal, make certain that you choose your words very carefully. So much depends on saying the right thing in the best possible way.

Section
Five

WRITING FOR
THE COMMUNITY

$\mathcal{T}$he poet John Donne wrote, "No man is an island. . . ." We might well paraphrase that line to read, "No school is an island. . . ." We all realize that no school, anywhere, exists in a vacuum. Schools are created to serve the community in which they exist, and they exist within the community they serve. This may seem like a small distinction, but it has far-reaching implications.

When a community is in love with its schools, it is a fine sight to see. When a community becomes disenchanted with its school system—or even a single school in the system—however, then it is rather like a couple on the verge of divorce; everything the other one does is suspicious, and the stress is incredible.

BLUEPRINT FOR POSITIVE SCHOOL-COMMUNITY RELATIONS

What if you had a school, and you put up a 25-foot concrete wall around it so no one could look in? What if students passed through a steel door and reemerged seven or eight hours later, and never said a thing about what happened in the place? What if teachers, administrators, and school employees, when asked about the school, took on the look of spy-novel secret agents and mumbled, "What school?" What about conditions like that? What do you think would happen?

It's obvious, isn't it? Given the ludicrous conditions just mentioned, the community would be in an uproar—tigers at the gates—demanding to know what unspeakable horrors took place behind those grim walls!

At the very least, you'll agree that this is an example of very poor school-community relations. We hope you'll also agree that it has a rather simple solution—communication.

The best school in the world—the one in which the best education takes place and student growth is a daily miracle—will remain an object of suspicion if no one knows about the good things that are happening there. In a like manner, even a school with problems can gain the support of the community if the members of the public have been kept informed and made to feel that it is truly *their* school. Effective school-community communication often spells the difference between acceptance and hostility within a community.

93

The model letters you are about to read in this section all aim at establishing a positive school-community relationship, where the members of the public will consider the needs of the school their needs. This is no easy task, nor is it accomplished overnight or with the use of a single letter. It can, however, be accomplished if you keep certain facts in mind.

First, remember that everything you write may be read by the community. We have seen letters written in confidence to individuals become the center of heated political debate, so watch what you write and make certain that whatever it is, it could be read and understood without damage to the school or the system.

Second, always present your school in the best possible light—*any* time it is presented to the public. This does *not* mean that you make things up, but it *does* mean keeping track of what is happening at your school and making certain that the community is aware of it, too. Be proud of your school, and take every opportunity to let the community know just how much you care.

Third, stand firm on your positions. Few things will engender distrust in a community more than an educator who changes opinions on a daily basis. If you believe that the community needs a new high school, then get your facts ready and stand by your belief. Even if you find yourself before a group of citizens who believe that local taxes are too high already, they may disagree, but they will respect you (and, by projection, the school) if they find you a person of resolve and honor. If you believe that you and your school are right, defend that position.

Finally, always encourage openness between school and community. If you are proud of your school, you will want others to see what is going on. If you limit access to the school, or so it is reasoned, you must have something to hide. A response to a letter, for instance, that accuses the school of not providing a proper lunch selection should always include a "would you like to come and see for yourself" sentence. Of course, this is just one example, but you get the idea.

In this section, you will read model letters between the school and the community on a wide variety of subjects. Notice that in each, whether positive or negative, the school is always paramount and that openness always encouraged. Moreover, strong, yet respectful, opinions are presented with an aim toward making a superior school (*yours!*) even better. Above all, they reflect an attitude of enthusiasm and pride in the accomplishments of the faculty and student body.

Following such a blueprint will go a long way toward establishing a school-community relationship that can only benefit both sides.

MODEL LETTERS FOR THE COMMUNITY

86. Letter Supporting Proposed Community Legislation

The school can benefit from legislation proposed for a community, or it can suffer from it. Therefore, when legislation comes along that will have an impact on your school, something like these next two letters would not be amiss. First, let's look at a letter that supports the proposed legislation.

Dear Chairperson Sayers and Members of the Township Planning Board:

I am writing in regard to proposed legislation Township 286.73-44. As you know, this particular legislation will be brought before the board for a vote at your next regular session. Before you take that action, I respectfully wish to make you aware of certain facts in the matter.

The proposed legislation would permit the construction of a new road between Nutswamp Road and Dwight Road along the southwest edge of the existing property of Tremont Elementary School. I would like you and the board to know that we at Tremont Elementary School are delighted with the proposal, and we sincerely urge you to vote in favor of the legislation.

For years, we at Tremont, where 87 percent of our students are bused to and from school daily, have fought the "battle of the buses" each and every afternoon. At present, the only access to the school campus is off Dwight Road. This is true for buses as well as emergency vehicles, should they ever be required. At the very least, it makes for monumental traffic jams in the mornings and afternoons when students are being transported. Moreover, to reach Nutswamp Road from the school currently requires a mile-and-a-half trip to reach a road that can be clearly seen from the second floor of the school.

The proposed legislation would provide immediate access to Nutswamp Road and would grant a second access to the campus that we could use to alleviate traffic difficulties, provide a safer environment for our students, and allow unhindered access to emergency vehicles. Certainly, the new road would make the quality of life at Tremont School a great deal better for all concerned.

Therefore, I respectfully suggest that the planning board approve proposal Township 286.73-44.

Please feel free to call if I may be of service to you or the board.

Yours sincerely,

NOTE: When writing about legislation, make certain you identify it correctly. A simple telephone call can get you that information. Also, notice that specific reasons why you are in favor of it are given clearly. Whether you are for or against something, make certain you give a clear reason for your point of view.

87. Letter Opposing Proposed Community Legislation

You will notice a great deal of similarity between this letter and the former one. One supports and the other opposes, and both give solid reasons for their position. Even though this letter opposes the legislation, it remains calm and matter-of-fact about the whole thing, never accusatory or vindictive.

Dear Chairperson Sayers and Members of the Township Planning Board:

I am aware that you are about to vote upon Township 286.73-44, a proposal that, if adopted, would expedite the construction of a new road, joining Nutswamp Road to Dwight Road along the southwest boundary of Tremont Elementary School property.

I am writing to respectfully state my personal opposition to that proposed legislation and to make you aware of certain facts pertinent to the matter.

At present, the only access to the school campus is from Dwight Road. Indeed, all buses entering Tremont School go through this entrance, as do all vehicles of parents, faculty, and visitors.

This has two advantages. First, it allows us to know and control the number of vehicles on school property at any given time. Second, while all vehicular traffic is relegated to the Dwight Road side of the building, it provides a safe and protected area for students on the Nutswamp Road side.

The proposed road would change all that. With access to school property from the southwest side of the school, the rear play and recreation area would no longer be safe for the students, requiring increased supervision and personnel. Moreover, we could never be sure that vehicles might not approach from that direction undetected. This is not reflective of paranoia, but reasonable precaution in today's unsettled world.

At the very least, this new road would require a great deal of attention and a diversion of our energies from valuable educational pursuits. We have functioned well with the current situation since the school was established, and I can find no reason to change that which obviously works.

Therefore, I respectfully suggest that the planning board deny proposal Township 286.73-44.

Please feel free to call if I may be of service to the board.

Sincerely yours,

NOTE: Again, letters in support or opposition may be similar in form. Notice, however, that each gives good reasons for the stand of the writer, and each point of view comes from an apparent desire to have what is best for the students of the school.

88. Letter Supporting a City/Township Decision

Because the school is such a vital part of the community, any decisions made by that community through its legal representatives will affect us in one way or another. Let's look at a "letter reaction" to two such decisions—one where the school would be helped and one where it would be hurt.

Members of the Township Committee:

It was just this morning that I learned of your decision last night, at your bi-monthly meeting, to permanently ban smoking anywhere within the public buildings of Manteneau Township. May I state that you have my complete support in this action, and I, for one, congratulate you for your wisdom in coming to this conclusion.

The dangers of smoking and the so-called second-hand smoke are best left to other forums. Needless to say, however, we at Carver High School have held a "no smoking" policy for our students since the school's inception, and have taught the negative effect of smoking in our health classes for decades.

Children learn by example far more than lecture. Being told not to smoke has very little effect when the student sees adults smoking all around him or her. By eliminating smoking anywhere in township buildings, you have set an example that will tremendously benefit the youth of our community.

Again, my congratulations on a well-made decision, and please know that we at Carver High School stand behind you.

Respectfully,

NOTE: This was a letter of full support for a township decision. Note the form: statement of support; reason for support; restatement of support. That's an outline that works well in a variety of letters.

89. Letter Opposing a City/Township Decision

In this letter, written in opposition to a decision, the form is the same, effective one used above; what changes is the content.

Members of the Township Committee:

This morning, I learned of the decision made by you last night, at your bimonthly meeting, to permit Funland Arcade, an establishment containing electronic games played for money and selling soft drinks and snacks and located in the

Manteneau Shopping Center, to remain open on weekdays until 11:00 P.M., a change from its usual closing time of 9:00 P.M., when most of the rest of the mall closes.

It is with regret that I write to you to state my personal opposition to your decision. As an educator, I share the concerns of my fellow educators here at Carver High School—teachers and administrators alike—that your decision on this matter will have far-ranging and negative effects upon our students.

Funland Arcade is a large attraction to the teens of our community. Indeed, recent articles in the *Manteneau Sentinel* have indicated that the place is virtually jammed with youngsters from 3:00 in the afternoon until closing at 9:00 P.M. All this time is time spent away from their studies in a fairly unsupervised area without the restraints and protection of the school environment. These are young people still in the process of developing maturity and responsibility. Many times, homework, studies, and other responsibilities are neglected and become secondary to Funland activities.

Now, with your decision, the place will be allowed to stay open another two hours. Does the committee honestly suppose that teenagers will voluntarily leave at 9:00 in order to get those homework assignments done? Do you suppose that an extended two hours of gathering at such a place will produce fewer of those unfortunate occasions where police have had to be called in to quell near-riot conditions? Is it probable that the situations involving the use and sale of drugs will *decrease* with the additional time your decision provides?

I and many of my colleagues at Carver High School believe that your decision was ill advised. We wish to state our strongest opposition to it, and we urge you to reconsider this action on your part before it turns into something quite undesirable.

If we at Carver may be of any help to you in this regard, please call upon us at any time.

Most sincerely,

NOTE: In a letter of opposition, be very careful not to let your emotions get the better of you. Even here, where it is obvious that the writer thinks the decision is potentially catastrophic, the committee is not railed at, and the entire situation is presented as if to say, "I think you overlooked a few things." Moreover, help is offered, and the concern for the students is prominent throughout.

90. Letter Requesting a Community Action

In this letter, you are initiating a proposed action for a community. It is being sent to a township coordinating committee, which is most likely the agency that would handle such a request. Do a little research first, and find the right person, committee, or agency to receive your request. That's half the battle right there!

Mrs. Shaido, Chairperson, and Members of the Township Coordinating Committee:

I send you greetings in the name of the eight elementary schools, three middle schools, and two high schools of Berkeley Township.

We deeply appreciate just how busy you are, as well as how heavily your responsibilities must lie upon you. With major budgets with which to contend, and the varied and often passionate opinions of all the citizens of our growing township, there must be times when you wish you had some help. That is what we wish to do—help out!

As you are aware, the school budget is up for a vote in two months. We all realize that it will be a highly contested vote, and we all likewise know that the future of many fine educational programs hinges upon its passage. That is why we are contacting you.

We would like to request that the township coordinating committee establish a "Pride in Rock Township Schools" day, to be held two weeks before the budget election. Under your auspices, we would produce posters, streamers, and the like, decorate the schools with student-made ornaments, and produce a flier detailing the accomplishments of the Rock Township Public School System. On the day designated by the committee, we would have a parade featuring the combined marching bands of both high schools, which would end up in Nash Stadium, where a proschool rally would be held.

That rally would consist of music by the high school choruses, bands, and jazz ensemble. There would also be speeches by educators, committee members, and—if she is available—the mayor. The rally would last about 90 minutes.

With this type of support from your committee and the opportunity such a day would present to show the public the great job we are doing in our schools, we honestly feel that the budget would stand a good chance of being passed by the ctizens who have had the opportunity to see the schools at work.

We anxiously await your replay. If we may be of any assistance in that decision, please feel free to contact us.

Respectfully submitted,

NOTE: This letter requested an action. The reason for it was explained, but not in detail. There was enough to spur interest, and that's what counts. If you are going to request a community action, you had best give some reason for it. Details can be worked out later between you and the committee.

91. Letter Granting Access to the School

The schools in a community are for public use, and time and again, various groups rent the school for a meeting. The group must follow certain procedures in applying, and is responsible for the condition of the place afterward, as is usually delineated in the individual school system's policy guide. Here is a letter granting access to a school.

Dear Rev. Jasko,

In reference to your application to use certain facilities of Rock Township High School for Sunday morning meetings of your organization, Rock Township Worship Center, I am pleased to inform you that the school board has granted your request at the terms agreed upon.

You are granted the use of the school "cafetorium," including the kitchen and storage facilities that are connected to it. Please note that there is to be no use of classrooms; these are not included in the permission.

I have enclosed a list of school board requirements for any organization using school property. You will notice that it is your responsibility to provide janitorial services and leave the place the way it was left for you. I am certain you will agree that all the listed rules are reasonable.

Welcome to Rock Township High School! Perhaps I shall stop by one Sunday morning just to say hello.

Yours sincerely,

NOTE: We did not list the rules, because your school surely has such a list, and it may differ from place to place. Note that the letter is friendly, but very professional.

92. Letter Denying Access to the School

Not everyone who applies to use the school automatically gets to do so, and for that, you should check your local school board policy. Here is a letter of denial for one such reason.

Dear Mr. Weir,

This is to inform you that the Rock Township Board of Education has met and considered your request to use the auditorium of Rock Township High School for a political rally on the afternoon prior to election day from 12:00 noon until 5:00 P.M. I regret to inform you that your application has been denied.

Part of the requirements for using school property is that the use "in no way interfere with or substantially disturb the educational process of the school." The time you request occurs during a regular school day at Rock Township High School. It was the feeling of the board that with the media coverage, the noise that would most certainly be generated, and the number of people entering, leaving, and generally in the hallways, there is no way that education could *not* be disturbed. This is no reflection upon you or upon your constituents—merely a matter of fact.

Again, I regret that I could not have had better news for you, but I am certain that you will understand that the education of our students must be our first priority.

Thank you for your understanding.

Most sincerely,

NOTE: The denial was made, a sound reason given, and all in a friendly but professional letter. That's the essence of a good school letter of this type—simple, factual, professional.

93. Answering a Positive Letter from the Community

Schools get letters; that's a fact. Sometimes these letters leave you wondering if you are in the same place they describe, sometimes these letters are releases of frustration simply aimed at the school because it's there, and sometimes they are wonderful, warmhearted letters telling you what you've done right. Here's a reply to one of the latter variety.

Dear Mr. Samopoli,

Thank you so much for your letter of January 21. It meant a great deal to us at Rock Township High School. In a world where the bad and the negative are plastered on the front pages of newspapers and TV news programs, it is so refreshing to receive a letter like yours, abounding with good will.

Let me tell you that after I read it, I showed it to a number of people in the school, including all the teachers who had had your son Nicholas in class. Needless to say, they were all delighted to hear of Nicki's progress at medical school, and they, as well as I, were humbled at your praise of this school and its personnel in preparing him for his transition to college. We remember Nicki with fondness, and we remember his service to this school while he was here. Everyone here is certain that he will make an outstanding doctor.

Again, let me tell you how much you brightened our day. We were privileged to have Nicki, and we are so thankful that you took the time to express your appreciation of our efforts. In a many times thankless job, it is good to know that someone cares.

Your graciousness will sustain us through many nights.

Yours most sincerely,

NOTE: If the writer had included anything specific or asked a question, you could comment upon that or answer the specific question, rather than giving a general return such as the letter above. In either case, be enthusiastic and genuine.

94. Answering a Negative Letter from the Community

As not every letter that comes in to the school from the community is one of encouragement and good cheer, let's consider ways to reply to the negative letters. Some are general letters of complaint or negativity, some are negative about various school personnel, some express negativity at a decision you or the school has made, and some may be just negative about you, personally. Let's deal with all of these, starting with the answer to a generally negative letter.

Dear Mrs. Patouli,

I am in receipt of your letter dated June 2, _____. I assure you that I, as well as several others, have read it very carefully—not once, but several times. To say the least, it was most disturbing.

Basically, you seem to take us to task for "failure to provide a safe place for children." You further claim that this "failure" is "a symptom of the neglectful and uncaring attitude the school has always had toward its students."

Since you did not specify any particular way in which we had been "neglectful" of our students' well-being and safety, we began to investigate. We found that your daughter Joellen sustained a sprained ankle approximately two weeks ago. The accident report and follow-up interviews with the teachers who witnessed the incident indicate that Joellen was running in the halls when she met up with another youngster coming around a corner. That student was walking; your daughter was running. Joellen suffered a sprained ankle, which was immediately treated here in school by a professional nurse. She was later transported by the first-aid squad to Meuller General, where it was further attended to before she was released.

Of course we care about the safety of our students, and of course we take a great many precautions to see to that safety. In the case of your daughter, for instance, you might wish to read page 47 of the student handbook. Paragraph 16 states in part, "Running in the hallways of this school is *not* permitted, as many serious accidents could occur unless all students walk to classes." I respectfully suggest that had Joellen followed this rule, the accident might never have occurred.

This is just one of many rules and regulation in effect to protect the students of our school from harm. In addition, we have faculty members on regular duty in places where such mishaps may occur, which is why your daughter received such prompt attention. If they are followed, these rules provide that safety you bemoaned in your letter. If they are not followed, then perhaps they can stand reinforcement both at school and at home.

We care about our students, and we care deeply. I hope that this reply can give you a new insight into just how much we care.

Sincerely,

NOTE: It is often effective to quote from the individual's letter and then answer those parts you have quoted, as was done here. No matter how bad the letter, you should never show a negative reaction in your own reply.

95. Answering a Negative Letter Concerning School Personnel, I

Negative letters that come in about school personnel, from teachers and aides to secretaries and cafeteria workers, seem to come in two flavors—the bad and the horrendous. Let's begin with the lesser of the two.

Dear Mr. Wasserman,

I have received your letter of March 12, _____, expressing your concerns about Mr. Sanchez, a teacher at our school. I assure you that your letter has been read thoroughly by myself and several others at the administrative level. Before we progress any further, we feel that it is necessary for you to completely understand several very important facts.

First, you maintain that Mr. Sanchez "gives too much homework, keeping the students up after their bedtime." You should be aware that the amount of homework given in a class is the direct responsibility of the teacher. On no evaluation of Mr. Sanchez over the past eleven years has this been noted as a problem. Indeed, Mr. Sanchez has several letters in his personnel file from parents praising the fact that he "makes his students work" as one parent put it. In short, what you mention as a detriment might well be considered an asset by others.

Then, you mention that you personally saw Mr. Sanchez come out of a place "that served alcoholic beverages." You then contend that this is "not fitting for a person who teaches children." I would remind you that Mr. Sanchez's personal life is just that—personal. Where Mr. Sanchez goes or what he does with his life outside school cannot, legally, be our concern. Indeed, if I saw you coming out of such a place, I would have no right to contend that you were not fit to be a parent, would I? We can only be concerned with the job he does, and constant evaluations have shown him more than adequate in that regard.

Should you wish to pursue the matter before the school board, I would advise you to retain legal counsel, to avoid any actionable statements. The decision, of course, is yours.

You may, of course, contact the school at any time, and I would even try to arrange a meeting with Mr. Sanchez and you and proper school representatives as you suggested, but I honestly do not believe that anything more substantive than what I have affirmed in this letter would be forthcoming.

Yours most sincerely,

NOTE: This letter was easily handled by merely stating a few truths. That alone can defuse a situation. Let that be your rule; don't go beyond what is required for answering the negative letter.

96. Answering a Negative Letter Concerning School Personnel, II

Now, let's get to a really serious complaint against school personnel. Of course, if the complaint contains anything that would be actionable under law, then the best policy might be to turn it over to the board attorney. Let's assume, however, that for now, just the suggestion of legal pursuit is sufficient.

Dear Ms. Castelli,

I have received, read, and studied your letter of September 30, _____, concerning the actions of Mr. Raymond Pettigrew, the chief custodian at our school.

Just to restate, in order that we both understand the content of your letter, you state that on September 27, _____, following the "Open House Night" at our school, you chanced to be alone with Mr. Pettigrew during what could best be described as cleanup activities. You state that at that time, while other women were attending to other tasks outside the custodian's room where you and Mr. Pettigrew were located, Mr. Pettigrew, to use your own words, "grabbed at [you] and touched [you] in inappropriate places." When you told him to stop, you claim that he laughed, and you were forced to flee from the room.

Needless to say, this is a very serious accusation, and one that, if proven valid, could lead at the very least to Mr. Pettigrew's dismissal. It must, therefore, be handled in the most sensitive manner.

I have spoken to Mr. Pettigrew before witnesses, and he claims that it was a misunderstanding. He states that you lost your balance, and he did place his hands on you, but only to steady you so that you would not fall. He denies that the placement of his hands was "inappropriate." He further claims that he laughed because he thought you were joking with him.

Obviously, this matter will require further investigation. I have set up a meeting for Friday, October 3, _____ with our board attorney, Mr. Pettigrew, and his union representative. I invite you to join us, and I advise you of your right to have legal representation present—or anyone else of your choosing.

Please contact me as soon as possible to confirm the date of our meeting. Your charge is serious, and I assure you that we will handle it in a serious and most responsible manner.

Most sincerely,

NOTE: This charge was far more serious than the previous one. You will never get into trouble checking it out with the board attorney first. The implications of a case of sexual harassment, as this purports to be, are so serious that you had better "get all your ducks in a row" first.

97. Answering a Negative Letter Concerning a School Decision, I

As the saying goes, "you can't please everybody." Perhaps that is more particularly true in education than anywhere else. Educators, from teachers to administrators, make decisions every day of their lives, for that is part of the job. Many times, these decisions do not set well with some people. Here's an example of an answer to a letter of complaint about one such decision.

Dear Mrs. Pease,

There are times when I truly wish that all the decisions that had to be made in a school could be pleasing to everyone. I am also aware that this simply cannot be, because of the wide range of views in this community that we serve. It is, regrettably, guaranteed that some decisions will please, while others will displease, any given person within the community. I believe that is what we have here.

I have very carefully read your letter to me of November 13, _____. I have also shared it with several administrators on staff here at the school.

As a teacher, part of my job is to set rules and make decisions regarding the work done in my classroom. Therefore, when the project in question was assigned to your son, with it came a sheet of criteria and a listing of rules for its completion. One of the rules reads, "The project is due on the day for which it was assigned. Late projects will receive one grade off for each day late." Troy had this sheet from the beginning, the project was mentioned daily, and the due date posted prominently on the board.

When Troy did not have his project in for three school days following the deadline, he received a failing grade, since the project was poorly done and would have received a *D* or *C* under the best conditions.

Of course, we are not heartless, and we realize that there may be extenuating circumstances. When Troy was questioned as to why it was late, he first said he didn't know and later stated that he "forgot" it was due. Under those circumstances, I virtually had no other choice than to allow the grade to stand.

If you wish to pursue this matter further, please contact the main office and arrange a conference where we can speak and have the principal present as well.

Thank you for your concern.

Very truly yours,

NOTE: Usually, most negative letters about pesonnel don't go beyond the expression of negativity in the letter, and most of the time a letter of response, particularly from the principal or someone in charge, seems to end the turmoil. Sometimes that just doesn't happen, as in this next letter.

98. Answering a Negative Letter Concerning a School Decision, II

The previous letter was used to handle a relatively easy complaint. Now let's look at a response to a negative letter concerning a major decision that affected the entire school. Here, we use our maxim from before, and answer the question without resorting to commentary—and certainly not reacting emotionally.

Dear Ms. Longbow,

I have read and understood your letter of March 10, _____. I have also shared it with others, including the assistant superintendent at the central administration building. I hope that my answer will be sufficient to solve the problem.

You state in your letter that my recent decision as principal of Rock Township High School to require all students to prove the reason for their absence in the form of a note that is subsequently checked by our office staff literally constitutes an invasion of privacy. You state further that the decision is evidence of distrust on my part which, you contend, is an example of how schools are destroying the free will of our students.

Those are very serious charges, and I am extremely saddened that you should even feel that this condition exists in our school, much less that I should be the one who, to you, is the instigator. Let's take these one at a time.

First, let me state unequivocally that the vast majority of our students have no trouble with absenteeism. They are absent only when they are ill; they are here when they are healthy. There is a percentage, however, who do not consider their education paramount—who have a history of cutting school. As long as they can get away with that, they continue to hurt themselves by their lack of attendance, and others by their example. The new rule was made to discourage absenteeism and to see to it that the majority of students do what they are required by law to do. The decision is no more arbitrary than the law requiring one to stop at red lights.

Furthermore, I deeply resent the implication that I, personally, do not care about the students of this school or that any decision made is aimed at "destroying" the minds of our student body. I tell you frankly that I will stand on my record, which has been approved by the board of education and validated by the student body time and time again.

If you wish to pursue this matter, please call for an appointment and we shall talk in the presence of the superintendent and board attorney. I advise you that at such a meeting, you have the right to be represented by counsel as well.

Perhaps this can be the end of it, but if you insist on carrying it beyond this, please be advised that I will not allow myself or this school I love so much to be so attacked without cause.

If you wish to carry this matter further, please contact me to make arrangements to do so.

Sincerely,

NOTE: This is a no-nonsense reply. In all likelihood, the charges would end here. If the complaint continues, however, you have clearly stated what you will do. There are some matters you cannot let go, and your reputation for caring for your students is one of those things.

99. Answering a Negative Letter Concerning Yourself

While there will be letters that attack your decisions, such as the last one, there may also be those that attack you on a personal level. Here is a short but effective answer to such a letter.

Dear Mr. McLeod,

I have received your letter of December 16, _____, in which you comment on both my personal appearance and my speaking ability. You refer to my appearance at a school function for a guidance activity here at Rock Township High School.

You claim that my appearance was "a disgrace, reflecting a sense of style that went out three decades ago." Furthermore, you claim that my speech was "uninspired" and "totally devoid of serious content."

Sir, my purpose in speaking that night was to introduce the other speakers on a very serious topic. That is what I did, and I feel that I accomplished my purpose for that evening.

As far as my dress was concerned, I assure you that my clothing was clean and comfortable, and served its avowed purposes of covering and warmth. Other than that, all I can say is that style is arbitrary at best.

In short, thank you for bringing those facts to my attention. I regret that my standards are wanting in your eyes, but that, sir, is life.

Please let me know if I may be of any further service.

Yours sincerely,

NOTE: Come on now, we've all gotten letters like the one just answered. A personal attack should be answered by calmness if it is to be effective. Getting angry, even with the most frivolous and picayune of negative letters, merely places you on the level of the writer and does no good at all. The letter above answers it well.

100. Accepting an Invitation from the Community

Invitations to do certain things or go certain places within the community come in to the school all the time. A community group wishes you to speak at a luncheon. A civic group wants you to represent the school at a tree planting. A dinner is being given for the mayor, and you are asked to speak. And so it goes. Let's begin with a happy letter, where you accept the invitation.

Dear Mrs. Quentin,

Thank you for your very kind letter of September 27, _____, in which you extend an invitation to me to be the guest speaker at the Betsy Ross Civic Association regular meeting and luncheon to be held on Thursday, October 11, _____, at 11:30 A.M. at the Waterfront Café here in Rock Township.

It is with a true sense of honor that I accept your invitation; I will be there at the time and date mentioned above.

My speech will be titled, "Inside the Schools; Inside Tomorrow." It is approximately 30 minutes in length, and all that I will require is a microphone and PA setup which, it is my understanding, the Waterfront Café supplies.

I shall be most happy to speak to your fine organization, and I truly look forward to being with you on that day.

Again, thank you for the invitation. I hope I will be able to justify your judgment in inviting me.

Sincerely,

NOTE: This is a rather clear-cut letter, but notice that in the reply, you have supplied all the information necessary for the event to which you were invited. By doing this, you give them the opportunity to use the information for advertising purposes as they may deem advisable.

101. Turning Down an Invitation from the Community, I

Not every invitation from a community source is one that you wish to accept. Turning down that invitation, however, should be done gently, with avenues left open for future contact. Here's an example.

Dear Mr. Leferts,

Thank you so much for your recent letter inviting me to be the guest speaker at the December 10, _____, meeting of your fine organization.

May I state that the Rock Township Betterment Society has, in my opinion, done a considerable amount of good for our community and our schools? Indeed, we consider your organization to be a friend of our schools.

That makes it all the harder to have to decline your invitation. I would love to accept, but a look at my date book confirms that I will be in Dallas, Texas, at a convention of elementary school administrators. Believe me, only the urgency of that meeting keeps me from attending the meeting of your group.

I hope for two things: I hope that you will forgive my having to turn down your invitation, and I hope that you will call upon me in the future to speak at a time when I am not otherwise engaged.

I assure you, that would be an invitation I would be quick to accept.

Yours truly,

NOTE: You can see how this letter turning down an invitation left it wide open for future contact. We sincerely doubt that anyone could be offended by such a refusal.

102. Turning Down an Invitation from the Community, II

The previous letter turned down an invitation and left it open that a future request would be welcomed and accepted. Now let's deal with an invitation you do not, under any circumstances, wish to accept. Here, we wish to leave no avenues open.

Dear Mr. Smith,

I have received and read with growing interest your letter of April 16, _____, in which you invite me to speak at a rally of the Purity League, in order that I might have a chance to "explain, if [I] can, the racial policies of [our] anti-American school system that proposes the mixing of mongrel races."

Those were your words, and these are mine. I decline your invitation, and choose not to associate myself with your group or its stated aims.

Sincerely,

NOTE: This very forceful letter makes both your position and your feelings perfectly clear. A letter this strong should be used sparingly, and only when you are convinced that circumstances warrant its use. It is important, however, not to become offensive nor to resort to name calling.

103. Replying to a Community Action Group, I

Any community is composed of a large number of individuals with individual opinions and viewpoints. Many times, individuals of like opinions join together to form groups for various purposes. Sometimes their purposes are lofty, and sometimes much more mundane. These community action groups can be very helpful to the school, and any letter to you or the school by them should be answered thoughtfully. First, let's look at a response to a letter that was very positive.

Dear Mrs. Kimanan,

I received the letter from your group, Citizens for a Better Rock Township, just the other day, and I am delighted to read that your group will be sponsoring a "Pride in Rock Township Schools" day just prior to the general budget election. I am certain that it will go a long way toward informing the public about the good job being done in our schools and exerting a very positive influence on the passage of this year's school budget.

Toward that goal, we at Rock Township High School stand ready to provide you with any and all assistance.

I, personally, can be of use in obtaining permission to use Nash Stadium and facilitate the marching bands, choruses, and special musical performances. Our graphic arts department will gladly provide whatever posters and streamers are deemed necessary.

In short, we stand ready to help.

I would suggest that our first step might be a meeting in order to get together and discuss the totality of this project and perhaps clarify our roles in this most worthy endeavor. Can we meet Friday, February 11, _____, in my office at Rock Township High School? Also at the meeting will be the vice-principal and the head guidance counselor, who can be very helpful in projects like this. I will also be advising the central administration of this, and they may wish to send a board representative to attend.

Should any representatives of your organization wish to attend this meeting, please feel free to bring them. I would appreciate your telling me in order that I may have some idea of the refreshments needed.

Of course, should that date present any difficulty, please let me know and we will reschedule immediately.

I am truly looking forward to meeting with you. I have every expectation that this project will prove of ultimate benefit to our schools and, by projection, to the children of this township.

Please call me and let me know your pleasure, and thank you for your continuing concern for Rock Township schools.

Yours sincerely,

NOTE: You'll agree that this is a very positive answer to a letter that you really wanted. Note the numbers of details mentioned as well as the extreme willingness to accommodate the request from the community group in any way possible. It is a truism that your enthusiasm is contagious in every situation, and your enthusiasm here can make others involved in this project catch fire as well.

104. Replying to a Community Action Group, II

Again, not all community action groups are positive and helpful to the school. The first reply was very positive, because the action group wanted to do something that was very proschool and that might even help with the school budget. Now, let's look at a letter in response to a group from the community that opposes what your school is doing. We are assuming the group, here, to be a "watchdog" organization whose concern is the ever-rising school tax. In today's economy, that is not a far-fetched assumption.

Dear Mrs. Trimmer,

Yesterday, I received copy of your "Open Letter to the Community" from your organization, Citizens United for Tax Reform. In that letter, you call for a public forum in which to discuss what you call the "misuse of tax revenues" in our schools.

Your "open letter" then goes on to state that "waste of the citizens' tax dollars" is "legendary in our township, and is nowhere more pervasive than in our very own high school." Finally, it is your contention that the "wasters of revenue be held accountable for their flagrant spending and unnecessary outlay of expenses" to the "detriment of the average taxpayer of our community."

I would like you to know that I take exception to both the tenor and content of that letter. If you wish a public forum to discuss this matter, I would like to offer one to you. If such a forum will bring out the facts of the matter, you will find me *most cooperative* in making it available.

If you will contact me at your earliest convenience, we can discuss a location and time for such a public debate. I will personally participate and look forward to the opportunity to place the case of the schools before the public.

As an educator in Rock Township for many years, I am well aware of the needs and expenditures of our school system. I can assure you that I shall not be hesitant in placing before the public facts that are substantiated by public records, and they tell quite a different story from that told in your letter.

I will await your call; I am eager to enter into public debate. May I hear from you soon?

Very truly yours,

NOTE: An action group aimed at "exposing" the school, for whatever reason, real or imagined, is a formidable force to work against. We all know that the possibility exists. The only way to handle such action, many feel, is by an equal reaction. In the letter just given, if your reply had been weak, there would only have been stronger attacks. With the answer given above, the wind is taken out of their sails, so to speak, and any confrontation will be on neutral ground where you stand an equal chance.

105. Replying to a Community Protest Group, I

Civic groups, community action groups, civic action leagues, and the like are a part of the school scene, because they so directly affect the school. Whether the influence is for good or for bad, however, they absolutely pale beside the impact that a community protest group can have upon a school or school system. A protest group, unlike most other community organizations, is single-minded. Usually, such groups are formed for one purpose or to achieve a single goal, and that directness of purpose may often manifest itself in legal forms of expression of dissent, or even acts of purposeful civil disobedience.

It is neither our purpose nor our desire to argue the rightness or wrongness of causes here, nor, in all reality, does that have a bearing on a protest group's interaction with the school. In any reply to a letter from such a group, it would be well to remember that your purpose is to mediate, not confront, which should always be a last resort.

Let's look at two replies to protest groups—one easy and one not so easy. Let's begin with one that might be handled fairly quickly, before it gets out of hand.

Dear Mr. Padden,

I am in receipt of your letter of October 25, _____, and I assure you that I have read it carefully and shared it with the vice-principal and the head of guidance at our school.

I wish to understand fully, so please allow me to restate what I believe to be the problem as stated in your letter.

The seventh-grade reading anthology currently in use here at Carter Middle School contains two short stories entitled "City Sun Rising" by Gary Connors* and "Aunt Maude's Porch" by Harriet Yancy.* You read these stories, shared them with "many other concerned parents," and found them to be "morally objectionable" to you. So much do you believe this that you and the other concerned citizens have formed a group you call Citizens Asking for Morality, Ethics, and Order, or CAMEO, for short. The aim of this group is to keep from your children such stories as the ones mentioned.

You mention that CAMEO will be willing to do whatever is necessary to bring "some sense of moral sanity" back to the classroom, and "protect [the] children from exposure to this type of material."

_____

* The titles and authors are fictitious and used as examples only.

In reply, let me first state that I sincerely hope that in this process we can also teach our children that adults may disagree without confrontation, and that willing spirits can always reach a satisfactory solution.

As to specifics, the stories mentioned are part of an anthology that was approved by the board of education for use in our school. Recourse to having such a book removed from the curriculum starts with a formal petitioning of the board, which will then hold hearings and work according to established procedures.

In the meantime, as far as your children are concerned, we have had a policy for quite a number of years to handle just this type of situation. If you will supply me with the names of the children of the members of your group, I assure you that they will be excused from reading those stories when such time comes in class. Instead, they will be given an equal, meaningful assignment that will be graded in place of any assignment or work on the stories mentioned. They will not receive more work—just different work in order that they may keep up with the class while not having to read anything you deem inappropriate.

I hope, sir, that this will prove sufficient to handle the matter at hand. I await hearing from you with the names of the children, and please contact me if there is any further need of discussion on this matter.

Most sincerely,

NOTE: This letter is an attempt to extinguish a brush fire before it turns into a forest fire. Should you receive a letter like the one that prompted the above response, you would be wise to share it with school board authorities before replying, just to make sure you are doing the right thing. The policy mentioned in the letter, by the way, of giving meaningful work in place of a contested assignment, has worked well in a number of situations, and has stopped many a protest at ground level.

106. Replying to a Community Protest Group, II

The worst thing in dealing with a protest group is when it comes to physical confrontation in spite of all efforts—perhaps on both sides—to prevent it. A school surrounded by angry parents or teachers or a special-interest group is not a pretty sight nor a healthy one for our students. Here is a "last minute" letter about just such an action.

Dear Ms. Parone,

I am aware that your group is to hold a formal protest at our school on Thursday, October 16, _____, from 8:00 A.M. until 4:00 P.M. if there is no action from the school board, which meets the previous evening. You have made it abundantly clear in letters to various school officials and the local newspapers.

I do not dispute for one moment your constitutional right of assembly and of peaceful protest. Rather, I ask that we join forces on the one issue that it seems we have always agreed upon throughout this entire process—we love our children, and we do not want to see them hurt.

We at Carter Elementary School will do our very best to see to the safety of our children as they enter and leave school and go about their normal routines. We do not intend to allow them to come near the fenced area where you will be protesting, and we ask, for their safety, that you do not encourage them to do so.

Moreover, we surely all want learning to go on in our schools. I would ask, for the sake of our children, that you consider this in the noise level of your actions. I also ask that you be judicious and allow supplies to enter and waste to be removed during your protest.

We wish nothing more than to get through that day in safety and in relative peace. Surely, you must have the best interests of the children of this township at heart as well. Therefore, we look forward to a peaceful protest that will allow our children to continue their education.

Thank you for your concern, and let us both pray that this situation may still be averted.

Yours sincerely,

NOTE: What we would do with a letter like this is send a copy to the head of the protesting organization, and a copy to the local newspaper. Protests frequently get out of hand, and a letter like this shows that you care and have tried your best to avoid any difficulties for your children.

Section
Six

EFFICIENTLY HANDLING LETTERS OF COMPLAINT

"How are things going?" asked the superintendent.

"I can't complain!" replied the teacher.

"Wonderful! You must be very happy here."

"Not at all!" stated the teacher. "You see, I *want* to complain, but that dumb principal just won't listen to me!"

You may chuckle or grimace at that old joke, but like most humor, it has the "germ of truth" that strikes that responsive chord in our minds. Everybody complains to one degree or another. With some, it is a verbal and a once-in-a-while event, while to others it is a constant process involving speaking and writing. Therefore, it is not surprising that you may be called upon to either write a letter of complaint or answer one that has come to your desk.

Let's see what we can do about that.

GETTING RESULTS WITH LETTERS OF COMPLAINT

Why do we complain? The answer is simple—to get results and have something changed. Sometimes, this is a relatively easy task. We write a simple letter, and results are forthcoming. Many times, however, it is much more complicated than that, involving a number of steps and a number of remedies. Whatever the occasion or details, the results you get will be quicker and more complete if certain basic rules are followed.

The three rules of good complaining are basically modifications of the so-called Golden Rule. If we "do unto others as we would have them do unto us," then we will have a letter of complaint that will get attention.

RULE ONE: Always Be Civil—This means be polite as well. Never resort to invective or name calling, no matter how frustrated you may be. Be kind, and if at all possible, be humorous as well. A cheerful letter, traditionally, gets noticed and gets answered. How would you answer a letter that began, "Dear Stupid"? Be gentle; this is not a power struggle.

RULE TWO: Always Be Specific—Give the part number that is missing or tell how the projector is broken or explain exactly what action you wish the recipients to take. Never assume that they are mind readers and automatically know what you are talking about. Be reasonable. If a bottle cap came off and stained the top of your desk, we seriously doubt that you are entitled to $50 million in compensatory damages.

RULE THREE: Never Threaten— Threatening gets your letter tossed out or turned over to a lawyer—both actions causing a considerable amount of delay. If it ever comes to the point where you do have to seek out legal action, it will be a last resort. Even if legal action becomes necessary, you should never offer the hint of a threat. Even something like "If I cannot find satisfaction, I shall have to resort to more aggressive legal means" should not appear in any letter other than the last one you, personally, write before your lawyer takes over.

Start by being civil and friendly. Be specific as to what happened and what you desire. Avoid being demanding or threatening. Combine these three, and you will have a letter of complaint that gets noticed, gets read, and gets acted upon.

In this section, you will find a number of examples of letters of complaint about every school-related subject from textbooks and supplies right up to letters of complaint about a class, a teacher, an administrator, or the school itself. In each of them, you will find those three rules at work. In writing a letter of complaint, you want the situation righted, and that is the intent of all the letters you'll find here. As you read them, try putting yourself in the place of the person receiving the letter, and try to imagine what your reaction might be to it. Putting yourself in the place of the person to whom you are writing will always help you write an intelligent, effective, and efficient letter that will be well received and well answered.

Read on.

MODEL LETTERS THAT HANDLE COMPLAINTS

107. Complaining About a Textbook

This first letter is meant to show you all the rules in action. Notice that, while it is relatively short and to the point, all of the elements we discussed are present— from identifying the textbook to the remedy that is desired. See the note that follows the letter for additional ideas.

Dear Mr. Dixon,

Recently, our school system purchased over 550 copies of your company's literature anthology for seventh-grade students. I refer specifically to *Imagination*, Silver Edition, copyright _____, by your company, edited by Maurice Alster, Ph.D., and others.

We ordered this book after a long search, and we are quite delighted with it. In fact, we would love our seventh graders to read the whole thing, except for one unfortunate fact—it's not all there.

By that, I do not mean to imply a mental aberration; I mean exactly what I say— it is not all there. Each of the copies we received is missing pages 177 through 197. These twenty pages make up most of the section you call "Imagine: The World of the Author."

We have dealt with your company many times in the past, and our relationship has always been satisfactory. I am certain that this oversight will be corrected just as amicably. We request that you replace our "less than whole" textbooks with ones that contain the missing pages.

We do have a bit of a time constraint here, as school starts in about three weeks, and the teachers will want to use their textbooks from the very first day. I know that you appreciate our situation, as we appreciate yours.

I would be glad of a call from you as soon as possible, therefore, so we can work out the exchange. I know from your past cooperation that we will be ready for the new school year with your wonderful anthology, whole and entire, for our seventh grade.

I am looking forward to hearing from you.

Very truly yours,

NOTE: While this was about missing pages in a new textbook, the complaint could have been about anything related to a textbook. The product and defect were very specifically noted, so the manufacturer knew precisely what was in question. The result wanted was explicitly pointed out, and the letter still remained positive, even a trifle humorous, and assumed cooperation. A letter like this will usually not have to have another letter follow it. Try it; it gets results.

108. Complaining About Wrong School Supplies

Mix-ups in school supplies are legendary, and so are the complaints about them. Even so, look for the pattern suggested earlier and the very specific listing in order to ensure that your wrong school supplies do not get replaced with supplies that are even "wronger."

Dear Mrs. Ballis,

As part of our school supplies for the _____–_____ school year, I ordered certain items that we need to continue the educational process as we have every school year, but I fear that something may have gone wrong—"gotten lost in the translation" as it were. I ordered some specific items and received items like those ordered, but they were not the same. In short, I received some very wrong school supplies. I refer specifically to the following:

We Ordered:	*We Received:*
#554R3—5 × 7 Yellow Pads	#554R2—3 × 5 Yellow Pads
#557R8—3 × 5 White Index Cards	#557R3—3 × 5 Gummed Labels
#58Q7A—No. 2 Pencils With Erasers	#58Q8A—No. 2 Pencils w/o Erasers
#59T77a—Manila Practice Paper	#59T76b—Colonial White Drawing Paper
#66YG23—Teacher Marking Books	#66YG28—Marble Composition Books

As you can see, the supplies received in these five cases were a number or a letter and number different from those listed by me on the original order form.

While some of the items you sent us are intriguing, and we might want to order them next year, we really do need the supplies we ordered for the beginning of the school year—which is coming in two weeks, as I am certain you are aware.

Of course, mistakes happen; that's why we ordered the No. 2 pencils *with* erasers, and we do understand how demanding your position must be, especially at this time of the year. We do, however, need our supplies for the quickly coming school year, and I am certain that you appreciate that as well.

May I look forward to a phone call from you when you receive this? I am certain that we can make arrangements to get this matter straightened out just as soon as possible, even before the first child arrives at school.

Thank you for your understanding and cooperation. I look forward to hearing from you.

Very truly yours,

NOTE: In a letter like this, you would also include the quantity ordered and delivered. Also, if your supplies come from a central supply office, you would, of course, first check out school district policy and follow that in your letter to the specific agent responsible.

109. Complaining About Insufficient School Supplies

The budget and the proportional school allotment—and therefore teacher allotment—fluctuates with the budget amount. Needless to say, teachers and administrators never complain about having too much to spend for supplies, but time and again, they bemoan the fact that their supplies will not outlast the demand for them in their classes. Here is a letter of complaint about a general insufficiency of supplies.

Dear Superintendent Harafa,

Education will continue in the classrooms of Tyler County High School. Teachers will teach and students will learn. What I write to you about, however, is not that education continues but that it continues under what I and many others feel to be an unfair and unnecessary burden.

I speak of the general insufficiency of school supplies that we face at Tyler. Certainly, the recent budgetary cuts have gone to the bone, and that "bone" seems to be the very classrooms of our schools.

The community, through the school board, tasks us with the education of its children. Then, when we ask for the essentials, we are met with the "necessity" to cut school funds. It is as if we were hired to paint a house and then told that we could use neither brushes nor sprayers, but had to figure some other way of getting the job done.

Nor do we think that an inapt analogy. We are not, when we speak of supplies, talking about extravagances. We do not need gold-tipped Mount Blanc fountain pens, but some pencils for our students would be nice to have, as would practice paper, and perhaps a textbook that understood what a "computer" was.

In short, the insufficiency of school supplies this year will hurt us at Tyler High School; it will hurt the teachers, and it will hurt the students most of all. Therefore, I feel that, in all conscience, I must voice my most serious objections to the budget cuts that so deeply affect the classrooms of our schools. I am hopeful that you will bring these concerns to the board of education and ask them to most earnestly reconsider the situation with school supplies as it currently exists.

In the meantime, understand that education will continue, and we will do our best as we have always done our best, with the goal in mind of a thorough and total education for each of the children of our community.

Won't you help us do our job?

Most sincerely,

NOTE: A principal, or a head of a teachers' professional association, might write a letter like this to a school board, or even as a public letter in a local newspaper. What it says is very basic, and the hope is that it will elicit the agreement of all concerned.

110. Complaining About Poor Quality of Materials

There are times when, to save money (what else?), the slightly higher-priced materials that are ordered are replaced by, shall we say, "generic" brands. While they may be the same type of item you requested, they are cheaper, and often that is because they are made differently, allowing the company to charge less. While this may be fine for the accounting office, it often poses a problem in the classroom. Take a look.

Dear Mrs. Pacalli,

Don't you love the "What If . . ." game?

What if you went to write on the blackboard and the chalk crumbled away as you wrote? . . . and the next piece? . . . and the next piece? What if you gave out practice paper for math, and the pencils went through the paper and tore it up, almost every single time, no matter how "gently" the children wrote? What if the children received bound notebooks, and three days later twenty out of twenty-seven of the notebooks had lost their covers or started to unravel? What if?

Well, we don't have to play the "What If . . ." game at all. All we need do is visit the classrooms of this school, because everything that I just described—and more—is happening right now.

I thought I heard you ask why this is taking place. Well, I'll be glad to hazard a guess. You see, all the materials I described above were those materials substituted for what had originally been ordered. The reason for the substitution, may one assume, was the lower price of the items. Unfortunately, the lower price also brought with it a lower quality of product, the partial results of which I just detailed. Indeed, those are not isolated instances, but come from all over this building.

We understand that it would be virtually impossible, at this point, to replace all the poorer-quality materials with the original orders, nor do we ask for that. Somehow, we will muddle through with what we have, but we will pay a price in having to require students to purchase materials, continued frustration with the poor results of low-quality materials, and time lost due to having to do the same thing time and again.

What we do ask is that the board of education be made aware of this situation and of our frustration at having to work with these materials. We would also ask the township purchasing officers to understand that the amount saved by these substitutions will be paid for in other ways that may not be so desirable. In subsequent years, perhaps the purchasing office will remember that in education there is and has always been a priority of quality over quantity, that "a penny saved" can often amount to "a dollar's worth of trouble and frustration," and that we *must* weigh one against the other.

With every hope that next year may bring with it chalk that writes and composition books that remain books, I am

Very truly yours,

NOTE: This letter, in spite of the obvious frustrations experienced, is reasonable. Perhaps our first reaction to a situation like this would be to demand that these low-grade materials be replaced, and replaced now! Well, that would simply be impossible. No school system can afford to do that on the scale that would be required. The best you could hope for would be to have the system changed for the succeeding years, and that's precisely what this letter asks for.

---

111. Complaining About Defective Materials

A poor-quality material is quite different from a defective material. You can live with poor quality; you cannot function with something that is defective. Your goal, since you obviously want to use the item in class, is to either get it fixed or get it replaced—as soon as possible. Let's take a look.

Dear Mr. Weston,

I am writing in regard to an item from your catalog, #322MI16J, the Weston School Microscope. As you may be aware, our school purchased twenty-five (25) of these just two months ago, in August of _____. Our difficulties began with the very first use by students.

Simply put, the lenses keep dropping out. We are extremely conscientious about the ways in which our students use materials that are expensive and meant to last a long time. Therefore, we are certain that the students did nothing to occasion the "drop-out" rate. To date, over sixteen microscopes have lost their lenses—the said lenses dropping out both while in use and sometimes while sitting on the shelf.

An examination by one of our science teachers yielded the following explanation. The microscopes that operate normally and still retain their integrity have a rubberlike grommet inside the microscope barrel where the lens is seated. The microscopes with the propensity for lens dropping do not have this circular part. Our investigation shows that seventeen of the twenty-five microscopes do not have the operative part.

We think you will agree that these microscopes are fairly unusable in their present condition. Consequently, we are certain that you will wish to either fix the microscopes in question or take them back and supply new ones. Either case would be acceptable to us. Whatever you might decide, however, I am sure that I need hardly tell you that we need these items in our science classrooms as soon as possible.

I look forward to hearing from you within the next week in order that we may discuss this matter further.

Sincerely,

NOTE: Make certain that you remind the supplier that you are a school and need the proper materials right away. Note that the last line sets a time limit—in a friendly manner—that is much better than saying "at your earliest convenience" or something of that sort. Being specific is a key to getting action.

112. Complaining About Delayed Delivery

When you need something for the start of the school year, you mean the current school year. Indeed, few things are more frustrating than to depend upon something for a specified time, only to find that it has not arrived, even though you feel that you have allowed more than sufficient time. A delayed delivery can cause a great deal of frustration and inconvenience, to say the least. Here is a letter that deals with just such a situation.

Dear Mr. Vetter,

We are aware of the fine student desks manufactured by your company. Your reputation precedes you, and that is why we placed a rather large order with your firm for 230 brand-new school desks. At the time of the ordering in April of _____, we were assured by your office manager, Mrs. Florence Kalapuch, and later in a separate letter from you, that delivery would be made in six weeks—certainly not to exceed two months.

It is currently the middle of August, four months from the original order, and the desks have yet to be delivered.

I am sure you are aware that school begins in less than three weeks. At the beginning of July, we got rid of 230 old desks, because we had been assured that the new desks would arrive shortly.

The question is, where do we place 230 youngsters when school opens if the desks have not yet arrived? That is a question we must deal with and you must answer.

We need the desks we ordered, and we need them within the next three weeks. While we are certain that you will do all in your power to expedite this matter, you can surely understand our concern.

Please call me by the end of this week, as this is a most serious matter, and we must have answers to it.

Sincerely,

NOTE: Here again, the end of the letter specifies a time frame for action. Also, although far from what you might call a threatening—or even an angry—letter, this is a no-nonsense piece of writing that states the matter clearly and succinctly, and expects action—immediately. One can be strong without being offensive.

113. Complaining About Inefficient Response

Let's say that the last letter was answered, but not in the way that you wished. For our purposes here, let us say that the company in question delivered 100 desks in time for the opening of school with the remainder promised, "as soon as possible." Here is a letter complaining about this highly inefficient and unacceptable response.

Dear Mr. Vetter,

You have placed this school in a most unfortunate position. Following our contact and conversation in early August of this year, I was assured by you of two things: first, that you would handle the situation "to our complete satisfaction," and second, that we would have the 230 student desks in our possession by the opening of school.

We took you at your word. We cleaned the rooms, made space for the desks when they arrived, and arranged for their quick distribution to the classrooms where they were so desperately needed. We waited—and we waited.

Three days before the scheduled opening of school, a shipment arrived from your company. A quick look at the shipping label, as well as a count by our custodian, attested to the fact that only 100 of the 230 desks had arrived, leaving us 130 desks short. A call to you produced nothing more than your secretary's assurance that the matter would be handled "as soon as possible."

When school opened without those additional desks, and students were forced to sit and work on the floor, we were quite upset. The parents of the children involved were also upset, and you may rest assured that I conveyed to them the full story of their children's unique seating arrangements.

We really cannot afford to wait any longer. Time and again, we have given you every opportunity to get the ordered and paid-for materials to us. To say the least, your response has been inefficient.

I respectfully request to know the exact date upon which our school can expect the remaining desks to be delivered, in order that I can reassure the parents, students, faculty, and administration of this school, as well as our school board.

Please call me upon receipt of this letter and let me know your disposition in this matter.

Yours most sincerely,

NOTE: The tone of the letter has become much stronger—even to including a veiled reference to taking the matter to the school board, which would mean some legal action in all likelihood. Even so, note the politeness and civility. Indeed, if something like this ever came to court, your calmness and control would go a long way toward strengthening your side of the argument.

114. Complaining About a Contracted Service

Many schools and school systems use services contracted from agencies and companies outside the school in order to perform functions within the school itself. This could be anything from cleaning services or lunch room suppliers to gardeners and groundskeepers. When a contractor fails to perform properly, the following letter might serve.

Dear Evergreen Plus,

Starting September 1, _____, your company, Evergreen Plus, has been contracted to perform the maintenance and landscaping of the grounds of Tyler High School. In the express written contract between your company and the Tyler School Board, one of the services you are to provide is the "cutting of all grassy areas on a regular basis."

Normally, I am not one to complain, but we are currently into the third week of school, and to my knowledge, the front lawn of the school has not been touched. Since the cutting of the grass on school property is a regular part of your contractual duties to the school, I ask that two actions be taken. First, we would like the front grass, at the very least, to be cut immediately. Second, we ask that you give us a written schedule indicating exactly when we may expect the grass to be tended to and cut. The reason for the first request is obvious, while the second will allow us to plan around your scheduled maintenance of the school's grassy areas.

I would like to see the first request handled by the end of this week, and the schedule as soon as possible thereafter.

I look forward to hearing from you by the weekend.

Yours sincerely,

NOTE: If you want a service, it is good to specifically mention the times you wish the service to take place, even if it is an all-inclusive time such as "by the end of the week." One thing this letter does is specifically state what is desired and the specific time frame for its accomplishment.

115. Complaining About a Scheduling Conflict

In many schools, space is at a premium, and scheduling of much-used areas is of paramount importance. Unfortunately, even in these days of computer scheduling, mistakes do happen. In this letter of complaint, a suggested solution is also given.

Dear Mrs. Pastuli,

At present, my fifth-period graphic arts class meets in Room 102 at the beginning of period 5A, which begins precisely at the end of Period 4B. My students have class and then proceed to Lunch D.

While this scheduling does allow for both period four and five classes to use 102, it presents a problem for me and my graphic arts class. The schedule allows just four minutes between the end of the class in 102 during fourth period and the beginning of my class for fifth period.

There are times when I would like to get into the classroom before my students and set up some displays or place a particular problem on the board. I would like to be able to place special materials on desks in order that the class could begin at once. I would like to make certain that the projects of the previous class were put away safely so they were not injured, and yet that my class had sufficient space to start. These are hardly feats that can be accomplished in the four minutes between periods.

I understand the difficulty of scheduling in a school our size, but this particular pattern presents a true conflict, in my estimation, between what I would like to do for my students and what I can do.

I have fifteen students in that class. If those fifteen were switched from Lunch D to Lunch C, they would come in half a period later, and Room 102 would be free for twenty-seven minutes. This would not upset any other scheduling in the school (I checked), and would give me the time required to prepare for that particular class.

I wonder, may we talk?

Yours sincerely,

NOTE: The writer here is complaining, but also offering a solution to the problem he or she perceives. Understand that something like this will not work in every situation, but it certainly brings the problem to the attention of the right person.

116. Complaining About a Physical Condition

Teachers have to teach somewhere, and there is such a thing as an atmosphere conducive to learning. It is virtually impossible to teach in a boiler room, for instance. Therefore, the physical condition of the actual school plant is an important subject.

Dear Mr. Oni,

I wish to bring to your attention a physical condition of this building which, I believe, should be tended to immediately.

Simply put, the thermal pane windows are filling up with water between the panes. Not only is this causing difficulty seeing out the windows; it is preventing the windows from properly insulating the rooms in which they are installed.

While this is not happening in every window in the school, enough of them are so affected as to cause a troublesome physical condition. Those with the water between their panes are obviously not doing the task of insulation for which they were intended, and when the really cold weather comes, they stand a chance of freezing and cracking or breaking outright, and then we would be hard pressed to keep the winter on the outside.

I am sure that you must see this as a problem as well, which is why I am contacting you. I am hopeful that something may be done to remedy the situation as soon as possible.

If I may be of any assistance, please feel free to call upon me.

Yours sincerely,

NOTE: Here is a straightforward complaint about an observed physical condition. Notice that it accurately specifies the condition, briefly explains why it should be looked after, and leaves it in the hands of the person being addressed. The observer has done his or her duty.

117. Complaining About a Dangerous Physical Condition

Physical conditions like the one mentioned previously, while they are a nuisance, do not pose a serious hazard to either students or faculty. There are other physical conditions that contain a potential for serious harm, and those have to be handled with more urgency. In this letter of complaint on one such condition, you have a letter of "complaint with caution."

Dear Ms. Lessing,

I wish to bring to your attention a most disturbing physical condition of this school. If left unattended for much longer, it may become a dangerous situation that could well affect the health and welfare of our students.

I direct your attention to the lighting fixtures in room 211. While they are functional at this moment, they have been observed to blink as well as dim out intermittently. What is more, several times within the last month, when several heavy trucks from the new construction site have passed by the school, they have been observed to literally sway with the pounding of the heavy machinery. I have personally climbed a ladder and looked at how they are attached, and have found dry chips of plaster as well as what I considered to be some badly frayed wires.

Certainly, I am no expert on lighting or lighting fixtures, but even as a casual observer, I am worried. I believe that a dangerous physical condition exists that could prove highly detrimental to the students and teachers who use that room on a daily basis.

I respectfully request that these fixtures be looked at immediately by someone qualified to assess their status, and that necessary repairs be made at once.

Should this situation remain untended for very much longer, I would not wish to be responsible for the consequences.

Very truly yours,

NOTE: When a situation is potentially dangerous, a complaint or report should be immediately forthcoming. Even if it comes to nothing, it has still been documented by you.

118. Complaining About a Developing Situation

Sometimes, you may be in a position to observe a situation developing that might be just as frustrating and troublesome as any adverse physical condition. Here again, a request for a change before the situation worsens is well within reason.

Dear Mrs. Frensler,

Because I am actually in a better position to notice such things, there is a situation here at Spaulding High School that should be brought to your attention in order that you may handle it while it is still a "small" thing.

The way it has turned out (and I truly do not suspect that it was done on purpose) is that Mr. Loponte spends periods 5, 6, and 7 teaching in room 97, while across the hall, Mr. Tyndale teaches in room 96 during these same periods. As you are very aware, this could pose serious problems.

Mr. Loponte and Mr. Tyndale do *not* get along. I ask you to hark back to a similar situation three years ago. Do you recall the virtually constant complaints about noise that each made about the other, along with the demands that you come down and stop it? Do you recall the shouting match when the student of one teacher waved at the student of the other while passing the room? Do you recall the accusations that each was taking the other's school supplies? In short, do you recall that any excuse that could be used for an argument *was*?

I believe that we even tentatively agreed then that these two should never be placed in proximity again, and I am suggesting that we find another room for one of them (take your pick) for those three periods in question. Since it is still early in the school year, we should be able to do that without any disruption of anyone's schedule, if we get on it right away.

For the good of all concerned, ourselves included, let's do that as soon as we can!

Yours truly,

NOTE: While this was almost humorous in tone, a situation where two faculty members (or staff members for that matter) who don't get along are placed in physical proximity for an extended period of time can get unpleasant for those around them. Although light in tone, this letter addresses a serious concern.

119. Complaining About a Potentially Dangerous Situation

Troublesome situations exist all the time in education, but when the troublesome threatens to become the dangerous, then it must be handled firmly and immediately. This letter offers an example.

Dear Dr. Bonner,

A situation exists in our school that I feel must be handled immediately and with dispatch before it becomes a very dangerous situation for all concerned. I speak of the lunch room; more precisely I am addressing the situation of Lunch C, which takes place from 11:57 through 12:27 each day.

As you may be aware, that particular lunch combines a good two thirds of the senior class with half to 60 percent of the sophomore class. What you may not be cognizant of is the growing rivalry between those two groups. Traditionally, the upperclassmen have looked down upon the new class in the school, and there has always been some degree of pranks pulled by one group upon the other. Usually, these are minor in nature and quickly run their course.

In the past, however, these groups have been separated in their classrooms, in separate sections of the school, and in separate lunch periods. This year, the lunch room situation, as previously described, has placed the majority of these groups into proximity for at least half an hour each day.

To say the least, the pranks have begun to proliferate. What started with a word a month ago has gotten to the point where the lunch duty teachers narrowly avoided a food fight last Friday.

It is my fear that if this situation is left untended, it could well escalate into a potentially dangerous situation for the students involved. When does the next prank end in a seriously injured student?

I strongly suggest that we get together as soon as possible to review our options as to the scheduling of students for the various lunch periods. I am making myself available to you to help in any way you see fit.

For everyone's sake, let's move on this one right now.

Sincerely,

NOTE: The suggested action here is almost in the form of a directive. The writer volunteers to help solve the potential problem. If you volunteer to help in your letter of complaint, expect to be called upon to do so.

120. Complaining About a School Board Decision

Decisions made by the board of education have far-reaching effects in every part of the school system. While the proper forum for objecting to such a decision is in the public board meeting, a time may still come when you must complain about a decision after it has gone into effect.

Mrs. J. Wanake, President, Bartley Board of Education

Dear Mrs. Wanake,

Recently, the Bartley Board of Education passed resolution 127.32A. This was done over some objections both by citizens of Bartley Township and a number of administrators and teachers. This decision has now been in effect for over a month. Regretfully, I must write to you once again to protest that decision and to request your immediate review of the situation.

Basically, and without any rhetoric, your decision removed all bus transportation from our school. All the students at our middle school were required to find their own method of transportation to and from school every day. In the month that this decision by the board has been in effect, it has caused near-chaos conditions at our school.

Parents bringing their children to school and taking them home in the afternoon have caused virtual gridlock on Dwight Road *every* morning and *every* afternoon. When it happens to rain, the situation is even more confused, and the Bartley Township Police have had to detour traffic around Nut Swamp Road in order to have *anything* moving. This does not please the parents nor the commuters who must use Dwight Road to get to the Thruway. Because of this, close to *one third* of our student body has been late to school *every day*. It's a mess.

Two days ago, a student injured himself in gym during the last period of the day. We had to call the first-aid squad to take him to the hospital. The ambulance *could not get through the traffic* that had begun to form to pick children up from the school. Finally, the police had to guide the ambulance over the field area to get to the injured student.

That is *not* acceptable, nor will the compromise of the safety of our students *ever* be acceptable.

I and a representative group of citizens and educators plan to be at the board meeting next Tuesday night. We hope that you will *very seriously* reconsider your decision on 127.32A.

Respectfully submitted,

NOTE: If there are certain written requirements before you can speak at a board meeting, you must, of course, follow them. Here, however, you have a serious situation, caused by a board decision, and it is of such a nature that it must be addressed quickly. This letter seems forceful enough for that.

121. Answering a Complaint About the School

Up until now, we have been writing letters of complaint about various subjects. You may, however, also be in a position where you will have to answer such letters of complaint. When you do, the remaining letters in this section may be helpful to you. Let's start by answering a complaint about your school.

Dear Mr. Uncasa,

I have read with interest your letter of January 21, _____, in which you state your strong objections to our recent placing of a signboard on the front lawn of the school. Your claim is that it is distracting to motorists passing by, and you fear that this may cause an accident, possibly involving a child from the school.

First, I wish to thank you for your concern. It is comforting and uplifting to realize that members of our community have the best interests of our students at heart. That you would take the time to notify us shows your attentiveness to the needs of our school and our students.

Although your concerns are well founded, what you had no way of knowing is that they have been addressed. A signboard outside a school serves two purposes: First, it identifies the school boldly, so that people searching for it will know they have reached their destination, and second, it informs the public as to events taking place at the school, which citizens might care to know about. Both these services help contribute to positive school-community relations.

The Wall Township Civic League, an association of citizens like you, donated the signboard to the school. Before they did that, they researched the project with the Wall Township Police. They could find no instances of a serious accident linked to a driver reading a school sign. In any event, we purposely keep messages short in order that they may be read in one glance. Moreover, the students of the school use exit and entrance routes a good 300 feet away from the sign, so there would be little chance of a student's being endangered.

In short, we have already checked out your concern, and we have the assurance of the police that we are well within the proper safety parameters.

Thank you again, however, for your obvious care and concern. Thank you for being a true friend of this school and its students.

Most sincerely yours,

NOTE: Complaints come into the school for a huge variety of reasons. Whenever you can answer a complaint in a positive manner, as was done in this letter, it is wise to do so. If there is a cardinal rule for answering a complaint, it is this: Whenever possible, try to make a friend out of the complainer.

122. Answering a Complaint About a Teacher

When a letter comes in complaining about something like the signboard in front of the school, it is one thing, but when that complaint is about a person, it is more serious. For elaboration, see the note following this answer to a complaint about a teacher.

Dear Mrs. Huang,

I have received and carefully read your letter of March 30, _____, in which you complain that one of the teachers at Rock Township High School has been unfair and even punitive toward your son Richard, who is currently a tenth-grade (sophomore) student in our school.

The teacher in question is Miss Fiona Dunne, who teaches Sophomore English. Miss Dunne has been a teacher in this school for the past five years, holds a master's degree in the teaching of English, and has received highly satisfactory evaluations for all her years at Rock Township.

What is obvious is that you have a disagreement with Miss Dunne. Generally, when we disagree, a reasonable solution is to talk it out—meet and discuss rationally the problem and its possible solutions. This we would be most happy to arrange.

Therefore, if you will kindly contact the school and speak to Mrs. Davenport, the school secretary, we will be happy to arrange a meeting. Miss Dunne has a teaching schedule, of course, but we are eager to have this matter settled, so we will arrange coverage for Miss Dunne in order that you may meet at your convenience. Mr. Jangi, the head of guidance, will be there, and I will attend if you so desire. I am certain that, working together, we can reach an amicable settlement of our differences. I have spoken to Miss Dunne and she looks forward to meeting with you.

Please call the school and let us know your desire in this matter.

Very truly yours,

NOTE: Before you write the letter above, it is to be understood that there may be some contractual restraints on what you may say or arrange when there is a written complaint against a faculty member. Of course, you would have to refer to that contract in order to know the precise actions you might have to take (such as meeting at the teacher's convenience, having a representative of the teachers' association present, and notification of certain central office personnel) in the given situation. You can personalize the letter to meet the requirements of your situation.

123. Answering a Complaint About an Administrator

When a written complaint against an administrator comes in, it is good policy to take it seriously. If you ignore it, it may come back to you during a school board meeting—and that can be quite a shock. It is always best to try to handle such a complaint at the time it is made.

Dear Mr. Lertowicz,

I have received and read your letter of November 17, _____, in which you accuse the vice-principal of this school, Mrs. Theresa Teranski, of being "arbitrary and capricious" in an action relative to your son Alex, an eighth-grade student at this school. You claim that Vice-Principal Teranski suspended your son for a period of three days for no reason other than a "personal hatred" for the boy. You claim that Mrs. Teranski decided to "make an example" of Alex by "suspending him for something others have been allowed to go free on."

I am certain that you feel strongly about your son, and it is good to know that you consider a suspension from school a serious matter. Indeed, that is the purpose of suspension—to make both student and parents reflect on the facts of the matter.

Therefore, let's talk about facts. Alex was caught by two male faculty members who, as part of an assigned duty, were checking the boys' lavatories. When they arrived, they witnessed a cigarette between his lips and smoke issuing from his mouth and nostrils. Immediately, Alex protested that he was "holding it for a friend." It was evident, however, that Alex was the only student in the room at the time. As they are *required* to do, the teachers escorted Alex to the main office, where he was sent to Mrs. Teranski.

Like any large organization, we have rules. Some of those rules are inflexible, approved by the board of education at public meetings and supported by the town council and the state board of education. One of these is that any student caught smoking on school property is *automatically* suspended for three days, minimum. The administrator handling the case *has no personal choice in the matter.* Any student who has told you otherwise either did not get caught or is outright mistaken in his or her report to you.

Therefore, I would consider the facts very carefully before any further action is taken. Mrs. Teranski did not act in an "arbitrary and capricious" manner; rather, she acted in a manner highly consistent with her position as vice-principal, and totally within board of education guidelines.

Alex's suspension should pass quickly, and he will have learned something about smoking on school grounds. I am certain you will be speaking to him about that.

We look forward to Alex's return.

Yours sincerely,

NOTE: The sooner you can handle a complaint, the easier and less complicated it will be. We all get letters like the one being answered here. When such a letter can be answered with the facts, it usually stops there.

124. Answering a Complaint from the Faculty

Sometimes, complaints from outside the school can be handled quickly, but a complaint from inside the school is something that you have to live with all the time. Depending on the nature of the complaint and the legalities of contractual restraints, your response will vary. Here's one example.

Dear Mr. Paulson,

Thank you for your letter of October 25, _____. I have read it carefully, and I understand that it is from the entire faculty, with you as their collective representative.

As I understand it, the faculty members believe that the current parking area assigned for faculty use is an unsafe place to park their vehicles. You point out that the area in question is on the "blind side" of the school—the east side of the building where there are only doors to enter and leave the school but no windows from which to observe. You point out that the area goes unsupervised much of the day (as attested to by the number of student instances of smoking in that unobserved area, and at least three cases of cars being the target of vandalism, and in one case broken into and personal property taken).

You further make a very strong suggestion that the parking area for faculty cars in some way be moved to a position where they could be observed from the school during the school day.

First, I ask you to recall that I park in that same area. I agree that the place cannot be readily observed. I think there should be a better place for everyone in the school to be able to park. The difficulty is where that might be. As a faculty member in this school, you are well aware of the physical location in which we work and the demands placed on us by existing traffic patterns, to say the very least. I do not see, in the near future, how the parking lot can possibly be moved.

If rational minds work together, however, I am certain that we can come to a solution we can all live with. Among other things, we might create a "duty" of lot supervision for each period, or petition the board for some closed-circuit TV coverage. I am certain that you have other suggestions as well. Therefore, I invite you to contact me and set up a meeting to discuss these matters. Please choose any members of the faculty you wish to meet and talk.

I am not insensitive to your needs, and I truly believe we can solve the problem together.

I look forward to meeting with you.

Yours sincerely,

NOTE: As we mentioned before, if there are legalities to be observed in your answer, you should check them and adapt the letter accordingly. As it stands, however, here is an answer to a complaint that is sensitive, understanding, and offers positive avenues to communication. Not bad.

125. Answering a Complaint from the Staff

When the staff has a complaint, your attention must be drawn to it quickly, since the staff is quite often in a position to see things that others don't. We all know that the staff of a school can be a tremendous help in the educational process, and we must be attentive to their concerns.

Dear Mr. Earlie,

Thank you so much for your letter of May 23, _____, in which you explain a difficulty with the existing lunch room setup. I am happy that you have brought it to my attention, and I appreciate your concern for our school that urged you to write in the first place.

As I understand it, the problem stems from the fact that at the conclusion of each lunch period, students must exit the cafeteria via the three double doors. At present, they are merely dismissed, and most students immediately use the north door, which has quicker access to the main hallways of the school. This presents a problem to you and your staff, since the supply room, with cleaning equipment, is also located near the north door, and the crush of students makes it virtually impossible for your crew to get into the lunch rooms in time to have the tables cleaned and the floor generally brushed up before the next group arrives. This has led to delays in the past and even to the necessity of having students wait in the hallways while you finish cleaning.

I certainly sympathize with you; a flood of students in the hallway can surely stall traffic.

I believe, however, that I have a solution. What if the lunch duty teachers divided each lunch into three segments of students and required each segment to leave by a separate door—some north, some south, some west? The traffic out the north door should then be cut by two thirds, and perhaps that would be more manageable.

Please advise me as soon as possible as to your opinion of this plan, or any other insights you may have, and we can start working toward a solution at once.

Again, thank you for bringing this matter to my attention. I am sure we can work together to solve it in short order.

Very truly yours,

NOTE: Notice how positive this answer is. It assumes cooperation before it hardly begins. Picture yourself as the staff member receiving this answer. Makes you feel good, doesn't it? That's a plus in any situation!

126. Answering a Minor Complaint from a Parent

The intent of the title of this letter is not to imply that any complaint is frivolous. Certainly, anyone who takes the time to complain considers it serious, and it should be answered seriously, but we all know that some complaints can be very easily handled while others may try us severely. Let's take a look at an easily handled parental complaint first.

Dear Mrs. Wachert,

I received your letter of February 2, _____, stating that your daughter is being marked late to sixth-period gym class when the fact is that she cannot help but be tardy due to the inordinate distance she must cover going from lunch to her locker and then to her gym class. You think it unfair that she be penalized for her inability (your words) "to run a four-minute mile!"

Well, we checked it out. We ran (actually, we just walked briskly) the same pattern of lunch room to locker to gym that your daughter is required to do, and guess what—we couldn't do it! With the size and shape of our school, it is simply too far for the time allotted!

So, our apologies to your daughter Megan. All tardy marks have been erased from the gym teacher's book, and tomorrow, Megan will be issued a combination to a second locker close to the lunch room, where she can store her afternoon materials and be in good time for the sixth-period gym class.

Thank you for bringing this to our attention. I wish all were as understanding as you have been and that all problems were as readily solved.

If we can be of any further help, please do not hesitate to contact the school.

Yours sincerely,

NOTE: The problem was hardly earth shaking, and it was very easily solved. You might even detect an undertone of good-natured humor in the whole thing. Oh, if they were all that simple, but as we well know, they are not.

127. Answering a Serious Complaint from a Parent

Now, let's look at a parental complaint that is anything but simple and note the vast difference in approach. For this example, let's assume one of the most serious of complaints a parent can make—sexual harassment of a child.

Dear Mr. Yanelli,

Your letter of December 2, _____, was disturbing, to say the very least. I assure you that the letter was read very carefully by me; by the head of guidance; by the vice-principal, Mrs. Turnbow; and by Dr. Wallazi, assistant superintendent for pupil personnel services. Other than these individuals, who must be advised in a case of this nature, the letter is being held in strictest confidence, and any reference to your daughter's name has been blacked out of your original letter.

You assert that your daughter Elizabeth was sexually harassed by a school professional employee—specifically, the school librarian, Mr. Donald Padula.

As you, yourself, state in your letter, this is a most serious charge. Not only would the alleged actions violate school rules, but they would constitute a violation of civil law as well. The repercussions of such acts could mean extremely serious consequences for Mr. Padula, from the loss of his job and educational certification all the way up to imprisonment. These are steps that no civilized person can take lightly. We must tread very carefully and with great caution—not only for Mr. Padula's sake, but for the sake of your daughter as well.

We have arranged a meeting in the office of Dr. Wallazi for Thursday, December 5, _____, at 10:00 A.M. Present at this meeting will be Dr. Wallazi; myself; the attorney for the board of education, Rita Bartlett, Esq.; and a legal representative of the township teacher's association. We are inviting you and your daughter to attend. I am required to advise you that you may bring anyone you wish, including legal representation should you so desire.

This is a preliminary meeting to determine the precise nature of the allegations. We will do our best to make your daughter comfortable, and you may terminate the meeting whenever you wish, but please understand that we must know the specific nature of what happened.

Please advise me at once if this meeting time is acceptable to you. If not, another will have to be arranged.

This type of thing is never pleasant nor easy, but I assure you we are as anxious as you to get to the bottom and know the truth. This, we will do.

Most sincerely,

NOTE: A serious subject demands a very serious, no-nonsense letter that "lays it all out" and leaves no doubt as to the solemnity of the subject and your desire to deal seriously with it.

128. *Answering a Complaint from a Student*

If we take every complaint seriously, then we will never pass one off as being unworthy of an answer. This is vital when we receive a written complaint from one of our own students. This type of complaint should always be answered with as much sincerity as the answers you gave to the complaints from any adults.

Dear Anthony,

Thank you for your recent letter expressing concern about the quality of the food served in our cafeteria. I have read your letter carefully, and I have checked your concerns.

The school cafeteria is checked periodically (at least twice a month) by representatives of the local board of health. If the cafeteria does not pass inspection, they do not operate. All facilities are checked for cleanliness, and the food is checked for nutritional value. I must report to you that they have passed every inspection this year. The food you are eating is safe and does contain required nutrients.

The taste is another matter entirely. You are used to certain tastes that you have grown up with in your home. The cafeteria tries to accommodate all tastes, and therefore the lack of spicing may lead some to claim that the food is tasteless. That may be unfortunate, but it hardly is grounds for the dismissal of the entire cafeteria staff, as you suggest in your letter.

In short, it is clean; it is nutritious; it is healthy. Beyond that, we simply do not have the authority to go. You are at liberty to bring your own food from home, and many students do. If you want the cafeteria to offer different items, organize a petition. Otherwise, I fear there is not much I can do for you except to speak to the head of the cafeteria, which I have done.

Thank you for your concern about this school and your fellow students.

Yours sincerely,

NOTE: Cafeteria food is probably the number-one target for complaint by the student body. If and when those complaints come, treating them with respect goes a long way toward affirming a positive relationship between you and your students.

129. Answering a Complaint About a Classroom

Teachers and students need a place to teach and learn. Sometimes, a particular environment can become a detriment to that process. The complaint referred to here certainly must be addressed.

Dear Ms. Alston,

I read your letter of January 14, _____, with great interest. I was unaware of the problem with Room 202, and I thank you for bringing it to my attention.

As I understand from your letter, Room 202 is located at the northwest corner of the building, it is now midwinter, and the heat in the room is intermittent at best. I further understand that even at its best, the heat maintains a room temperature of around 52 degrees, more or less, depending on the outside temperature and the power of the winds striking that northwest corner. It is clear that you and the classes that meet in that room are cold and getting colder. Certainly, this is not a scenario conducive to good education.

I have contacted maintenance, and they have examined the heating unit in Room 202. They have found it defective, with a key part malfunctioning. I am assured that it is quite fixable, and that they can do it just as soon as they get the part they need. It is on order.

They assure me that the part should take no longer than a week to ten days to arrive, and I have asked them to tend to the matter the moment the replacement part gets here.

In the meantime, please advise me if you want to stick out the week in the room, or perhaps make some arrangement to take your classes to the library, or even the cafeteria when it is not in use. That decision is yours, and we will be happy to try to accommodate you if we can.

Try to stay warm; spring, like the missing part, is on the way, but let's hope the part gets here first!

Very truly yours,

NOTE: Here's another insight, particularly when you are dealing with colleagues and people you work with in the school. If you can, try to make life comfortable for them while the complaint is being handled. No act of kindness is ever in vain in terms of interpersonal relationships.

130. Answering a Complaint About a Class

Sometimes, you can handle a complaint, and all is taken care of in a relatively short period of time. We all understand, however, that the existence of a question does not necessarily imply an answer. There will be times when the complaint cannot be handled. For the last letter in this section, let's look at one of those.

Dear Mr. Tassenari,

Thank you for your recent letter detailing the problems that exist in your period-three, general English class. I am glad that you feel free to share these problems with me, and I want to be of as much help as possible.

As I understand it, this third-period class contains a number of students who, you state, are "known discipline problems." Indeed, you go on to identify twelve of your twenty-three students in that class as such. You further state that trying to teach with them in the room is "virtually impossible." Finally, you express your opinion that these students were purposely placed in your class because of some sort of enmity that exists between you and the head guidance counselor, who set up the schedule.

First, the twelve students you mention are not "known discipline problems." I have had previous experience with three of them, but even so, we like to give every benefit of the doubt, especially at this age level. If a child misbehaves, we handle it, but we cannot go looking for an infraction before it takes place. Moreover, it would not be wise to stigmatize a child before any wrong act has been committed.

Next, as far as your teaching goes, I have no doubt that it would be difficult and challenging to teach in such a highly active class, but that is part and parcel of what we do as educators. I, personally, know that some of the best teaching I ever did was in the effort to reach kids who did not want to be reached. Yes, I understand the effort and frustration it takes, but I urge you to keep your eye on the sense of accomplishment when you manage a breakthrough with such a class.

As far as your statement about the head guidance counselor is concerned, you should be aware that he did not schedule your classes; I did, along with the vice-principal. I assure you that I have only the deepest regard for you, and the nature of the children in your class never entered into the decision.

I cannot take twelve students out of your class. There is no other place to put them, and should I do it for you, I would be deluged by requests to remove every troublesome student from every class in the building.

I hope you understand, as I hope that you can make that super effort to get to all the students in that class and all of your classes. You know, I hope, that we stand ready to provide whatever teaching equipment and assistance we can. Please call on me, and I'll be glad to share some of that with you.

Yours sincerely,

NOTE: When it is necessary to deny a complaint, it is a good policy to follow up, several days later, with a personal call or another very friendly letter asking how things are going. Basically, you want to show the person that even though you must refuse the request made in the complaint, you are still interested in the individual and his or her problem.

A GUIDE TO LETTERS DEALING WITH THE MEDIA

A local newspaper writes an editorial condemning you and your school, and calling for major reform. So what? That's just one opinion, isn't it? A local TV station manages to sneak a camera onto the campus, and catches one student doing something he or she shouldn't. Who's going to believe that reflects on the whole school? Just how powerful are the media, anyhow?

Well, Napoleon Bonaparte, who was extremely powerful, once wrote, "I would rather fight three hostile armies than one hostile newspaper!" Does that give you an idea of how powerful and how destructive to a school—or even to a school system—the "hostile media" can be?

APPRECIATING THE POWER OF THE MEDIA

We all grew up with the cliché, "The pen is mightier than the sword." Today, we might wish to add that the local newspaper, community bulletin, local TV, radio, a local web page, and all the advances of technology have made the media even more powerful than in Napoleon's day. The power of the media is awesome.

For us in education, this can be good and bad. A newspaper that is on your side can help pass a school budget. A TV station that is proschool can make a community look upon your school as something just short of Camelot. A radio station that supports the local schools can uplift the school's image virtually beyond belief.

Conversely, a school in a community where the media have taken a stand against it fights an uphill battle every day of the year. Budgets get defeated; every decision of the school is circumspect; "school spirit" is barely alive.

Fortunately, there are ways of presenting your case to the media in the best possible light. That process starts with three basics:

1. **NEVER LIE TO THE MEDIA:** Those whom the media catch in a lie, they do not forgive. Be honest with the media, and if you don't know, say so, Never try to bluff. Just look at what has happened nationally to those who tried to do so.

2. **KEEP THE MEDIA INFORMED:** Don't wait for the media to show up on your school's doorstep with cameras and microphones. If you inform the media first, you stand an excellent chance of having your story heard. Moreover, they are more likely to print or air the stories you send them about the good things going on in your school.

3. **MAKE THE MEDIA WELCOME:** If at all possible, try to make friends (or, at least, good acquaintances) with your local media. Try to accommodate them as much as possible without interruption to the school. If you have a newsworthy event, ask them to come. Remember, if you invite them first, you can make up some ground rules (*see letters 146, 147, 148*).

In this section, we will take a look at letters that aim at establishing and maintaining a good school-media relationship, and even repairing damage that may come your way through adverse media coverage.

Let's try to keep it very positive—for our own sakes and for that of our students and our schools as well.

MODEL LETTERS INVOLVING THE MEDIA

131. Informing the Media of an Impending Media Event, I

Let us suppose that you are going to have an event at your school that you think would feature well in the local newspaper. You have two choices: You can inform the media of what is about to happen and leave it at that, or you can inform the media and formally request coverage. Let's begin with two examples in which you are merely informing the media about the event.

Dear Community Editor:

Two weeks from today, October 15, _____, Pasteraux Middle School will be holding a unique event at the school. I refer to our "Candidates Speak" assembly, scheduled to begin at 1:00 P.M. in the school auditorium.

Present will be Township Mayor Allison Balderich and her opponent, Councilman James Gerhart, both of whom will speak as well as answer questions from our student body. Also present will be several members of the town council, as well as all members of the township board of education.

This is our fifth annual "Candidates Speak" assembly at Pasteraux Middle School. In the past, we have had candidates for virtually every position in the township address our student body. Moreover, our students have been known to ask some rather pointed and even difficult questions in the past, and this year should be no exception.

Every year, our students have conducted a "mock election" immediately following the assembly, and the results have forecast those of the actual election three out of the past four years.

If you should wish any further information or clarification, please feel free to give me a call at the school. I think you'll find that we can be most cooperative and accommodating.

Yours sincerely,

NOTE: If you were the community editor of a local newspaper, would you respond to a letter like this? More than likely you would, for while it does not ask for coverage, the story speaks for itself. This is something special; this is newsworthy; this is something that the people of the community will want to know about!

132. Informing the Media of an Impending Media Event, II

Now, let's inform the media of an event that is not quite so dramatic as the candidates for mayor battling it out in the local school auditorium. This time, let's tell them about a simple, child-oriented event. The challenge will be to whet the appetite of the press for the event.

Dear Community Editor:

We know of your commitment to the citizens of this community. We are aware that you do your best to reflect, within your publication, the life and times of our township and the people who live in it. We understand that not everything goes into your newspaper, of course, but that you concentrate on those stories that touch the hearts and minds of our citizens.

That is why we at Pasteraux Middle School like to keep you informed about what is happening at "our place." We think that you join us in the belief that a community's schools are its greatest assets. Therefore, what happens there is of paramount concern and interest to the majority of the community, especially since their children—tomorrow's citizens—are so deeply involved.

Ten days from now, on April 16, _____, at 10:30 A.M. in the school auditorium, we will be holding the Pasteraux Middle School Spring Fashion Show, hosted by our PTA and involving students from our seventh- and eighth-grade home economics classes. The students will be modeling clothes that they have made themselves, and in some cases, designed and made. This year, we will also feature a number of fashions made and modeled by the boys in those classes.

This presentation is traditionally well attended, and we expect over 300 parents and local community leaders to be in attendance.

If you want to call me at school, I'll try to be more specific. We were sure you would want to know about this upcoming community event.

Very truly yours,

NOTE: Again, a good rule in writing letters like this is to put yourself honestly into the position of the person receiving it. Would you, as an editor, have your curiosity aroused by something like this? Would it make you start thinking of ways you might use such a story? Let that be the criterion for letters such as these.

133. Letter Requesting Media Coverage of a School Event, I

The previous letters merely "informed" the media of an upcoming event. There may be times, however, when you really want coverage, particularly if the school is going to come off in a positive light. Let's take the same two events we just wrote about and revisit them. This time, however, we are not informing; we're requesting!

Dear Community Editor:

With the understanding that your newspaper wishes to cover the strongest and most important news stories relative to our community, I am formally requesting that you provide news coverage of an impending event at Pasteraux Middle School to be held on October 15, _____, at 1:00 P.M. at the school.

At that time, incumbent Mayor Balderich and Councilman Gerhart, opponents in the local race for mayor of our township, will be debating and answering questions from our student body as part of our school's fifth annual "Candidates Speak" assembly. Our student's questions are incisive, and in the mock election held by the students following this assembly, they have chosen the candidates elected in the actual election three out of the last four years.

While you may be aware of this event from the candidates' schedules, I am writing to request that you make this a definite item for news coverage, as it is so obviously newsworthy.

Please contact me at the school at your convenience, but certainly within the next week. We will be able to provide a private room for interviews with the candidates, as well as exclusive photo opportunities, but we must know when—and how many will attend.

I look forward to hearing from you soon, in order that we may accommodate your needs.

Yours sincerely,

NOTE: Here, you are requesting media coverage, but you are starting with the assumption that of course they will want to come and cover this event. Note also how you are providing for their special needs, thereby adding even more incentive for them to cover this event and, of course, your school as well.

134. Letter Requesting Media Coverage of a School Event, II

Sure, you are thinking, any newspaper would come if the mayor were going to be present, but what about the smaller school event? How can I request coverage of something like that? Well, let's take that fashion show again, and this time, let's request coverage for it.

Dear Community Editor:

I am going to request something of you that may appear somewhat shallow on the surface, but all I ask is that you dig a little deeper. I am formally requesting that your newspaper cover a student fashion show to be held at our school on April 16, _____, at 10:30 A.M. in our school auditorium.

Ordinarily, this might not be of great interest nor might it be the type of thing that you would want to cover in the space allotted in your newspaper. However, this is going to be no ordinary event.

Hosted by the PTA of Pasteraux Middle School, this Annual Spring Fashion Show involves students from our seventh- and eighth-grade home economics classes modeling clothes that they have made themselves, and in some cases, designed and made.

An added feature, for the first time this year, will be the presentation of a number of fashions made and modeled by the boys in those classes. This overcoming of stereotypical gender-biased thinking should be enough to assure you of a most newsworthy event.

In addition to that, however, this is a traditionally well-attended affair, and we expect approximately 300 parents and local community leaders to attend.

We would be happy to detail those local dignitaries who will be in attendance, as well as provide special photo opportunities for you. We hope you will agree that our request for coverage by you is hardly frivolous and will provide you with material that will be well suited to the needs and desires of our community.

Please call me soon, and we will be glad to accommodate you in any way we can.

Sincerely,

NOTE: It is a matter of attitude, isn't it? It is an old maxim that if you are on fire, those around you cannot help but feel the heat. The same is true here. If you are enthusiastic, that enthusiasm will carry over. You "know" it is a newsworthy story; you feel it, and you're saying so. That heat cannot help but be felt, and you stand a good chance of getting that coverage.

135. Letter Responding to a Positive Newspaper Article

Not everything that the media say about schools in general, or your school in particular, is necessarily bad or negative. There have been many fine and positive articles on the good things that go on in our schools. The following letter is written to the editor of a paper in which one such article appeared. Read it, and make certain you read the note at the end of the letter.

Dear Editor:

I would like to draw your attention to the article, "An Apple for the Teacher Ain't Enough!" by Gloria Nusbaum of your staff, which appeared in the March 28, _____, edition of your newspaper.

Thank you for publishing such an inspiring and uplifting article! Ms. Nusbaum's often humorous, and often poignant, detailing of a typical teacher's day revealed an insight and an understanding that could have come only from honest research and a true heart for those involved in dealing with the community's most precious asset, our children.

So often today, many of us see only that which is wrong, because that seems to be the thing that pushes its way to the foreground, that screams and demands our attention. That is why it is so refreshing to read an article such as Ms. Nusbaum's and realize that there are people who deeply appreciate the glory and the pain of day-to-day work with children. Her article brought that out with sensitivity and heart. It was, for me, a pleasure to read.

Please extend to Ms. Nusbaum, my personal thanks as well as the thanks and appreciation of everyone at Mintina Elementary School. The article is prominently posted in the school office, and every comment I have heard is positive and appreciative of her efforts.

Again, thank you for printing such a fine and honest appraisal of the work of the educators of our community.

Sincerely,

NOTE: The letter you just read is written to the editor of the newspaper, but it is also written with the knowledge that it might be published as well. Consequently, all that is said must be written so that it could be read by every citizen who reads the paper where the original article appeared. Certainly, you are writing to an individual, but you are writing for the public as well.

136. Letter Responding to a Negative Newspaper Article, I

Of course, there will be positive articles about you and the schools, but, unfortunately, there will be negative ones as well, and we have read plenty of them over the years. When you respond to one of those, keep in mind that you are writing for the public, and fight falsehood with fact—not emotion.

Dear Editor:

It was with great interest that I read the article in the September 26, _____, edition of your newspaper. It appeared on page 4 and was headlined "Public Schools: How Much Is Too Much?" There was no author's credit given.

In that article, the author uses example after example of waste of time, work force, and money in various public school systems. Indeed, the article lists those examples of waste and fraud that we, sadly, have almost come to expect—a box of chalk that cost taxpayers $450.00; school maintenance workers putting a new roof on the principal's home; teachers and other school employees sitting around and doing nothing for many hours of the day.

All of that is, I am certain, true, shameful, and a cause of great concern, but what I take exception to is the fact that these actions seem to be held up as the norm of our public schools rather than the rare exceptions. Of course these things happen, but I know that if you take them in relationship to the schools systems where these do *not* happen, they represent a very small percentage of the public school employees—both nationally and in our community.

I have served in the public schools in this community for over twenty-two years, and I can personally testify to the honesty, dedication, and deep concern for the schools that exist within the ranks of all school employees. If such misdeeds occur here, I have yet to see or hear of them, and I assure you I am in a position to know.

I would hope, if there are to be future articles about the schools, that the full story will be told—and that includes the good deeds of the vast majority as well as the misdeeds of the few.

Most sincerely,

NOTE: It is important to identify the article at the beginning of each letter; this is just good, common sense, since there is no profit in talking about something if the other person is in the dark as to what you are talking about.

137. Letter Responding to a Negative Newspaper Article, II

The previous letter was about an article that might be misinterpreted. Now, suppose that the article was factual, and named your school specifically and in a negative light. Let's also assume that the facts mentioned were accurate. Here, your aim is to make certain the readers get a proper perspective on those facts.

Dear Community Editor:

I read with great interest the feature article on page 12 of the Thursday, November 2, _____, edition of your newspaper. The article, "Readin', 'Ritin', and Drugs in Your Desk," by staff writer Henry Hallace, went into detail about a sad situation that exists in our nation today—the use of drugs by students in school.

In general, the article was accurate, including many statistics to prove the points made. What I wish to bring to your attention deals with one sentence in the article, appearing in the fourteenth paragraph. It reads, "Even our own middle school has had two recent instances where police have taken student drug dealers from the school grounds in handcuffs."

I take exception to that sentence for two reasons: First, the two instances referred to took place over the last three years. Personally, I would hardly call three years "recent instances." Second, these statistics show that our drug policies at the school are working. You see, five years ago, we had six such instances in a single year. Four years ago, we went through seven in a year. Over the past three years, we have had only two.

I feel that this drop is due to the "zero tolerance" policy adopted by the school board, as well as our new, required "antidrug" classes and our highly publicized crackdown on drugs in the school.

Certainly, two referrals where, in the two years previous we had thirteen, indicates some sort of hard-won progress. The article makes it look like a condemnation. What's more, it gives, within the article's context, the feeling that our middle school is rife with drugs, with drug dealers behind every locker in school. This is simply not true, and I am personally saddened that you would release an article that, in my opinion, implied such a thing.

While it is certainly worthwhile to understand the problem of drugs in our public schools, is it not also wise to appreciate the work that is being done to change the situation and to note the progress that has been made? I trust that any future articles will reflect all the facts and appreciate their true significance.

Sincerely,

NOTE: Benjamin Disraeli, Prime Minister of England under Queen Victoria, once wrote that there are three kinds of falsehoods, "lies, damned lies, and statistics." It is well to remember that bit of wisdom. Facts do not always speak for themselves; quite often they require interpretation. When you catch a misuse of a fact, your letter should concentrate on other conclusions—perhaps those more positive in your behalf—that may be drawn from the same material.

138. Letter Responding to a Positive Newspaper Editorial

Whether it is a newspaper editorial or one on local TV or radio, the difference between an article, which we dealt with in the last three entries, and an editorial is that an article is usually an exposition, something written after research on an item, while an editorial is simply one person's opinion—usually that of the editor of the paper. Since an editorial does express opinion, you, as the reader, are free to agree or disagree. First, let's deal with an editorial that was very positive about your school.

Dear Editor:

I wish to both thank you and congratulate you for your editorial entitled, "Removing the Mask and Seeing the Smile," which appeared in the Tuesday, December 3, _____, edition of your newspaper.

In an age and at a time where it is increasingly easy to criticize and find fault, it is both rare and refreshing to find a person who is willing to espouse something positive and stand out from the fault-finders and critics who point fingers but offer no positive suggestions.

The essence of your editorial, I believe, is the observation that if one takes the time to go beyond the outside appearances of our schools, one will find a dedicated staff at work, and that the work is far from easy. You further illustrate your point with examples drawn from Hapwell High School itself. Your conclusion states that looking beyond the sports events and well-kept lawns, we find even more to make us happy and proud of our schools.

As one who has spent the greater part of her life involved in education, and particularly here at Hapwell, I wish you to know that my heart confirms the words you have set on paper. I have been privileged to work with a dedicated staff of teachers and counselors who constantly place the needs of the students above their own. I count it an honor to associate with individuals who so obviously have a single objective—the welfare of the students placed under their authority.

I have known that for years and years; it is so good to observe someone else come to the same conclusion.

Thank you once more for you concern; it is so refreshing to know that there are people out there who are watching—with love and with care.

Sincerely,

NOTE: An answer like this stands a good chance of being printed in the next edition. Also, it is a positive stroke to the local newspaper, which may be more inclined to print more positive articles and editorials about your school because of your very positive response.

139. Letter Responding to a Negative Newspaper Editorial

As with a child growing up, there comes a time when you realize that not everybody thinks that everything you do is cute and wonderful. When that happens and a negative editorial appears, the best you can hope for is to turn the negatives into something positive for your school. This next letter is just such an attempt.

Dear Editor:

It was with a great sense of wonder that I read your editorial on page 17 of your newspaper of January 21, _____. As you undoubtedly recall, that is the editorial in which you take to task the faculty and administration of Halsey High School for their "frivolous waste of taxpayers' money." That is the editorial in which you talk about "overpaid teachers and administrators" using the township funds "to provide luxuries that have nothing to do with the education of our children."

I read your editorial with a growing sense of wonder—wonder as to where you got your information. As to overpaid teachers and administrators, may I remind you that everyone working at Halsey High School receives no more and no less than what is proper for their placement on the salary guide approved by the board of education and further acknowledged by the township committee? May I further remind you that a bit of research at the state department of education would have shown you that this township's salaries are sixth in our county and seventy-seventh overall in our state? That is hardly what one could call "overpaid."

As to the "frivolous waste" of money, you refer to our "providing luxuries" instead of education. If you are referring to the new programs introduced this fall, I would remind you that they are state required, and that the funds are being provided by the state. If you mean for ourselves, we did get a new refrigerator for the faculty lounge, but that was bought by the teachers' own money—contributed privately by them.

Perhaps, however, you are speaking of other luxuries, and to those we should plead guilty. Yes, we believe every student should have a textbook that isn't falling apart, and we managed to achieve that. Yes, we think teachers should have such supplies as paper and chalk and maps, and we did spend toward that end. Yes, we think it is valuable to have tutoring and after-school activities and plays and concerts, in which students can showcase their special talents for parents and friends to appreciate, and money was laid out for these things. Are these the "luxuries" to which you refer?

I feel you have done us a disservice. Perhaps, however, you have done this because you have been misinformed. Therefore, I invite you to call me as soon as possible in order that a day may be arranged when you can visit our school and see for yourself. You will have free rein, and may speak to whomever you wish.

Yours sincerely,

NOTE: The "challenge"—the invitation to visit—is an effective way to combat a negative editorial or article, but make certain that you do not issue such a challenge unless you are truly ready for it. Even if that were left out, the letter would still be effective.

140. Letter to Staff About a Negative Newspaper Editorial

We will assume the editorial answered in the last letter. Such an editorial has an effect upon everyone in the school—students, teachers, administrators, cafeteria workers, and maintenance personnel. This open letter to the school, therefore, would probably be posted on the school bulletin board, in the custodian's room, in the teacher's lounge, and anywhere else you think it might be necessary.

To the Students, Faculty, and Staff of Halsey High School:

As you probably know by now, the January 21, _____, edition of the *Courier* printed an editorial on page 17 that was, to say the least, less than complimentary to us. Basically, it accused us of wasting the money of the taxpayers of this township by inappropriate spending, being frivolous with school funds, and purchasing "luxuries" for ourselves.

Right now, if you are scratching your heads and murmuring "How frivolous? What luxuries?" you are right up there with the rest of us. We provide a good education for our students within the limits of our budget. Our record stands for itself, and we are proud of it!

That is precisely why I have issued an invitation to the editor of the *Courier* to come and visit our school and see for himself the good work that is going on. If he should accept this invitation, I want you to do nothing special for his visit. Let school progress as usual. Should he ask you questions, answer honestly; should he visit your classroom, conduct your normal class; should he come to the cafeteria, provide the same lunch students and teachers consume. In short, show him our school as it is, for we are justly proud of that.

So—don't worry or fret about that editorial, for the editor will soon be discovering the truth, and even if no one ever showed up and the editorial stood unchallenged, we would still know that Halsey High School is a great place, with great students and a great faculty and staff!

That knowledge will surely carry us through.

Workers together,

NOTE: Acknowledging the hurt is the first step toward making the sting go away Moreover, this not only strokes the workers in the school but gives guidelines for dealing with such a visitor on campus. Also, your injunction to complete openness and honesty cannot help but be taken in a positive light by everyone, including the visiting editor.

141. Sample Editorial for a School Newspaper

The newspaper of a local school can be anything from a single sheet done on the school's copy machine right up to a several-page, professionally printed model. Often, and particularly in the larger publications, you may be asked to write a "guest" editorial. Here's an example of just such an editorial in a student news publication.

Welcome back!

I understand that those words may not be ones that cause you to jump up and down and yell, "Whoopie!" I understand that "Welcome back!" means "Welcome back . . . to school!" That's where the problem comes in; the start of school has traditionally meant the end of summer; the end of those great days with family and friends, beaches and ball games; the end of that "free time" you cherished so greatly, and the start of classes and study and homework and routines.

Yet, I would like to think that it means something else as well.

I would like to think that the start of school means a return to friends you left behind last June; a return to those activities you cherish and enjoy such as the publication of this newspaper, the drama presentations, the band, the sports teams, and all the other activities that make up your school year; a return to dances and assemblies and the orange and red of fall leaves on our campus along with the sweet green of spring and the infamous snowmen of our white winter season.

I would like to think it is all that and much more. I like to believe that the start of the school year is also an open door through which you walk to find new knowledge, new insight, new understanding; an open door that leads you to still more doors and places where you will be challenged, you will be tried and tested, and you will learn and grow; a door that will inevitably lead to something called "your future," which lies within your grasp; a door that leads to attainment, and joy, and satisfaction, and success.

All this and more are here at Rock Township High School, just waiting for you to step forward into these halls of your school.

Therefore, I can say it, and mean it, and it sounds wonderful: Welcome back!

NOTE: It is well to remember that any editorial you write in a student newspaper will not be read only by students. Parents and all kinds of people in the community get to read it as well, and they do so with some interest. Therefore, choose your words carefully and remember that you are writing for at least two audiences.

142. Responding to a Negative Student Editorial

Student newspapers can do everything from telling about the harvest party held in Miss Simmons's third grade to writing editorials that excoriate the administration, or the school, or you individually. Assuming such an editorial got through, here's one example of a response to it.

To the Student Editor:

I wish to thank you for this opportunity to reply to your editorial in the last issue of "The Tiger's Tale." I read the piece with great interest, especially since it basically charged that the administration of this school did not take student opinion into account when making decisions that affected the student body.

I feel that this is a serious charge, and I would like to take the time to answer it seriously.

In making decisions relative to the operations and good of Tyndale High School, it has always been the policy and practice of the main office to first solicit opinions from our students, to advise them of the situation requiring change, and to involve the students in the decision-making process wherever and whenever possible.

To those ends, we have placed suggestion boxes in the main office and guidance office, and all signed suggestions are answered, as many of our students are personally aware. Moreover, we have a process for making a complaint. In addition, the student council, which represents the students of our school, has been consulted on all matters that concern the student body. Finally, a student advisory committee has been established, whose functions include investigating student response to various suggestions and directives from the main office.

To me, this spells student involvement in every possible manner. I cannot see how we could better include the student body in the decisions that affect this school. If any student has further suggestions in that direction, I will always stand ready to discuss the matter with him or her.

My office is open to the students of this school.

NOTE: We must apply the same caution we mentioned in the previous letter. Not only the students will read your response, but your faculty, the school board, parents, and members of the general community will see it as well. Straight-forwardness, truth, and never saying anything you don't really mean should be your watchwords and guides.

143. Sample Editorial for a Community Newsletter

Many community governments publish some sort of public relations vehicle which, for our purposes here, we'll call a community newsletter. Basically, it tells what is going on in the community, and since the schools are a big part of any community, they have to be represented. This is an excellent opportunity to let your light shine for your school!

I hope you are reading this!

This is the first issue of the Tyler Township Community Bulletin, and I have been asked to write this first editorial about our schools. That's why I really hope that you will read it, since our schools are so much a part of what makes a community special; they are so much a part of what makes a community a good place to live; they are so much a part of the justifiable pride in our children, their achievements, and their place as a part of the future of our community.

That's what we'll be investigating in this section of this bulletin each month. Here in Tyler Township, we who are a part of your school system are proud of what we do, and we burst with pride at what our students have accomplished, are doing today, and will be achieving tomorrow. We want you to know and understand what's going on.

We have no secrets, nor do we want to have them. We think that the more you look at our schools, the more you'll find to like and appreciate. We think you will find a great deal to be happy about right here on these pages as we begin to unfold one of the most significant stories ever—the story of your children's education.

You're going to be amazed!

NOTE: That was a fine editorial, full of promise, but don't write it unless you are prepared to deliver. The community will remember what you say in these publications. If used properly, a community newsletter is an excellent vehicle for gaining the public's support of their schools.

144. Responding to a Negative Community Flier

Things seem to be going well, and out of nowhere, or so it seems, there is placed on your desk a flier that is being mailed to every home in the community. It is published, we will assume here, by a group that is dissatisfied with the school system. You have already received ten calls asking what you are going to do about it. Well, here's one approach.

Dear Parents,

I had a most unpleasant experience this morning. I opened my mail.

There was a flier with the title "Reading, Writing, and Blindfolds." It was, basically, an attack upon the schools of this township, claiming that our schools are doing "nothing of substance" to "prepare our students to face the challenges of tomorrow." More specifically, it berated us for our "limited number of out-of-date computers" and for failing to offer courses in TV production. The flier further suggested that we in the schools must be "held accountable" for this "almost criminal lack of foresight."

I write this letter to you, the parents of our students, only because it is my understanding that this flier is being mailed to every household in the community. What a waste of perfectly good paper!

The computers called "out-of-date" are not this year's model, it is true, but they do accommodate all the software we have available, and with the replacement each year of those that are beyond repair, we do manage to keep current enough that we now offer six different computer courses to our students—at a significant savings to the taxpayers of this community. As far as the courses on TV production and design are concerned, these courses were approved by the board of education and await the purchase of the necessary equipment to implement them. There, yes, we do have a problem.

You may be aware that the school budget has been resoundingly defeated for the past five years running. Well, each defeat entails a reappraisal of monetary allotments, and the purchase of TV equipment (not even considering the replacement of all computers in the school as the flier implied) had to be weighed against possible cuts in the basic curriculum. I hope that flier isn't suggesting that we cut back courses in English or math. Personally— and I think most would agree—I'll take an English or math teacher over a TV camera any day!

Therefore, parents and friends, when you get this flier, remember that we cannot offer courses or extras beyond our fiscal possibilities.

Yours sincerely,

NOTE: Here's a case where you have the facts on your side, and they should be hammered as hard as possible. This is also a case where a good offense is the best defense. Something like this takes the power out of the negative flier before it has a chance to start causing trouble in the community.

145. Responding to a Negative Community Advertisement

Not all negative criticism comes on the editorial page of the daily newspaper or in letter form. As you are undoubtedly aware, community groups opposed to the schools have taken out full-page ads in local papers and even hired highway billboards to voice their complaints in the most visual way. Here's a letter to parents about such an occurrence.

Dear Parents:

I'm a little shaken as I write this. I almost ran my car off the road this morning.

I was coming to school as I usually do, and I had just passed the intersection of Dooley Street and Port Road, headed north on Dooley, when my eyes caught the huge billboard in the lot just before the hardware store. Usually, that means nothing, for I am merely being informed about the merits of a particular brand of lemonade or how I should vacation in the Bahamas. Today was different.

There, in what I imagine are thirty-foot-high letters, was the legend, "Your Schools Have Lied To You!" That was the point at which I began to head into the nearest curb at an alarming rate of speed!

Fortunately, I was able to straighten out my car, but my mind remained a bit off course for the next several minutes. First, I deny emphatically that we at the schools have lied to community, parents, or students. Second, that statement is so nebulous and without form that it could mean anything. Next, even though it states no facts, the very implication of dishonesty on the part of our schools is personally distasteful and offensive to me. Finally, if it is just left there, enough people are going to pass by and look at it that they may begin to respond to the tenor and feeling of that sign without ever looking at the facts. There is much wrong in that eye-catching billboard.

Of course, there will always be groups within a community of our size that will disagree on any number of matters. That is to be expected, and the debate of issues along with the expressed will of the people is the hallmark of our democracy. When these disagreements arise, however, I think it only right that we explore these differences face to face and not try them by inference or unfounded accusations placed where they can ruin an otherwise pleasant drive.

I would ask you, the parents of this community, to realize that. By all means, take a drive and see the sign—and when you do, remember that we at the schools stand ready to debate, to place the facts openly before the public, to place ourselves before the people we serve.

Ask yourself, do we deserve to be shot at from ambush? We will trust the answer you come up with!

Sincerely,

NOTE: It is very difficult to fight unsubstantiated accusations. The best thing you can do in a case like this is to plant equal seeds of doubt in the minds of those who will be affected. Of course, if the advertisement gets specific ("Principal Smith went on vacation using school funds!"), then you answer the specific allegation.

146. Establishing Rules for Media on Campus

If you have a newsworthy event at your school, the media will be coming to visit. If, for example, a candidate for governor comes to speak, the media will be all over your school. Unless you want chaos—and a total disruption of the educational process—you had best establish some rules going in. Here's a sample.

Welcome to Tyler Middle School:

I am certain that you are interested in getting a suitable story for your agency and following sound journalistic practices. I am also certain that you wish to go about that task without causing undue disruption to the educational process that is taking place in this school. Indeed, if I thought that the education of our children would be adversely affected, you would not be here. Therefore, I have a few guidelines about which we in our school are very particular. You will surely understand.

1. Please inform the main office of your presence in the building. This procedure is required of all visitors to our school. We would also appreciate it if you would inform the main office when you are about to leave school premises.

2. Without the express permission of the main office, no student is allowed to be removed from class.

3. Teachers are *not* to be disturbed during an assigned teaching period. Teachers are available for interviews during their professional periods; a copy of any teacher's schedule is available at the main office.

4. Finally, please remember that there are always many sides to an issue, and while we have no desire to interfere with journalistic freedom, we would hope to have the entire story presented, with equity to all sides.

I hope you have found these guidelines reasonable and to the point. If we all adhere to them, there is no reason why your time at our school should not be profitable for all concerned.

Yours sincerely,

NOTE: The guidelines above are reasonable. They serve well in actual school-media situations, and are highly unlikely to cause conflict. Of course, if you have any special conditions at your school that need particular attention, specify them in your particular set of guidelines.

147. Letter Detailing Guidelines for Media Contact

Of course, we do not tell people what they may or may not say to the media, but it is well within our rights to suggest guidelines for contact with the media, especially when the guidelines are common-sense approaches to the matter. The following letter to the faculty suggests some approaches to media contact.

To the Faculty and Staff:

You are surely aware of the recent interest in our schools in the local press and on the community TV station. You are also aware that next week, we shall have the media in our school when Mayor Allerton visits to speak at an assembly program. Related to her appearance, members of the media may wish to speak to you, and to ask questions, opinions, and the like.

Should you be interviewed, I suggest the following guidelines only for your consideration:

1. Be honest. Personally, I am very proud of this school and our faculty and staff. We have nothing to hide.

2. Please tell the entire story. Most certainly, we have problems and we fail from time to time, but we also have had some fantastic successes. Please try to make certain that the person interviewing you is aware of these pluses, along with the minuses, within our system.

3. I would ask you not to make a personal grievance seem to be reflective of the school as a whole. We all complain, we all have difficulties, and we all have procedures for handling these difficulties within our system. Is it right, therefore, to air a personal grievance in the newspapers?

4. This is your school, and you have made it the fine institution of learning that it is; be proud of it.

These are nothing more than suggestions, and you are free to accept them or not as you see fit. I sincerely believe that our school can step into any spotlight and be proud. I know you believe that as well.

Sincerely,

NOTE: In this kind of letter, it is important to remember that you cannot obstruct any individual's right to freedom of speech; that is why these are called "guidelines" and "suggestions." Even so, they cannot help but have a positive effect when the media come to call.

148. Letter Detailing Guidelines for News Releases

Many times, teachers and administrators will write stories that they intend to send to local newspapers. Sometimes these get published and sometimes not, but it is always good to establish some guidelines for these news releases from the people involved. Here is a short example from one school.

To Faculty and Staff:

There seems to be what I consider a very positive change in our local newspaper. They are providing more and more coverage of the events at our schools throughout the township, and at our school in particular. This provides an excellent opportunity for us to present ourselves to the citizens of this township, whose children we serve.

Many of you have written news releases for the local papers before, but for everyone involved, I thought you might be interested in a few suggestions for the very next article you feel led to write.

1. Try to emphasize the positive. There are many outstanding students and activities in our school, and the public should be aware of this.

2. Don't make an effort to hide the negative. If we have had something unfortunate happen, we do not cover it up. Rather, we present it honestly, stating our opinions in a positive manner.

3. Please tell the whole story; be certain that you provide all sides of the story or issue. For instance, if 62 students stage a walk-out protest about something, please be sure you mention that the remaining 620 students did not follow them, but stayed in class. Let fairness be your guide.

4. If there is ever a doubt in your mind, I will be most happy to review, make phone calls, and generally help you decide what you want to write or say.

Please remember, we do not have to manufacture news, nor do we have any intention of telling you what to say. There are sufficient positive, energetic, and encouraging activities going on in this school to supply materials for many fine news stories.

Let's let the public know the wonderful and good things that are happening here at our school.

Sincerely,

NOTE: Again, your purpose here is not to tell people what to say, but to give them something to think about when it comes to presenting the truth about your school in the most positive and effective manner possible. If you get everyone to think first, that alone will help your school come forth in the best light.

149. Letter Suggesting Guidelines for Newsworthiness

You can overload a local newspaper with stories about the school. After a while, it has a negative effect, in that the local press might begin to ignore those stories that are worth reading. To avoid this, it might be well to detail what makes a story "newsworthy." Here's an example.

To Faculty and Staff:

Many of us have stories about our classes or extracurricular activities that we believe are worthy of publication by our local newspaper. Before such a story is written by you or sent out to the paper, here are some guidelines for newsworthiness that you should review as objectively as possible. Simply put, if you can answer "yes" to seven of these questions, your story may be newsworthy. If not—well, would you want to rethink?

1. Does the story you propose involve something that goes beyond the day-to-day operation of this school?

2. Does your story emphasize some positive interaction between students, students and faculty, students and the community?

3. Will your story emphasize the positive aspects of school life?

4. Are there aspects of your story that take it beyond the ordinary and mundane?

5. Besides the students involved and their parents, would anyone be interested in the story, or need or want to know about it?

6. Are there any heartwarming or humorous aspects to your story?

7. Has every single fact in your story been checked for accuracy?

8. Does your story contain material with which a significant number of the general public could identify, or in which they would be interested?

9. If desired, could photographs be provided?

If we all follow these guidelines, we will save many hours of valuable time while seeing to it that those wonderful things that happen here get spread around the community.

Keep writing,

NOTE: If, and that's if, these guidelines are followed, they will provide a very good basis for the objective evaluation of the newsworthiness of a story. Sending a limited number of really good stories to any paper gets a much better response than a deluge of run-of-the-mill material that will end up discarded anyhow.

150. Requesting TV Time for a School Event

If you have a local TV station, it is a highly effective medium to use to show the good points about your school. To get the station to cover a school event with cameras and spokespeople, and the like, will require a bit of asking. Here's an example of one such request.

Dear Ms. Folkner,

I am well aware of just how busy you must be. I can also appreciate that a TV station like yours must receive a hundred requests for coverage each week, if not more, and perhaps most of those requests are to photograph the opening of the begonias in Uncle Willie's backyard or to cover the opening of a lemonade stand constructed by the child of the writer. I don't envy you that!

That is precisely why I refuse—absolutely refuse—to bother you with the mundane or the ordinary that is happening at Tracey Elementary School. Oh, no! When I come to you, it is with something that you can use on TV, something that the people of this community will want to tune in to see; something that will jump right off the screen at them.

That's why I knew that you would be interested in our "Celebrated Jumping Frog Contest" to be held at our school next Thursday, May 17, _____. Does the name tell it all? We will have our students interacting with those little green creatures as they jump for a trophy and provide an almost inexhaustible opportunity for coverage by the TV cameras.

You know, I might even get down on my hands and knees and spur a frog on to victory. Moreover, Mayor Richter has agreed to be the judge, and I am certain that he will have something "froggy" to say about the event.

I sure hope that you will want to send coverage of this exciting and uplifting (not to say "hopping") event! We know how newsworthy it is, and we would love to have you with us.

Please feel free to call me at my office, and we'll try to accommodate you in any way we can. Need I say that I am "hopping" to speak to you soon?

Yours sincerely,

NOTE: Yes, there was a definite sense of humor in that letter, but it is likely to get results, because it gives some very good and practical reasons why it would be worth the time of the TV station to provide the coverage—a principal who is ready to be cooperative, the mayor of the town as a judge, a chance to get pictures of kids and teachers, all tied up with frogs. A story like this definitely meets the criteria for effective local coverage that might be part of the TV station's mission statement.

151. Requesting Assistance for an Impending Media Event

In the letter establishing rules for media on campus, a visit from a candidate for governor was mentioned. If you are planning such an event, you can be sure that you can't handle the volume of traffic nor the amount of media personnel that will be coming. This is one of those times when you just have to ask for help.

Dear Superintendent Scalzo,

As you are aware, two weeks from today, October 23, _____, the Hon. Dunbar Q. Welton, candidate for governor of our state, will be visiting Tyler Middle School and addressing us in a special assembly. You are also aware of the township dignitaries who will be present, as well as certain state officials and, of course, the media. At present, it is our understanding that between the newspaper, radio, and TV coverage, we expect close to 50 media people alone. This figure does not include the candidate's secret service personnel, campaign manager and staff, personal photographer, helicopter pilot, and many other people—not to mention members of the community who may wish to visit their school.

It is only reasonable, therefore, that we at Tyler approach you at central administration for help. We will need the cooperation and aid of our local police force, if for nothing more than parking control and crowd management. Certainly, we can provide assistance from within the school, but it will not be sufficient to cover all that will be going on.

I therefore request a meeting with you and Chief of Police William Greer at the earliest possible moment in order to discuss and determine what assistance will be required at the time of the event, and how all peripheral difficulties such as parking, crowd control, preparing the back field for the helicopter, and so on may be handled with dispatch and for the safety of all concerned.

I am sure that you will agree that this is a most serious matter, worthy of our immediate attention, in order that this upcoming media event may go as smoothly as possible for all concerned.

I look forward to hearing from you.

Sincerely,

NOTE: It is far better to ask for the assistance you need to keep the media event running smoothly than to enter into it and find yourself frantically treading water as the storm mounts. Good preparation, plus a feel for dealing with the media, will help you to get through.

LETTERS THAT RELATE TO YOUR JOB

*I*n school, we write all kinds of letters. We praise students; we suspend them. We inquire about supplies and books and assembly programs. We write thank-you's and apologies and congratulations and the like. It seems that we do an awful lot of writing; it just goes with the job. If we were to analyze all these written efforts, however, we might discover that the vast majority of these letters concern the children we teach or the functioning of the school we administer. Few of us would say that we write a great deal about our jobs.

We do write about jobs, however, and we do it more frequently than we think. We evaluate others who are doing a job, from teacher to custodian; we request transfers from one position or school to another; we resign from one job to accept another; we even have to write a letter on that long-anticipated retirement.

THE DELICATE MATTER OF JOB-RELATED LETTERS

Any letter related to your job can be extremely difficult to write and may require great delicacy. You would not, under any circumstances, write a letter of resignation that merely stated, "I quit!" As ludicrous as that may sound, that is the impression that a poorly written letter of this type may create. It is well for us to take some time and make certain that all our "delicate" job-related letters are fully thought out and reasonable when looked at from any point of view.

Toward that end, there are a few guidelines you might want to follow:

1. **NEVER GET ANGRY:** Whatever the circumstances, and even if someone has really done wrong by you, control that anger in the letters you write. A letter filled with rage or anger burns in the reader's hand, and that reader is going to want to stay away from the heat.

2. **NEVER GET VINDICTIVE:** If you begin to blame others for your troubles, even if you are being accurate, it could well backfire and look as if you were just trying to shift blame or point fingers. This may not be taken well by the person or agency to whom you are writing.

163

3. **PRESENT YOURSELF IN THE BEST POSSIBLE LIGHT WITHOUT DENIGRATING OTHERS:** In letters about your job—and particularly in those you send looking for a new job—always present your accomplishments in a straightforward and positive manner. The feeling should always be "look at what I have done." Never, never should there be the implication of "I could have done better if . . ." Let what you have done speak for itself, and even if there were any extenuating circumstances—we guarantee—the people you are addressing will find out on their own, and you will come out the better for never having brought up any unpleasantness.

Keep these suggestions in mind as we look at this section of letters. Whether you are seeking a new job, rebutting a negative evaluation, or writing that letter of resignation or retirement, those principles apply almost universally.

Perhaps you will never have to write any of these letters (other than the one for your retirement), but if you should, here are some models that will be effective in a wide variety of situations.

MODEL LETTERS THAT RELATE TO YOUR JOB

152. *Letter Announcing Your Availability for a Position*

There are a variety of reasons why you might wish to move on to another position that has suddenly become available. Without delving into those reasons, here is a letter that might be used to investigate the system's interest in you for that new position, and to announce your availability for it.

Dear Superintendent Ortiz,

It has come to my attention that you have created a new post within our school system, to be effective as of June 1, _____. The position is to bear the title "Superintendent of Summer School Classes and Activities."

I would like you to know that I can be available for such a position, and I feel that I could serve this township well in such a capacity.

As to my qualifications for the position, those I would gladly supply, and I know that you will be quite satisfied with them. The purpose of this letter, however, is to assure you that I would be available for the task as of the times designated by you.

My duties at the school officially end on May 31, _____, and do not resume until August 15, _____. Since the term of the new position is from June 1 through August 14, _____, I would be readily available to devote my full time to our township's summer school classes and activities.

I felt that I had to write to you to express both my availability and my interest in that position. I would be most grateful if you could send me any further information you might have, as well as requesting any further information from me concerning my personal or professional qualifications.

Thank you very much for your time and consideration. I look forward to hearing from you soon.

Yours sincerely,

NOTE: This is not exactly a letter of application, is it? It assumes that, of course, you would be acceptable for the job, but in addition (happy thought) you just happen to be available for the times specified. In any school system, people know what jobs are going to be available long before they are ever published, so a letter like this one is not out of line.

153. Letter Expressing Interest in a Position

The last letter expressed your availability; now, let's look at one that shows your definite interest in the position. Here, you are really interested in the job, and you wish the person to whom you are writing to understand that. Previously, we expressed availability, with interest implied, but here we will reverse the process and show interest, with the implication of availability.

Dear Superintendent Ortiz,

It has come to my attention that you have created a new post within our school system, to be effective June 1, _____. The position is to bear the title "Superintendent of Summer School Classes and Activities."

I would like you to know that I am extremely interested in such a position, and I feel that I could serve this township well in such a capacity.

As perhaps you know, my past record indicates my satisfactory performance of such duties for the summer school program in the Belknap County School System. There, for three summers, I was in charge of some 40 teachers and activity directors, as well as supervising the educational progress of well over 350 students on seven different grade levels.

I loved it! I thought at that time, as I do today, that it was challenging, interesting, and very rewarding work. I got to know every one of the kids by name, as I did the teachers, and that established a rapport that served all of us well during the regular academic year.

That is why I am so interested in the new position you have established. Of course, it must be advertised and interviews given, but I wanted you to know that when you receive my application, you will be dealing with someone who truly wants that job because he feels that he could do an outstanding job for the children of this community. Moreover, my commitments to the school contractually end and begin at such a time that I would be readily available to devote my full time to our township's summer school classes and activities.

I felt that I had to write to you to express both my great interest in and my availability for that position. I would be more than grateful if you sent me any further information you might have.

Thank you very much for your time and consideration. I look forward to hearing from you soon.

Yours sincerely,

NOTE: If you are questioning whether a letter of this type can help you with that new position, then let us put it this way: "It sure can't hurt!" Even if there are 20 applicants for the position, a letter such as this, written and sent early on, at the very least places you in the forefront of the mind of the superintendent or hiring agent. Certainly, when it comes time for an interview, this will be in your folder along with your application, and it cannot help but positively impress those who read it. This letter and the previous one are similar, yet both serve a really positive purpose in getting you to that new job.

154. Letter Requesting an Application

Some time has passed, and you have come to the point where you must apply formally for the new position. This may be handled in a number of ways inherent to your school system, but let's assume that you will have to make a formal application. Here is a letter requesting that formal application. Notice, however, how your former writing efforts are used to reinforce your position.

Dear Superintendent Ortiz,

May I formally request that you send me, at your earliest convenience, an application for the newly named position of "Superintendent of Summer School Classes and Activities" for our township, which will be available through the period beginning June 1, _____, and ending August 14, _____?

Thanks to your kindness in sending me the criteria for this position and the formal job description, I am more interested than ever. All of that has certainly whetted my appetite and, should I be selected, made me very eager to begin.

While I shall certainly complete the application at once, I want you to know that if there is anything I can do to expedite the matter, I will be happy to cooperate.

Of course, I will be available for interview by you or anyone you designate whenever you shall determine. I am certain that I can accommodate any request, and, indeed, I am looking forward to sharing my ideas with you.

Some time ago, I wrote you a letter expressing my interest in this position. The time between then and now has not lessened that feeling but added a keenness to it—an even greater desire to get on with it.

Thank you very much for your time and consideration. I assure you that I shall return the application as soon as possible.

I look forward to receiving the application material soon.

Sincerely yours,

NOTE: You've made it clear here that the intensity of interest still remains very high, and you have reminded the superintendent about your previous letter. Basically, you are doing things to make yourself special and noteworthy in the eyes of the person who must consider you for the post—and that's not a bad idea.

155. Personal Statement on Application

The trend on many applications nowadays is to have applicants write a short, personal statement as to why they want a position; why they feel qualified for the job; what they intend to do that makes them uniquely suitable for the position; what they feel they have to offer to the school system; and the like. Assuming that the application requested in the last letter contains something of this sort, here's an example of one such statement.

I view a position such as Superintendent of Summer School Classes and Activities as something that would have a tremendous impact upon our school system, not only during the summer, but for the entire school year. I believe that a student's academic needs are both supplemented and improved by summer school classes, and that can often spell the difference between academic success and a disaffected student.

Moreover, a student's attitude toward regular school is often affected by the quality of his or her experiences with the system, and the summer activities offered by the school can, if properly organized and supervised, foster an attitude toward school and learning that can inculcate in a student that spark of identification with success that equates with an outstanding record during the regular academic year.

Without undue modesty, I know that I am a person who could handle a situation like this and make certain that its full potential is realized. In both my personal ideology and my professional background, I adhere to these principles and give all my effort in philosophy and practice to make it the success it deserves to be and can become.

Indeed, I administered the Belknap County School System Summer School program for the previous three years. I supervised 40 teachers and over 350 students representing some seven grade levels. To say the least, the program was tremendously successful, and that may be attested to by contacting the references I listed previously. The only reason I am not returning there for a fourth year is that the program was canceled due to certain factors of economics and the loss of some of the physical facilities to fire. Were it not for these unexpected obstacles, the program would still be in existence and producing the stellar results it had before.

If I am selected for this post, I fully intend to give all the energy I put into the program in Belknap County to the Summer School and Activities that this township plans to offer. I want to tackle it with the same enthusiasm and drive; I want others to be as fired up with this opportunity to reach kids as I am; I want to lead the way by taking the first steps and shouting, "Follow me!"

For the children of this township and their ultimate academic and personal success, I truly feel that I can do no less.

NOTE: Since this is a statement, there is no salutation or friendly closing. Also, you should read carefully what the individual application requires and speak to that. If, for instance, it merely asks for your academic qualifications, you concentrate on them. Speak to what is required.

156. Letter of Acceptance of Position

Let's assume that you have gone through every letter so far in this section, and that you got the position. You could stop writing there, since you now have what you have sought, but that would be a mistake. Write one more letter, and formally—in writing—accept the position offered. Such a letter is a good way to start a new relationship. Here's an example.

Dear Superintendent Ortiz,

Thank you so much for your recent telephone call and subsequent follow-up letter of April 16, _____, advising me that I had been approved by the board of education at its regular meeting for the position of Superintendent of Summer School Classes and Activities, for the period June 1, _____, through August 14, _____. It was wonderful to hear from you, and I enjoyed our brief conversation. Your letter, needless to say, gave special meaning to my day.

I accept this assignment most humbly. Of course, I am overjoyed to be working with you in such a responsible position, but it also is quite a sobering thought to take upon oneself the responsibility for so many children, knowing that—to a large extent—what happens during the weeks of summer school may have a profound effect upon their futures. It is something that I do not take lightly.

Please convey to the board my deep thanks for their trust, and the assurance that they will have my full devotion to the task ahead, a task that I consider most important and worthy of my strongest efforts.

Personally, I thank you for your support throughout. I look forward to serving under your guidance, as I look forward to the meeting we arranged during your phone call. I am certain that we will have a productive session.

Again, thanks for your confidence, and please believe that I will work to confirm your confidence. I am eager to get started.

Yours sincerely,

NOTE: Speaking in terms of your own career, a letter such as this stands a good chance of getting noticed and being remembered. Moreover, it helps to build a good working rapport with the superintendent, or whoever will be your superior. As the old saying goes, if this letter can't help you, it sure can't hurt, either.

157. Request for Transfer (Nonspecific Reason)

A time may come when you wish to transfer to another job or another school or another level. Your desire for that transfer may be for a wide variety of reasons, none of which it is our purpose or desire to go into here. Suffice it to say, you desire a transfer, and for this first letter, let us assume that you do not wish to give a specific reason.

To: Assistant Superintendent for Personnel

Re: Request for Transfer

At the outset, may I assure you that I am quite happy with my position in the Cuthbert Township School System. A glance at my record will attest to the fact that I have served adequately in this system for the past sixteen years. My recent evaluations portray a person who is actively engaged in the education of the children of this township and greatly enjoys the privilege of touching young minds. Indeed, it was this enthusiasm that drew me into education in the first place and keeps me ever enjoying the process even today.

The question that follows is obvious: "Then, why do you wish to apply for a transfer?"

In answer, first allow me to state that the transfer I am looking for is to another school within the township at the same or similar grade level. If this transfer can be accomplished, I shall leave my current school and position without the slightest degree of animosity to anyone and with only the most pleasant of memories of students, faculty, staff, and administration.

I have been at this school for sixteen years, and lest I become set in my ways; lest the slightest degree of intransigence begin to creep in; lest I become effective only with one kind of child or class, I would like to transfer to a place where I can meet new challenges and new people.

I would, of course, continue to give my all no matter where I am assigned, but I really would appreciate a new start and a new school this coming September.

Thank you for any consideration you can give to my request.

Respectfully yours,

NOTE: Unless your contract has specific agencies for dealing with transfers, most transfers require that a reason be given. This letter, however, is as nonspecific as you can get. Also, note that it is completely nonthreatening and nondemanding as well.

158. Request for Transfer (Specific Reason)

A time may come when you will have to or want to give a specific reason for your request for transfer. When that happens, you will wish to phrase that reason in the most positive manner that you can. Always remember that what you write down has a nasty habit of following you around for the rest of your life. Be circumspect. Try something like this.

To: Assistant Superintendent for Personnel
Re: Request for Transfer

Please be advised that I am requesting a transfer from my current school and duties to any other school within the township. I would like this transfer to be commensurate with the beginning of the new school year, August 25, _____.

If it is at all possible, I would like to remain at the same grade level, and I truly do enjoy and appreciate the elementary school, so placement in either of the other two elementary schools within the township would be greatly appreciated.

I am requesting this transfer in order to make a new start after a somewhat unsettling incident that occasions my desire to leave my current school. A parent was told by his son that I struck him in the face, producing a split lip and a black eye. The truth of the matter was that the boy had been in a fight that afternoon, and when he was questioned by an angry parent, he made up the story about my striking him. The test he had failed in my class that afternoon may or may not have had something to do with it. In any case, subsequent investigation showed that I was with an extra-help class of students when he claimed the incident occurred. Confronted with that fact, the boy confessed he was lying.

This did not occur, however, before the father had sworn out a warrant for me on the charge of assault on a minor. The police came to my house, and I was brought to the police station for questioning. The boy's father was there and became so abusive, the police asked him to leave.

Within the next two days, the problem was solved, and the boy had confessed. During that time, Mr. Benson, my principal, was of great help and comfort, as was Mrs. Paloni, our vice-principal. I have only the highest regard for them.

The incident, however, left me shaken, and I had to take off several days to regain my perspective. This I feel I have done, but the boy remains in the school and will be there for the next two years. While I bear him no enmity, I really do not feel that I can work with him or even in proximity to him.

I believe, therefore, that a transfer would probably be the best course. I still love children, I still love to teach, I still want to make it my career—but I also wish to put this incident behind me.

I know you will understand, and I thank you for the kindness and consideration that you extend in this instance. I look forward to hearing from you soon.

Respectfully yours,

NOTE: Certainly, this request for transfer would get results. Wouldn't you act on something like this? Notice that, while the reason was traumatic in nature for the writer, it was handled matter-of-factly and without any vindictiveness. That should be your watchword in anything of this sort that you might have to write.

159. Request for Transfer to a Specific School

Both of the previous requests for transfer were nonspecific to the extent that they asked for a transfer to "another school" and did not name the exact place. A time might come, however, when you want a transfer to one—and only one—specific school.

To: Assistant Superintendent of Personnel

Re: Request for Transfer

I respectfully request a transfer from my current location at Haverford Middle School to the same or similar position at Thompson Middle School, effective with the start of the new academic year beginning August 25, _____.

I am requesting this transfer for two reasons. First, with the start of the next school year, Thompson Middle School is beginning a special program for Gifted and Talented children that will involve drama and children's theater for the elementary schools in the district. As you may be aware, I have a background both in the teaching of G&T and in drama as a communications tool. I would like to be able to contribute to this program, which I will be unable to do in my current position.

Next, I understand that Melissa Freedman will be administering the program. Ms. Freedman and I have worked together in the past on just such a program in another school system, and we have discovered a unique ability to cooperate in supporting both students and teachers in their efforts. I would be most willing to assist.

I find my current school a pleasant place to be, with fine and lively students, excellent faculty members, and a fine administration. I ask for a transfer to Thompson Middle School only because of the existence of the new G&T program and its administrator, and because I sincerely believe that I can make a decided contribution to that program and to that school.

Thank you for your efforts on my behalf. I look forward to hearing from you soon.

Respectfully yours,

NOTE: Never should there be any enmity left behind. Notice that the former school was complimented, even though the request is clear that you wish to transfer to a specific place for a specific reason. Even if you are required to fill out a form for transfer, you can still write a paragraph or two somewhere to bring home your point.

160. Request for Transfer to a Specific Job

Again, there may be times when you wish for transfer to a specific job. That is usually because you have heard that the person currently there is moving out. You may have to write a letter of request or fill out an application for the position. Here, we will handle it as we did the previous requests, and you can amend it to the form that fits your needs.

To: Assistant Superintendent for Personnel

Re: Request for Transfer

Please be advised that it is my desire to transfer, effective with the end of this current academic year, to the guidance department of Mantenberg High School.

I understand that Mr. Wilbur Goodman, who currently serves as head counselor, will be retiring at the end of this year. While I do not necessarily see myself in his position, I would like to get into that guidance system and work in it in order to learn and develop on the senior high school level.

I am quite qualified for such a position, having served for five years in the guidance department of Herzenwalk Middle School. As a member of the high school guidance department, I will undoubtedly see many of my former clients and have occasion to counsel with them there.

During my time at Herzenwalk, I have received nothing but superior evaluations and I have a portfolio of letters from parents and teachers, attesting to the kind of job I have done. Now, with the well-deserved retirement of Mr. Goodman, I feel ready to step into a position at the high school level that will not only expand my horizons but allow me to continue to counsel many students I know, as well as give me the opportunity to meet new challenges.

This is why I specifically wish transfer to a position on the guidance staff of the high school. Such a move would, I am certain, be good for all concerned.

I thank you in advance for all your efforts on my behalf, and I look forward to hearing from you.

Respectfully yours,

NOTE: There is no reason why this could not be put in the form of a letter, or parts of it adapted to the space for personal comment on a formal application. In a school system, word gets around rather quickly, and it is often the one who is aggressive who takes the lead in the race.

161. Request for Transfer (Difficult Reason)

Not everything in life is cheerful and wonderful and happy. Unfortunately, we get into situations and develop negative relations, and are misunderstood in a wide variety of situations and in a plethora of circumstances. Here, we are talking about the "difficult" reason you may have to request a transfer. How can you give a bad situation as a reason for transferring without getting tied up in it? Look at the following, and be certain to read the note at the end.

To: Assistant Superintendent for Personnel

Re: Request for Transfer

Please be advised that it is my desire to be transferred from my current school to any other school in the township that has an available position similar in duties and assignments to the one I now hold. Of course, I understand that positions such as this may not be readily available, but I would greatly appreciate it if you would expedite this matter as much as possible.

I know this appears hasty, but I assure you that I have thought a great deal about the matter, and I see it as the only viable solution to a situation that is best left to itself—and it would have been, except that a request of this nature requires that reasonable cause be given.

As head guidance counselor, I must work very closely with the vice-principal on a great number of matters concerning students and other problems relating to the school. That working arrangement, if it is to be effective and to the benefit of both students and the school, must be one of mutual cooperation and trust.

Regrettably, I do not have that type of relationship with the current vice-principal, nor, as far as I can see, is it likely that one will develop in the near future. I make no accusations nor offer any explanations other than our seeming inability to get along with each other. Indeed, the vice-principal does her job well, seems well liked by faculty and students, and is a reasonable person. I honestly believe the same may be said about me.

Mrs. Occupinti, the principal, has tried holding conferences with both of us from time to time, but to no seeming avail. The fact remains, we may respect each other professionally, but on a personal basis, we simply do not get along.

Therefore, without blame being placed anywhere, I believe that the simplest solution is for us to be parted. I think that would be best for the school, for each of us individually, and ultimately for the children with whom we must deal.

Most certainly, we will continue to do our best for those under our charge, but I urge you, and I believe the vice-principal would agree, to try to find an alternate placement for me as soon as is possible for the sake of all concerned.

Thank you for your concern and understanding.

Yours respectfully,

NOTE: Please note that even if the two of you were the worst enemies in the world and you developed a situation in which each moment was a lifetime of torture (which a personality clash certainly is not), you would still speak of the other person in the manner used in this letter. To make accusations or to use invective of any kind is a bad move, since what you write in public letters such as this one is often seen and analyzed by any number of people, and you could find yourself in an untenable position.

162. Letter Concerning Positive Job Evaluation of Employee

While you are an employee yourself, you may be in a position where you are responsible for the evaluation of someone under your supervision. When that happens, you will, of course, suit your evaluation to the individual and the particular circumstances of his or her employment. The following is just an example of the kinds of things you might say if you were writing a very positive evaluation.

Re: Evaluation of Russel Deitler, Teacher

One of the best things about watching Mr. Deitler teach is observing the fantastic rapport he has with his students. He is a master at working that class, and the students respond to him by granting their attention and respect. Mr. Deitler can spot a potential discipline problem from across the room, and in most cases, a mere look is enough to stop it in its tracks. He operates with a sense of humor that warms the classroom and makes students want to be there. His grasp of the material taught is obvious, as well as his fascination with it and love for it. The result is learning at its best.

He teaches to his students' individual differences, and every child is called upon to do something during the class period. A sign on the bulletin board reads, "Every Student Every Day!" and it is a motto Mr. Deitler adheres to with great regularity. With those students who answer correctly, he is effusive with praise, while for those who do not answer well, there is still praise for trying—with offers of help later.

In short, it was an enjoyable experience for me, even as an evaluator, to be present in Mr. Deitler's classroom.

Mr. Deitler is a master teacher, and his students are fortunate to be in his classes.

Respectfully submitted,

NOTE: Certainly, you include all else that you are required to do, but this "statement in summation," if you will, is an example of some positive things to say when you are evaluating a positive and masterful school employee like the person described here.

163. Letter Concerning Negative Job Evaluation of Employee

Unfortunately, you don't evaluate master teachers or wonderfully positive school employees all the time. In fact, the opposite is just as likely to be true. There will be times when you must give a negative evaluation, because that is what the situation calls for. While this may be an unhappy experience, it is a part of your job. Again, you would indicate specifics, but here is a very general example to go by.

Re: Evaluation of Vivica Wrensler, Teacher

During the fifty minutes I observed Ms. Wrensler in class, I did not see her walk away from the front of the room, or go to a student at his or her desk. Indeed, there seemed to be a separation between Ms. Wrensler and her students.

Ms. Wrensler sat at her desk as students entered the room. When the bell rang for the start of class, she stood and began to call for attention. The class did not quiet down; rather, they continued talking and privately interacting. Ms. Wrensler, after a good two minutes of calling for silence, finally slammed a dictionary upon her desk, and this quieted the class for a moment.

Page numbers of the text were given orally by the teacher, and six students did not have their texts. These were sent to their lockers, without passes. Several other students called out questions about various topics, ranging from the homework to whether the class could watch a movie on Friday. It was a good ten minutes before these questions were answered, the bookless students returned, and class got underway.

The class thereafter consisted of student after student reading orally from the text. Every so often, Ms. Wrensler would comment upon the text being read. I observed no students taking notes. During the reading, there was a great deal of general misbehavior. The teacher significantly raised her voice to quiet the class no less than eighteen times. At the end of the class time, the students rushed for the doors, while the teacher shouted the pages of a homework assignment at them. I estimate that a good 80 percent of them never got the assignment. One student tried to speak with Ms. Wrensler after class and was informed that the teacher was busy and perhaps he should write her a letter if he needed to discuss anything.

I deeply regret having to say that this class was one of the worst examples of teaching that I have ever witnessed. Students learned very little except, perhaps, how to ignore what was being taught. The only learning that went on in that class was what the students learned from each other, and none of us can be positive as to how good or bad that may have been.

Ms. Wrensler has been given a number of opportunities to improve her teaching skills, all of which were rejected by her. She has had numerous run-ins with the faculty, and the school has had several parental requests to remove their children from Ms. Wrensler's classes. This is her second year with us, and we have seen no evidence of change or improvement.

Therefore, I regret that I cannot do less than recommend that Ms. Wrensler's contract not be renewed for the next academic year.

Respectfully submitted,

NOTE: We hope that you will never have to write a letter such as that more than once in a career. A truly bad educator can have a powerfully negative effect upon both students and school, and a truly conscientious educator should have no problem calling it as it is. After all attempts to help, if this is what is called for, then this is what you must do.

164. *Acceptance of Positive Job Evaluation*

Technically, you do not have to answer a job evaluation, but you might want to in two instances. If it was particularly bad, you might want to rebut it; if it was particularly good, you might want to acknowledge the kindness of your evaluator. Let's look at the latter.

Dear Dr. Philhower,

I have received and am returning herewith the signed office copy of the recent evaluation you did of me. Naturally, it is signed without comment, and since it is so positive and so good, I think I broke a land-speed record getting it back to you. Perhaps you could help me decide whether I should enclose it in acrylic or just place it in a gold frame to show to my grandchildren!

Seriously, I cannot thank you enough for your kind words. Your insights, warmth, and genuine concern for education are evident throughout, and what you said about me personally has helped make me feel very positive about any efforts I may put forth in behalf of the students of this school. In short, it is nice to be appreciated, and I am very, very grateful for your evaluation.

If I am, as you say, a "master" teacher, it is because I have learned from masters and had the help and the friendship of masters like you and other members of the faculty for all these years. It is their experience and their willingness to share that has rubbed off, and they must take a large share of the credit for any "master" status I may carry in this school.

In short, it is a delight to teach here, and the best I can say is that I look forward to each day, being with everyone here—from administration to faculty to the student body. If I am a good teacher, it is because this is a good place to be.

Thank you, again, for the wonderful evaluation. I am very happy to be here, and I look forward to many more very happy and productive years.

Yours sincerely,

NOTE: Certainly, this is a gracious letter following a very positive evaluation. Letters like this get remembered. They can do a great deal of good for your reputation, as well as build a positive rapport with the administrator who wrote the evaluation, and is very positive about you at the outset.

165. Rebuttal of Negative Job Evaluation

All is grand and wonderful when everything is running smoothly, but suppose a negative job evaluation was written about you. It doesn't have to be horrendous, but any negative aspect of an evaluation should be addressed. Read the following, and be certain to follow up by reading the note at the end of the letter.

Dear Mr. Migliore,

Recently, I had a rather unpleasant experience, and since we are both involved with it, I feel that I must bring it to your attention. The unpleasantness I experienced was reading the evaluation of me you wrote for my yearly observation. It was unpleasant because nobody wants to believe that his or her work is unsatisfactory, and nobody likes to be misunderstood.

I truly feel that you misunderstood much of what you observed in my classroom. Your observation, for example, that I spent too much time with certain individual students in my class, to the detriment of other students, could only be made because you did not have all the facts. Did you know that many of the students in that class are students whom the world would call "troubled"? Of course, you understand that these student have extra needs that often must be addressed as they occur, for if they were put off to a later time, the acting out or self-destructive behavior might already have taken place.

It was to these students that I was speaking, and the time I spent with them was hardly "inordinate"—not for them! I asked for an aide earlier in the year for just that reason, but the request was denied. I do not think it equitable, however, to claim that I am ignoring the rest of my class, when I am merely dealing effectively with those students who have been given to me.

I would like to have a conference with you as soon as possible to discuss this in greater detail; I will keep the evaluation and bring it with me.

I am certain that we can work this out and that, once you are aware of certain factors (some of which, in all honesty, you could not have known), perhaps there are certain aspects of the evaluation that we could reconsider together.

Thank you, sir, for your understanding. I really look forward to speaking with you soon.

Sincerely yours,

NOTE: Whatever you do or say in such a rebuttal, do not become angry and do not get personal. An angry letter will not get you very far and will, in fact, only harden the resistance to you. Always assume a misunderstanding. That way, your aim can be to clear up those issues that were not clear.

166. Letter of Resignation for Health Reasons

One resigns from certain positions and jobs for a very wide variety of reasons, and for the next several letters, we will investigate some of them. One major reason for a resignation has always been health, or, rather the lack of health required for the job. That's the first one we'll look at.

Dear Mr. Shada,

It is with regret that I must herewith tender my resignation from the position of coach of the girl's field hockey team at Dannemore Middle School. My resignation shall be effective immediately, and I am requesting that you drop the customary 30-day notice period, which would require me to remain at my duties during that time. I understand that this time period is discretionary on your part, and I would very much appreciate your waiving it in order that I may leave my coaching duties at once.

This rather drastic move on my part is occasioned by an automobile accident in which I was involved as a passenger in a car that was hit by another car that had run a traffic signal. Although I am all right in all other respects, I suffered a double fracture of my right leg. Currently, I am still in a cast and the leg is being held together by two steel pins. I am advised by my orthopedic surgeon that it is critical for me to follow her direction and allow the healing process to progress uninterrupted if I wish to regain the greater part of the mobility I once had.

While I fully understand my doctor's reasoning, I am upset that this will mean the curtailment of many of the activities that are so intrinsically a part of my personal and professional life.

You surely can understand both my resignation as coach and my request that the resignation be honored immediately. Believe me, I do not wish to go, but the sooner you get another coach in there, the better it will be for the young women on the team.

I will be more than happy to speak with my replacement at his or her convenience, and—who knows—I may be asking for this job back in some not-too-distant future. Thank you for understanding.

Sincerely,

NOTE: When you are resigning for health reasons, it is best to be straightforward and explain what is happening. School boards and superintendents of personnel are almost invariably sympathetic where the health of an employee is concerned. In fact, they are most likely to bend over backward to accommodate an employee who has had to resign for health reasons.

167. Letter of Resignation for "Personal" Reasons

There are times when people want to stop what they are doing for a variety of reasons that can only be called "personal." This may include such things as personal difficulties in coping with the situation or job, difficulty with a spouse at home, or a personal tragedy involving one or more of your children. More precisely, these are difficulties that may occasion a resignation but that you do not wish to share with anyone at the present moment. Here's one example of addressing that kind of situation.

Dear Dr. Lenada,

Please be advised that it is my intention to resign from my current extracurricular contract as faculty advisor to the yearbook committee. My resignation shall take place November 15, _____, hereby granting the full 60 days' notice required by the contract. I shall stay and work with the yearbook committee up until that time, and that should provide you with more than sufficient time to find a replacement.

In fact, I am personally aware of two or three faculty members who are both willing and able to take charge.

I have served as yearbook advisor now for the past four years, and I have enjoyed it greatly. I thank you for giving me that opportunity. Lately, however, there have been some changes in my life—particularly with my home and family—that require my after-school and weekend time to attend to them. You undoubtedly know that we all have personal matters that must be handled within our families. Since they are personal, I am further sure that it is sufficient that I mention the situation without going into extensive detail.

I thank you for understanding, and while I regret the necessity of resigning, I am certain that you will find someone to replace me, and that the yearbook will be as good as ever—perhaps even better. Thank you, also, for understanding the personal nature of this decision.

I shall be glad to help in finding my replacement if you so desire.

Sincerely,

NOTE: In this letter you have honored your contract, even offered to help find your replacement, and advised them of your personal reason for the resignation, yet refused to go into it in any detail other than the fact that it was about home, and it was personal. All told, that's pretty good for such a short letter.

168. Letter of Resignation for a Better Position

Most school systems understand about such things as personal careers and advancement. There are few, indeed, who would criticize you for resigning from one position to take another that either pays better, gives you better working conditions, or helps to advance your career. Therefore, as always, be honest, and people will respond in kind.

Dear Ms. Li,

It is with both regret and anticipation that I now formally resign from my position as head guidance counselor of Cook High School. My resignation will be effective January 31, _____, which constitutes a proper 60-day notice as required by contractual obligation.

I regret the necessity of this decision, because I have served for ten very happy years as head guidance counselor of this school, and over that time I have established many bonds that press upon me to remain. Nonetheless, there is an equally strong reason why I must be moving onward.

I am leaving Cook High School to assume the duties of vice-principal of Power Memorial High School in nearby Reston Falls. You are aware that I have been actively seeking advancement in the field of school administration, and when this opportunity presented itself, I felt I could not, in all conscience, turn it down.

I leave with only the highest regard for my colleagues and for our school system. I carry many fine memories with me.

You will remain in my thoughts.

Yours sincerely,

NOTE: This is a straightforward letter that could be read and understood by almost anyone—certainly by the administrators of your school system. Congratulations, along with heartfelt offers to "help you get started" in your new responsibilities would surely be forthcoming. Career advancement is something we all understand!

169. Letter on the Resignation of an Employee

Not only may you be in a position to write a resignation, but you might, some day, have to reply to or recognize the resignation of an employee who is under your jurisdiction. You should be cautioned, in such a case, not to allow any negative personal feelings to enter into the letter you write even if you are rather happy that the person is retiring. Keep the letter simple and polite, and what you say won't come back to haunt you later.

Dear Mrs. Wexler,

Please be advised that at the regular meeting of the Coslow Board of Education held on Tuesday evening, January 17, _____, your resignation as chief librarian of Coslow High School was accepted with regret by the board, to be effective as of April 1, _____.

Shortly, you will be contacted by our personnel office to make all necessary arrangements and to facilitate all the paper work that must be done. Rest assured, however, that the major part of the process has been taken care of, and the details that remain will be largely handled by our office. On this, you will receive clear direction via mail in the next few days.

The board of education was most emphatic in directing me to inform you that your resignation was accepted with the deepest regret. Your record here at Coslow Township has been one of impeccable service to the children of this community, and the board deeply appreciates the years you have given, as well as the care and concern that have gone far beyond the outlines of your contract.

Toward the goal of expressing our appreciation, the board has further directed me to compose a "Statement of Appreciation" for your many years of loyal service. That statement will be presented to you during part of the year-end closing ceremonies at Coslow High School.

Further, the board wishes to express their heartfelt good wishes on your new position as Chief Librarian at Mainford College. A copy of the "Statement of Appreciation," approved by the board, will be sent to the personnel director at Mainford as soon as it is prepared.

On a personal note, I add my congratulations to those of the others in wishing you continued success in your new position and offering my thanks for the competent and conscientious manner in which you performed your duties here at Mainford.

Again, you will be hearing from us soon regarding the necessary paper work. May your future be bright!

Sincerely,

NOTE: This is a pleasant letter, in which the board has accepted the resignation of a good educator who is resigning to go to a better position. Not all will be that nice. If the resignation were offered under adverse circumstances, then this letter would be much more matter-of-fact, such as, ". . . the board accepted your resignation . . . certain papers will be mailed to you . . . thank you for your cooperation in this matter. . . ." You get the idea. The letter would be polite, but it would also be without all the personal thanks and recognition that boards usually offer to someone who resigns after good service.

170. Letter of Retirement

Of course, there are people who retire early, vest their pensions, and go into another career, but that is probably the exception. Most educators who retire do so after a fairly long career and, for many, one of distinguished service to the community. When the time comes for you to do so, and after you have checked all the legalities concerning pensions and the like, you'll be writing your letter requesting retirement. Note the difference from a letter of resignation.

Dear Superintendent Laughlin and the Board of Education,

Please be advised that it is my intention to retire from teaching at the end of this current _____–_____ school year, and I hereby tender my resignation for the purpose of retirement from the employ of the Middletown Township Board of Education effective with the expiration of my current contract, July 1, _____.

At retirement, I will have spent 37 years of my life teaching in Middletown Township. Certainly, not all of that time has been trouble-free, and there have been times that were "trying" to say the least. However, I can honestly add that the time I spent as an educator in Middletown Township has been amicable, productive, and, for the most part, gratifying.

I leave with a mind overflowing with magnificent memories; with a heart beating with positive feelings toward everyone; with no feelings of enmity or bitterness, and—perhaps most important—no regrets whatsoever.

My 37 years in Middletown have led to many changes. There have been physical changes, of course, but there have also been mental and spiritual changes as well. I have come to deeply appreciate the fine and outstanding work of my colleagues, to understand the significant impact a good administrator has upon a school, to realize the burden that a conscientious member of the school board must carry. I have seen it all and come to appreciate the grand array of dedicated individuals working with the youth of today and affecting the world of tomorrow. That is an image I shall carry with me as I walk through the school doors that final time.

Please convey to the board of education my gratitude for the many kindnesses Middletown has shown me over the years; tell them of my sense of privilege at being allowed to touch and be a part of so many young lives; and let them know my sense of honor at having been allowed to be a part of something truly significant. Also, convey the fact that the entire educational system of Middletown Township will remain in my thoughts and in my prayers.

With affection,

NOTE: Certainly, you could write something like, "I am retiring on . . ." and leave it at that. However, your letter of "resignation for the purpose of retirement" is a place in which you get to sum up, if you will, your feelings about the process after so many years.

Lest you think that such a letter would go unnoticed, let us share that the letter above (and we have changed names, places, and dates) was an actual letter of retirement that so impressed the members of the board that they demanded that it be read into the minutes at public session, and commissioned a special retirement plaque for the writer.

171. Letter on Retirement of Employee

When someone you know is going to retire, that is generally well known, since board matters are usually published in the local newspaper, or through a town newsletter or the like. Many times, you will be asked to join in as part of a retirement dinner as a speaker or master of ceremonies. All that is fine, but a personal letter written to the retiree often comes to mean as much as or more than all the public demonstrations of affection and appreciation. Here is one such letter.

Dear David,

I have been advised that you will be retiring at the end of the current school year. I must tell you that I greet that news with a strange mixture of happiness and regret.

I am happy that you will finally be getting that "well-earned rest" we so frequently talk about, and that you will finally have time to yourself to pursue those interests you have always wanted to develop but never had the time to do.

I am regretful only of the fact that you will no longer be here to grace the halls of this school, to be a vital and vibrant part of the faculty, to be someone to whom I could always come for a wise word or a shared laugh.

Therefore, please allow me to be among the first to wish you a happy and enjoyable and peaceful retirement. It is my sincerest hope that the years ahead will be a time of joy and accomplishment for you.

Over the years I have worked with you, it has been my honor and pleasure to get to know you both professionally and on a personal basis. On both accounts, I hold you in the highest esteem. Indeed, I consider you not only an outstanding human being, but the epitome of a professional educator.

I know that the faculty and students will miss you, as will I. You have left behind you a rich legacy of competence and affection, the memory of which shall stand us all in good stead in the years to come.

Again, my friend and colleague, best wishes on your retirement, and please remember to come back and visit us often. There will always be a time and place for you at this school.

Sincerely,

NOTE: You can tell a person all of this, and it will be done once and gone forever. Write it down, however, and put it in a letter like this, and it becomes a keepsake—something that the person will keep and cherish and perhaps take out to read again and again. That would be a fine gift to give to a fine educator who now walks the path of retirement.

WRITING EFFECTIVE LETTERS OF THANKS AND APPRECIATION

*D*id anyone ever do something really nice for you? Something that was unexpected? Something that shocked you with the kindness that was involved in the very act itself? You surely have had that experience at some time, as have we all, and it is truly one of life's grander moments.

We know and appreciate what it means to have a kindness done for us, and our hearts want to return the favor, or at least allow the giver to know what it meant to us, the receivers.

This is true in virtually all aspects of day-to-day life—and within the world of professional education as well.

EXAMINING THE ELEMENTS OF THANKFULNESS

If we look for opportunities to write letters of thanks and appreciation, we'll find that many are presented each day to the professional educator. Another educator takes over a schedule he or she didn't have to in order to save you some time; a colleague takes a class down to the assembly so you can make a phone call; someone from central administration backs you up in that problem you are having with that certain parent who is threatening to sue; an administrator recommends you for a position of trust and respect; you find that a community group wants to present you with a special award.

Yes, the occasions for being thankful—for showing appreciation—are many, and it is wise to take advantage of them. The most common way to do it is the letter of thanks or appreciation, which can be a most powerful reward.

Let us consider three elements of extending thanks in such situations:

1. **EVERYONE LIKES TO HAVE HIS OR HER GOOD DEEDS ACKNOWLEDGED.**
   Now, don't misunderstand—there are some really good people in this world who, when they do you a favor, do it from the goodness of their hearts, with no thought of reward. Even those people, however, enjoy being acknowledged by the person for whom they have acted. It is an acknowledgment that what they have done is right and has reached the right person.

185

2. **MEMORIES FADE; WRITTEN RECORDS DON'T.** Written responses to acts of kindness are often kept for a long time, and the writer is appreciated every time they are read. A verbal "thank you," no matter how impassioned, fades with time and memory. The written tribute keeps you ever on their minds.

3. **LETTERS OF THANKS ENCOURAGE FURTHER ACTS OF KINDNESS.** If I am appreciated for what I do, then I am encouraged and empowered to do it again. Put another way, kindness responds to kindness with kindness. That's not complicated—just a fact of life. A person you acknowledge as having done you a kindness is much more likely to repeat the process in the future than someone to whom you have not responded.

Of course, you don't want to overdo it. The loan of a dollar does not warrant the sending of a fifty-dollar bouquet to the person's home. That's ostentation, and it really does not evoke a good response. However, if the person went out of his or her way to deliver a special letter for you all the way across town, a thank-you note is quite reasonable.

There is also a difference between a thank-you letter sent to an individual and one sent to an agency, between one sent to a close friend and one to a mere acquaintance, between a formal note of appreciation and that which comes directly from your heart.

Let your words say what you honestly feel and try to put yourself in the recipient's place, and you will never go too far astray.

Oh, by the way, thanks so much for reading this book. We appreciate it—we *really do*.

MODEL LETTERS OF APPRECIATION AND THANKS

172. Appreciation for Offering a Prize or Award

No one would ever get a prize or award if someone had not thought it up and facilitated its development. He or she would welcome your appreciation.

Dear Mrs. Pashula,

I read with great interest your recent letter detailing the criteria for the award that you and your group are offering to a high school senior this year. I know that there are many deserving students at Craney High School who will be able to meet those criteria, and I am very happy to tell you that your committee will have a very difficult time trying to choose from among so many fine young people.

We at the school deeply appreciate people like you and, of course, the group you represent. In offering awards such as the one you describe, you help set standards for our youth and guidelines for those of us who educate. It has been truly said that if you aim at the stars you will surely rise above the mud!

Therefore, please allow me to thank you and your organization for considering and developing this fine award and tribute to our young people and citizens of tomorrow.

Very truly yours,

NOTE: Not only would a note such as this assure the cooperation of the offering group in the future, but they would certainly be inclined to work toward the good of your school and its students. Everyone likes to have his or her efforts acknowledged, including those who strive to acknowledge the efforts of others.

173. Appreciation for a Prize or Award Given to You

A time may come when you are the recipient of a particular award. Here is a letter of appreciation to the agency that issued and awarded you the honor.

Dear Mr. DeLuca,

As I write this, I am seated at my desk, on which the most beautiful and wonderful trophy in all the world is glowing and making the furthest corners of my office bright and alive with its warmth and grandeur. In case you can't tell, I like it!

What I like even more is the thought behind it, and the kindness of heart that would even have considered me for such an honor. To be considered was an honor; to have been awarded this trophy was beyond what I had dreamed.

I want you and your organization to know how deeply you have touched me, personally, through this gesture. It means a great deal to understand that there is someone who recognizes the work and cooperative effort that goes into a modern and functioning high school. I am gratified that you and your people are part of those who do see beyond the walls, and I was sincere in saying that I accepted the award in the name of the entire faculty and staff of this school.

I would also like you to know that this award will spur us on to even greater efforts on behalf of this community, our school, and—most important—our children.

Again, thanks to you and your group for caring. It is deeply appreciated.

Sincerely,

NOTE: Whatever you may think about humility, it is a good practice never to make light of the award, regardless of your actual feelings about it. Some people went to considerable trouble to present it to you, and it is their feelings you must consider as well as your own.

174. Appreciation for a Prize or Award Given to a Faculty Member

If you serve as an administrator, you represent the whole school, and when something happens to an individual member of that school, it happens to you as well. In this instance, we will take the scenario that a member of the faculty has just received an award.

Dear Ms. Vaneris,

As principal of the Greeley Elementary School, I am privileged to work with Miss Denise Panchette, a fifth-grade teacher here in this building for the past thirteen years, and an invaluable member of this faculty.

Recently, on behalf your organization, the Greeley Citizens Association, you presented Miss Panchette with an award, "Outstanding Citizen of the Year." I am writing to let you know just how much we appreciate the honor.

We have known Miss Panchette for many years, and there is not, I believe, a student, parent, faculty or staff member who has not been touched by her generosity, concern, and warmth of heart. I have had the pleasure of sitting in on classes given by this master teacher, and I can only envy the students who sit under her teaching.

In short, I wish to express my personal feelings, as well as those of the faculty and staff who have contacted me, that you have made a very worthwhile decision in presenting the award to Miss Panchette, and we are deeply appreciative of that fact.

If we may be of any service to you or your group in the future, please do not hesitate to call.

Most sincerely,

NOTE: A note such as this not only bolsters the presenting organization, but it also gives them direction in singling out your school in the future. In addition, it affirms the accuracy of their decision.

175. Appreciation for a Prize or Award Given to a Student

When an outstanding student gets an award, it reflects positively upon the school as well. It is a positive move to let the awarding agency know this.

Dear Mr. Denczak,

On behalf of the entire faculty, staff, administration, and student body of Jaggerstown High School, I wish to express to you our thanks and our deep appreciation for presenting the Newman Award for Academic Achievement to Kyle Shawn, a senior at our school.

Those of us who know Kyle understand how deeply she is committed to her own education, as well as to learning for tomorrow, when the world will benefit from the fine qualities of mind and spirit that she is even now developing.

That you would recognize these points in Kyle is to your credit, and that you would single her out for the award you present makes us deeply appreciative. We, who have dealt with her over the past several years, know that your decision could not be more perfectly suited to a recipient.

Again, on behalf of the entire school, you have our gratitude.

Most sincerely,

NOTE: If the award has impacted the entire school, as in this case with a student, it would be proper for you, as an administrator, to respond for the entire school—and make that clear in your letter.

176. Appreciation for a Prize or Award Given to a School Athletic Group

School is composed of many differing groups. Football is different from performing arts, which is different from fine arts, which is different from an English class. Letters of appreciation for awards given to each would be different as well. Let's look first at an award to the football team.

Dear Dr. Shasti,

I take this opportunity to contact you, to express the feelings of the entire school on your recent award to our football team, the River Bend Eagles.

Your organization, Committee on Sane Sports Medicine, is known for its attention to making all organized sports a safe place for youngsters to play and develop both physically and emotionally within the parameters of the sport. Your work within our area is appreciated, and I doubt that there is an administrator or parent within the community who has not taken your words to heart.

That is why we so appreciate the award to the River Bend Eagles as the "Safest Team of the Year." Indeed, we are very proud of our record of no serious injuries over the current season. Outside of the normal scrapes and bruises, there were no injuries requiring hospital time or recuperative therapy. We believe that is due, in large part, to putting into practice some of the methods you have described.

Please accept, therefore, our heartfelt appreciation for the award as well as our promise that we will try to sustain the title for as long as we are able.

Please continue in your very worthwhile endeavors and know that we do understand and appreciate your work.

Yours sincerely,

NOTE: Athletics are high-profile activities in any school. High school games are covered by local media as a matter of course. An award such as the one mentioned, as well as your response to it, could well be part of the next edition of the local newspaper.

177. Appreciation for a Prize or Award Given to a School Performing Group

A band, a chorus, a jazz ensemble, a drama group, and the like are constantly entering competitions—some of them statewide or even national. This letter is to the presenting committee from you as representative of the school from which the performing group came.

Dear Dr. Prechter,

Being a principal has its rewards. For instance, I often get to drop by the afternoon rehearsals of the Hillman Middle School Chorus and Glee Club. There, I am treated to magnificent music presented by enthusiastic young voices, and I am privileged to watch Mrs. Vonda Williams, the choral director, at work with her group. The music lifts spirit and takes me away for a moment from the rigors of everyday administration, and watching Mrs. Williams work fills me with pride that she is an educator in this school.

Recently, that group left for a day of excitement and competition at the state fairgrounds. They returned with the State Music Association's First Prize trophy. Needless to say, the next day was one of rejoicing throughout the entire school. Indeed, we arranged for an impromptu recital so we could become enthusiastic all over again.

It is so good to see hard effort and talent rewarded. There are not sufficient words to describe that feeling. To the chorus, it was the vindication of all that hard work, and to the rest of the school, myself included, it was a delirium we shared in most willingly.

Please accept our thanks and our deep appreciation for offering and presenting this wonderful award. You may be assured that it will have a featured spot in our school's showcase.

Yours sincerely,

NOTE: Now, that was an enthusiastic letter, and the awards committee, we feel, could not help but be impressed that they had made a very right decision. Next year, you will be the standard to beat.

178. Appreciation for a Prize or Award Given to the School

If you should be fortunate enough to have your school, itself, win an award or prize, there should be immediate follow-up. Along with all the media notification, don't forget to offer appreciation as suggested in this next letter. The community needs confidence in its schools, and this is one such opportunity to foster it.

Dear Professor Quentin,

How can we at Framali High School ever adequately show you our thanks and appreciation for what you have done? For a considerable time, we, like all secondary schools in this state, have been aware of the department of education at Kass College and the studies it has made of the educational strong points and needs of the various high schools in our state. Indeed, your annual reports are eagerly awaited by administrators throughout the area.

Therefore, when we received notice that Framali High School was to receive your award as this year's "State Outstanding Secondary School," we were overcome with joy. Such an honor is uplifting to say the very least, and there was not an individual in the school who was not affected by the announcement.

How deeply we appreciate your attention—and particularly, this encouragement. You have our assurance that this award will act as a beacon to light our way as we strive even more enthusiastically to provide the best for our students and our community.

Again, our thanks, our appreciation, and our personal assurance that you will never have to regret presenting this award to Framali High School.

With deep thanks,

NOTE: It would be a good idea to send a copy of that letter to the local newspaper as an "open letter" for the community to read. You would probably want the public relations officer of your school system to prepare an article on the award. And don't forget to mail the original to the presenting agency!

179. Appreciation for a Prize or Award for Academic Achievement

Here, we embrace the scenario of an award presented to your school for some form of academic excellence. That might be high school-wide achievement on standardized tests, a particularly good showing on the SAT's, or even an exemplary class average upon graduation.

Dear Senator Hamulczak,

How profoundly we appreciate your recent letter explaining that we at Rensler Middle School were to be honored by receiving your office's "Recognition of Academic Achievement." Your letter explained that the overall grade average of our eighth-grade class was the highest in the state, and the award is in recognition of "this outstanding achievement."

We thank you, and we do appreciate the generosity and striving for excellence that is part of the award's makeup. We want you to know that we shall cherish it, make it a very prominent part of the display that all visitors to our school see, and try our very best to live up to the high academic ideal it represents.

In accepting this honor, I do so for our school and in the name of the faculty, administration, and staff of Rensler Middle School. All have played a part in fostering the spirit of learning that is so integrally a part of our institution, and we humbly, and with great appreciation, accept this as one body.

Beyond that, we also accept it in the name of the students who worked so hard, and the parents who supported and labored with undaunted effort as their children learned and grew.

Thank you for *our* reward; it touches us deeply.

Yours sincerely,

NOTE: A reward for academic excellence is something that the community should know about. It would be a good idea to have this reply published as well. Something of this nature can only have positive ramifications within the area served.

180. Appreciation for a Personal Award

If you, personally, get an award, you must acknowledge that as well. Even for an award that takes you away from the school scene, it is always good to include in your acceptance that which is such an important part of your life.

Dear Mr. Larcuso,

I must say that I am overwhelmed by your letter informing me that I have been named to receive the Barden Chamber of Commerce "Citizen of the Year" award. Such a prestigious honor was beyond my consideration, and your letter truly knocked me off my feet.

First, I wish you to know how much I appreciate your letter and the award. Perhaps this is the reaction of those in the past who have been in this position, but I find it humbling to know that you in the community wish to recognize the work I am doing here in the schools, the community's greatest asset.

Next, you should understand that I do not take this award for myself alone. Rather, it very truly belongs to all the students who have listened, the faculty who have worked and taught and counseled, the staff who have maintained the school as a functioning entity, and my fellow administrators who have graciously shared their insights and reflections.

Finally, in the name of those just mentioned, I do accept your award with humility, with very deep appreciation that I would even be considered, and with the conviction that, working together, we can continue to achieve the academic excellence we want for every child of this community.

Someday, we would like to see them all become "Citizens of the Year." Now, that would truly be an award!

Very truly yours,

NOTE: Even though the award is to you, personally, this letter makes it clear that you had "help" in your achievements, and you are doing a little "recognizing" of your own.

181. Appreciation for a Specific Act of Generosity

Generosity need not refer only to money or a financial transaction. Many times, members of the faculty, staff, and general community can be generous with their time, their resources, and their talents as well. Here's a letter of appreciation for something like that.

Dear Mrs. Hastar,

It hardly seems enough to write and tell you how much we appreciate your generosity last Friday, May 17, _____. If there were an award for heroes connected to this school, I would most certainly be presenting one to you. Truly, for a class filled with expectant first graders, you saved the day.

The spring picnic for our first-grade classes had been planned for weeks. Everything was going fine, and even the weather seemed to be cooperating—until the Department of Public Works showed up on our back field with a work order to do some digging for old pipes, effectively canceling our picnic. The children were so disappointed, you could feel their energy draining on the spot.

Then, you were there—our neighbor—and you offered us your back lawn for the picnic. Of course, we gratefully accepted, and the children enjoyed their outing, as was attested to by their ready laughter. We all had a wonderful time, and didn't I see you playing tag with one of the groups?

I must tell you how very much we appreciate your act of generosity. The children, the teachers and parents who were present, and I wish to thank you for making a happy time for our first grade out of what might have been a disaster.

Again, thank you, and know that you are cherished in our hearts.

Most sincerely,

NOTE: Any act of generosity toward the school or its students should be acknowledged and widely publicized. All that was said above would come directly from your heart for this day-saving act on the part of a school neighbor. Let people know about it.

182. Appreciation for a Contribution to the School

As we inferred in the last entry, a "contribution" need not be an amount of money. Indeed, it can be anything from a piece of science equipment to making time in a busy schedule to come in to talk to a specific group about a job or profession. Whatever the contribution, it is your task to see to it that the deed is acknowledged and appreciated.

Dear Ms. Hyerwicz,

How deeply we appreciate your recent contribution to our school! We realize how valuable your time is and how tight and exact your schedule must be. As a performer of classical music, you are in various places both near and far, and that makes us doubly grateful that you found time to present a program to our lower elementary students.

Those children were positively enriched by what you played and the thoughtful manner in which you introduced them to the classics. Anyone with the least degree of perception could see how enthralled they were and how deeply it affected them all. I think that many of them will not fully comprehend the gift you have given them until the day when they realize that their appreciation for the great music of the world is so much fuller and deeper.

We thank you for your personal contribution to our school and to the future of these children, and we want you to know that around this place, you are profoundly appreciated.

Sincerely,

NOTE: Here, the contribution has been one of personal time and effort. Whatever it may be, let the person know that it is appreciated and what it will mean to the school or the students or their future, as was done in this letter.

183. Appreciation for an Individual Act of Kindness

In this letter of appreciation, we will use a poem, written for a previous book, that we think is appropriate here. See the note following the letter for further ideas.

Dear Ed,

I came across a poem some time back that struck a responsive chord in me. I saved it, not knowing why. I think I have the reason now. Let me share it with you.

> A single act of kindness,
> Like a stone thrown in a pond,
> Sends rings of ripples outward
> That travel far beyond;
> And joining other ripples
> Flow outward to the sea;
> A single act of kindness
> Affects eternity.

It was your kindness on that day when I truly needed someone to be kind that has affected my personal "eternity." Not to write in clichés, but if "a friend in need is a friend indeed," then you are, indeed, a friend, and someone I am privileged to know.

I greatly cherish your act of pure kindness in my behalf. I just want you to know how deeply you are appreciated.

Most sincerely,

NOTE: Notice that we have not specified the act of kindness, since this is but a suggestion and a sample. In your actual letter, however, it would be proper to do so. It doesn't have to be involved—perhaps something like ". . . for fixing my flat tire in the pouring rain. . . ." Make it clear what act of kindness you are appreciating.

184. Appreciation for an Individual Act of Helpfulness

There may be times when a faculty member, administrator, or staff member offers help, just when it is particularly needed. Anytime something like that happens, it is well to acknowledge the act and your appreciation of it.

Dear Mr. Janiak,

I have to write so many letters on so many subjects that some of them are bound to be negative. When, therefore, I have the opportunity to write to someone about something very positive, then my day is made all the happier for it. Thank you, for making my day!

Of course, I am referring to last Tuesday, November 23, _____. If you recall, that night there was to be a recital by our Jazz Ensemble. Somehow, the orders to set up chairs in the all-purpose room had gotten lost, and when Ms. Lanoka, the ensemble director, came in after school, not only were there no chairs, but it was late enough that there were no students to help.

She reports that as she, personally, was trying to set up the 150 chairs, you, our night custodian, happened by, assessed the situation, and personally offered your help, proceeding to set up all the chairs for the evening's performance. You did this in addition to your regular tasks as night custodian, even though it was not, officially, a part of your duties.

Well, on behalf of Ms. Lakota, the Jazz Ensemble, and the students and parents of this school, I wish to thank you for that act of helpfulness, and I want you to know that it is deeply appreciated by all concerned. I wish to add my personal appreciation as well.

A copy of this letter will be sent to the board of education for inclusion in your file.

Again, thank you. What you did is noted and appreciated.

Yours truly,

NOTE: For a school employee, you might want to consider sending a copy of a positive letter of appreciation to the board, for inclusion in the employee jacket or folder. It is a good gesture, usually well appreciated by the employee, and very appropriate for a positive letter like those in this section.

185. Appreciation for Outstanding Leadership

Leadership is vital at every level within any educational system. From the central administration in larger systems to the leadership of a teacher in a classroom or a student as captain of a team or squad, there are examples of leadership in action. It is a fine thing, therefore, to acknowledge that leadership—particularly if it has been exemplary.

Dear Mrs. Po,

For some four years now, you have served not only as a teacher in this school, but as director of the Phillipstown Players, our school's drama organization. Over that time, we have had the honor of observing our students present a rich variety of dramatic works to both the school and the community. These performances have been highly enjoyable and conveyed the highest degree of professionalism. No one has ever been disappointed in a production from our school.

I know, as do the faculty of this school, the parents of those involved, and the students who have participated, that the success of these endeavors has been due in an extremely large part to you and to your tireless and competent leadership. Through every problem, through every difficulty, through every triumph, you have been there; you have led them through rocky places. You have pointed the way through hard work, saying, "Follow me!"

Therefore, on behalf of the faculty, staff, administration, and students of this school, I wish to acknowledge your outstanding leadership in this area and express to you our unbounded appreciation for your many efforts to benefit the students of our school.

It has been a leadership effort from which we have all benefited.

Yours sincerely,

NOTE: Again, this type of letter could be placed in the director's personnel file, or it could just stand as it is, for it is certainly powerful enough in showing appreciation for the outstanding leadership of this individual teacher.

186. Appreciation for a Job Well Done

The following is a letter of appreciation to a student in the school who did a particularly good job at something. Word of such a letter gets around in the community, and it is very effective. With the necessary adaptations, this type of letter could be sent to anyone in the school.

Dear Marusca,

Here you are, just ending your junior year at Mt. Kane High School. It is my understanding that you have also reached the end of your tenure as editor of the *Mt. Kane Sentinel*, the official newspaper of our school.

Your year of service in that capacity has not gone unnoticed by the administration, faculty, or students of this school. Everyone has noticed and remarked upon the professionalism, hard work, and dedication that has obviously gone into each issue. Your editorials have been insightful, the layouts and features have held the interest of everyone, and the overall quality of the newspaper has been apparent to all—even to the winning of the state award for outstanding school journalism!

All of this indicates a job well done by a dedicated and talented individual. We at the school wish you to know that we thoroughly and deeply appreciate what you have accomplished. We are proud and happy that we may count you as a valuable part of this school.

Sincerely,

NOTE: As we indicated, this letter could be written to a teacher who has taken on a special project, a custodian who saved money for the school, a librarian who ran a special book display, or anyone who made some kind of special contribution. Just change the details.

187. Appreciation for an Outstanding Assembly Program

What would school be without its assembly programs? We are not going to expound on their worth or value, for you already know that. There can, indeed, be some really bad ones, but we have also been delighted by many outstanding programs. It is for one of these latter programs that this letter is written.

Dear Mrs. Jefferson,

What a delight! The assembly program given by you and your class recently was just outstanding. From the laughter and the genuine, heartfelt applause, you could tell how much the kids enjoyed it—and from the heads nodding in agreement, you could tell that the teachers and parents present understood that something good, something significant was going on.

There is an old adage that the best instruction is that which teaches as it pleases. I have always believed that to be true, and your assembly program was a prime example of just how effective that method can be. Certainly, the children will remember the songs, the skits, and the way in which they laughed and participated, but deep inside, they have also learned valuable lessons that every aspect of your program was geared to convey. It was teaching at its best.

Please accept my thanks and that of the entire school for your outstanding assembly program, and please understand how deeply we appreciate your many efforts in behalf of this school.

Very truly yours,

NOTE: We did not mention specifics of the program, but you certainly could if you wished to do so. Moreover, if the program included some outside source (a parent who did magic tricks, for example), you would want to write to this person as well.

188. Thanks for a Personal Gift

When we talk about personal gifts to you, we should advise you that you must be circumspect about taking such gifts. Obviously, if a colleague gives you a coffee mug with your name on it as a birthday present, that's all right, while a "gift" of a $500 savings bond from a supplier who has a franchise in your school might well be returned. Check with your school policy, of course, but here's a letter of thanks for a gift that is not suspect.

Dear Mr. Sawyer,

I have just received the name plaque for my desk that your woodworking class made for me as a birthday present.

I am overwhelmed by it. The workmanship is outstanding, and if I had seen this in a store, I would have been drawn to it for its fineness and richness. It is obvious that a great deal of time and talent went into the making of this item.

Please convey to your class my very deepest thanks for this fine gift. If they had done nothing on my birthday, that would have been all right, but someone let them know the day (was that you by chance?), and the result is this desk plaque which, I assure you, already has a featured place on my desk.

Thank you also, Mr. Sawyer, for your fine teaching of these skills, for your guidance, for your inspiration.

Again, I cherish your thoughtfulness. Thank you for the gift!

Sincerely,

NOTE: You might change the tone of this letter if the gift were from a colleague alone or a parent or a group, but the basic format would remain the same. Identify the gift, tell how much you like it, thank them for it. Be genuine.

189. Thanks for a Personal Gift to the School

People do give things to schools. The schools have received everything from money and land to portraits and sculpture. Here, an individual is thanked for a personal gift that has been presented to the school. It's a good model of a thank-you letter for such an occasion.

Dear Mrs. Weller,

How pleased and delighted we at Framehurst High School are with the thoughtful and wonderful gift you have just given to our school. It is not every school that is privileged to have the original deed for the land on which the school is built, especially when that deed is dated 1764!

Certainly, this is an historical document, worthy of a museum, and of great value. To think that you would present it to our school as a gift, for the edification of our present students and all those who will follow, fills us with thankfulness and appreciation for your selfless gesture.

Just as soon as we have the opportunity to have a proper presentation case made, we would like to hold an appropriate ceremony, and we would be most honored if you would attend in order that we may thank you properly. I'll let you know the details.

Until then, please accept the personal thanks of everyone connected with this school for your unique and timeless gift.

Most sincerely,

NOTE: Whether it is something of the stature just mentioned, or a few used books for the library, every gift to the school must be acknowledged. A gift such as the one described should also be acknowledged by the school board, and a separate letter might well be written by them.

190. Thanks for Visiting the School

The following letter was sent home to every parent following an "Open School Day," in which parents were invited to visit the school and attend classes as they chose. You may consider this a follow-up to that activity.

Dear Parents/Guardians/Relatives:

It was quite a day around here yesterday! You filled the halls and the all-purpose room and the classrooms . . . and it was wonderful!

I tell you, I was overjoyed to walk down the halls and look into each classroom and watch you enjoy the classes your children attend every day. I know that the students were excited because you were coming in, and their enthusiasm was catching. I think everyone in the school, from teachers to cafeteria workers, knew that this was a special day, and we were looking forward to our very special visitors.

We want to thank you for visiting. We do appreciate you and the children you have lent us for a little while, and we want you to know that we appreciate your kindness in dropping by and letting us show you what we are doing in the school.

Thanks again for coming. Please remember, you never need an invitation; you can drop by and visit anytime—you'll be most welcome.

With many thanks,

NOTE: Yes, this is a letter of thanks, but it is also a public relations vehicle. You might write such a letter to an individual who visited the school, but written to the entire group, it is highly effective in establishing proper school-community relations.

191. Thanks to a Colleague

Know what happens if a colleague keeps on doing nice things for you, and you never acknowledge the fact nor thank that colleague for his or her efforts? He or she will stop doing the nice things—that's what. This letter would go a long way toward avoiding such a situation.

Dear Ellen,

I want to thank you for pointing out my omission on the program for the awards assembly. I don't know what I must have been thinking, but if it had gone out the way I originally had it, I think I would have tasted the wrath of many.

You know, your sharpness and ability have helped me so many times that I think I have come to depend upon your friendship. That is hardly a bad thing, and I am both proud and happy to call you a colleague and a friend.

If I don't say it enough (and I am certain I don't), I thank my colleague for all the professional help and understanding she has sent my way; I thank my friend for being a friend—so many times.

How wonderful it is to work with you! Thanks again, for everything!

Very truly yours,

NOTE: If what you write in a letter of this type is from your heart, and you really mean it, then whatever you write will be wonderful. A letter such as this helps to establish a true working rapport that will make the jobs and tasks of both parties a great deal easier and more effective.

192. Thanks to an Administrative Superior

When you write a letter of thanks or appreciation to an administrative superior, you have to be careful that it does not sound like toadying. Your aim is to genuinely thank the administrator, not to personally ingratiate yourself with him or her. Here's an example you might want to consider.

Dear Dr. Danneman,

Recently, I needed a reference from someone who was in a position to know of my professional capabilities and the standard of my performance. I included your name, because I felt that you were in a position to know all that was required.

I have been contacted by the agency to whom you wrote your appraisal of my professional standing, and it is my understanding that your report was quite complimentary. As one person later told me, it was "glowing."

I wish to thank you for taking the time to compose, write, and send that report. I also wish to thank you for the obvious kindness and positive statements that it must have contained.

If I have performed well in our school system, it is truly because of people who encourage others, help them to grow in the position, and are always ready to help and instruct rather than demand and criticize. You, Madam, are one of those people.

Again, please accept my heartfelt thanks for all your efforts in my behalf.

Most sincerely,

NOTE: We think you will agree that this letter is far from ingratiating. It is matter-of-fact, straightforward, and genuine—highly appropriate for the situation described.

193. Thanks to a School Board Member

The same caution applies here as with the previous letter. It cannot appear to any reader that you are writing this letter to ingratiate yourself with the recipient, who, in this case, is a member of the board of education.

Dear Mr. Sinclaire,

It is my understanding that, at the last meeting of the Quillcasin Township Board of Education, you voted in favor of reworking the existing entrances and exits to Hill High School in order to better facilitate the entrance and leaving of student vehicles and school buses. Unfortunately, you were the only board member to so vote, and the motion was defeated.

Nonetheless, I want to personally thank you for acknowledging the need for such revamping now that the Main Street turnoff is in place. This is something that I have been advocating since the inception of the plan for the turnoff.

As principal of the school, I find it most disturbing that we shall have to wait until damage has been done to vehicles, or individuals have been injured, before the need for the restructuring becomes evident to all.

I thank you, therefore, for sharing the vision. It is only a matter of time, I feel, before the entire board will recognize what we have come to know.

Again, thank you for your vote, and if I may be of any assistance in the future, please do not hesitate to call upon me.

Most sincerely,

NOTE: Here, again, note the strength of the letter. It is evident that you are not trying to gain favor but are rather thanking someone who sees things the same way you do.

194. Thanks for a Positive Job Evaluation

Again, here is that caution. The letter has to be one of strength, without any appearance of an attempt to curry favor. The best technique is to be honest and merely state what you feel about the matter.

Dear Dr. Gasanali,

I have just received a copy of my professional evaluation for the _____– _____ school year. I will sign the appropriate copies and return them to your office at once. Why would I do otherwise with such a positive and absolutely encouraging report?

I could, of course, sign the evaluation and let it stand at that, but I really find that insufficient. What I want to do is to thank you for both your kind words and your understanding. In your report, I believe that you have captured the essence of what I have been trying to do at this school, and I am grateful for that.

I am honest in telling you that I would do the same job no matter who might be my superior, for I can do no less than the best I have to offer. It is gratifying, however, and extremely encouraging to know that my immediate supervisor is a person who shares the vision, understands the process, and can offer constructive guidelines that help build up rather than tear down.

Again, I thank you for that very positive evaluation—and for all the help you offer in so many positive ways.

Sincerely,

NOTE: A letter like this one does have an effect upon the recipient. He or she cannot help but be disposed to offer positive help to someone who believes in him or her. We tend to bend over backward for those who show gratitude for our help. This is operative in education as well as in the world in general.

195. Thanks for Supporting the School

Of course, the faculty and staff as well as the administration support the school, but what we are speaking of here is community support, when parents or a community group get together to support the school in a program or decision, or something the school has done that has met with opposition. Here's a sample letter of thanks for that support.

Dear Mr. and Mrs. Miller,

I wish to thank you and your group, Concerned Parents of Garfield Township, for the support you have shown our school during the recent difficulty. Please believe me when I tell you that everyone at the school is extremely grateful for all you have done to promote a sense of balance.

Certainly, it was a tragedy when one of our teachers drove onto school grounds one morning while under the influence of alcohol. It was even more tragic when he hit and very seriously injured one of the children. All of us were shocked and overwhelmed by this behavior, and we grieve for the child and pray for her recovery.

Your newsletter helped a great deal in allowing us to place this incident in proper perspective. The manner in which you contrasted the actions of one individual with the untold good that all other faculty members in the school provide for our children was indeed enlightening, and it helped many people to understand that this was the problem of one, not of the many.

Certainly, there will be investigations, and the offender is even now being held on high bail. We must make certain that this sad incident never happens again, but we must also remember that it was one person's fault, and the school continues to function and teachers continue to teach.

It is obvious that you understand this perfectly, and we thank you for your support of this school, which clearly belongs to the community it serves.

Most sincerely,

NOTE: One good base of support in the community can mean a great deal when such a tragedy happens. Even if it is nothing more than helping to get the budget passed, support for our schools should receive recognition and appropriate thanks.

196. Thanks for Personal Support

Here, we are going to look at personal support for you as an individual that might come from the community. If you have ever been the target of one person's or one group's animosity, you understand just how important this personal community support can be.

Dear Mrs. Lambering,

I want to thank you for your personal support during the school board debate of candidates, held last night, February 15, _____, at Meadowview Elementary.

When one of the candidates spoke out so vehemently about the need for a change of leadership at the high school level, he left little doubt as to whom he was referring. Of course, I felt that he had less than the truth, and that his rashness of judgment was due to his misunderstanding of the situation, but he seemed determined to "play that record," if you will, for all that it was worth.

That is why it was so gratifying to watch you rise to your feet and proceed to refute him on every one of the points he had erroneously made. I believe that the audience was greatly impressed by you and what you had to say.

Personally, I thank you for your support and your strength. It is good to know that someone in the community appreciates the truth and is willing to speak out for it.

Thank you for the edification and the support—and for being there.

Sincerely,

NOTE: One person on your side who is willing to speak out for you is a real treasure—particularly if that person is part of the community you serve. Whenever you receive support personally, it should be acknowledged.

197. Thanks for Friendship

Friendship is a wonderful thing. We once heard a person say that a school administrator should have no friends, but we cannot agree to that. Here's a letter written from one friend to another that says it all.

Dear Bob,

You know something, Bob? Over the years, I think I have had many occasions to thank you for all sorts of things. I have thanked you for lending me money, for giving me advice (even when I didn't want it), for taking over for me when I had to be elsewhere, for making me look good on more than one occasion, and a host of other things.

There remains one thing for which I have not thanked you properly, so please, let me do it now. Above all, thank you, Bob, for being my friend.

Each of us walks through life and meets up with obstacles and frustrations and brick walls that seem insurmountable; each of us knows the loneliness of trying to go it by ourselves; each of us understands the sting of criticism and the incredible burden of leadership and responsibility.

A few of us are blessed, even in these inevitable situations, with someone to whom we can turn, on whom we can lean, in whom we may trust. I count myself one of those few, Bob; I have someone who shares my concerns, and whose concerns I share. I have a friend.

So, I thank you, Bob, for all the kindnesses over all the years; I thank you for always being there when you were needed; I thank you for your frankness and honesty and genuine concern; I thank you—for being my friend.

With great affection,

NOTE: True friendship is a rare and beautiful thing, and happy are they who are blessed with it. May you be ranked in those numbers.

198. Thanks for Understanding

Sometimes, you must take an action that others may not understand. At those times, one person who understands what is going on and can communicate that to others is an invaluable aid. This letter is about such an individual.

Dear Liz,

There are times when it is difficult to go ahead and do what must be done, especially if those around you do not understand the reason for that action. Recently, I found myself in just such a situation.

The need to hold three fire drills in one day was never fully appreciated by many. They saw it—and rightly so—as a gross interruption of the school day, taking well over an hour out of the school day, out of their instructional time. What could not be told at that time was that, while the first one was planned, the other two were a matter of necessity, both responding to phone calls that indicated that a bomb had been placed in the school. Fortunately, both calls turned out to be hoaxes, but we certainly could not take the chance.

While others, on that day, were assailing the office with complaints, you were there and offered your help and assistance in whatever way you could. You perceived that there was something wrong; you understood that classes would never have been so disrupted had there not been a real cause; you offered your help rather than your criticism.

Thank you for that understanding. I do appreciate your insight and your offer of help at what you almost instinctively knew to be a difficult time.

Yours sincerely,

NOTE: If you find someone on your job who does, indeed, "understand rather than criticize," then you have found a very valuable ally, and certainly someone worthy of being acknowledged.

199. Thanks for Effective Handling of Situation

Many times, situations develop when you are not there to handle them. The situation, however, does not care that you are absent; it demands handling then and there. If someone steps forward and does that effectively, that is worthy of your acknowledgment.

Dear Marcia,

I picked a fine time to be out of the office, didn't I?

I understand that I had hardly left the parking lot yesterday afternoon, when the doors of the main office burst open, and a very irate parent entered, screaming as he came. I have been told that this gentleman pounded his fists on the counter, used considerable profanity, and was threatening everything short of World War III if he did not see me five minutes ago.

If I have described the situation lightly, I do not mean to, because such a display has the potential to become most serious in very little time. The scene was set for disaster.

That, I am told, is where you stepped in. It is my understanding that you calmed down the furious parent—taking him from blind rage to civility—sat him down, even got him a cup of coffee, explained my absence, and made an appointment for him when I would be available. When he left, I believe, he apologized to you for his actions and language.

Marcia, how do I say thank you for handling that situation so effectively, calmly, and well? I greatly appreciate the many, many efforts you make in contributing to the efficient running of this school. This is just one more instance of your competence, concern, ability to work under pressure, and genuine understanding of what needs to be done.

Thank you for so effectively handling that situation. I am grateful.

Yours sincerely,

NOTE: In a case like this, you might well want to have a copy of your letter placed in this secretary's personnel folder.

200. Thanks to Volunteer Workers

Face it, without volunteer workers, the school might still function, but a great deal would be missing that would be very difficult to replace. Volunteers may work for selfless reasons, to be sure, but everyone needs to be acknowledged, as this open letter does.

To All Volunteer Workers:

I want you to know just how much I appreciate the volunteer work you have been doing for our students and our school. Your contribution of time and energy have helped make our school a vital, harmonious, and happy place to be, and you must take a large share of the credit for this.

I have had many favorable remarks about you from faculty and students who appreciate your services, as do I.

Because you are volunteers, your pay is nonexistent and the work is hard. Your reward is the knowledge that you are doing a service for our students and our school, and you have our thanks for your invaluable help.

Please know that each and every one of you has our deepest gratitude for your services in our school.

Yours most sincerely,

NOTE: This letter could be sent out to each volunteer worker by mail, or it could be part of the program at a volunteer workers' dinner. However it is presented, honoring the efforts of those who volunteer is something you want to be sure to do.

201. Thanks to Staff Workers

Anyone who neglects the staff of a school, from cafeteria worker to teacher's aide to custodian, has neglected a vital part of the school—a part that keeps it functioning on a day-to-day basis. It is proper to acknowledge the efforts of your staff.

To the Staff of Greene Elementary:

How often it is that what we do tends to go unnoticed. We work hard, it seems, only to find our actions taken for granted or perhaps ignored altogether. Yes, that has happened to all of us at one time or another, and when it does, we all feel a bit sadder for the experience. That is why I, personally, want to make certain that it is a very rare occurrence at Greene Elementary.

I want you to know that your efforts are deeply appreciated. Whether you are a cafeteria worker or a custodian, a lunchroom attendant, a teacher's aide, or a classroom aide (which covers it all at this school), you should know that what you do is very valuable, and we recognize it as such. We applaud your skills and abilities, and we admire your warmth of heart and concern for the children that often causes you to go well beyond what might be expected of you.

Along with the faculty and students of this school, I want to extend my deepest gratitude for your many and valued services to Greene Elementary.

Most sincerely,

NOTE: If you take the time to look, you can find much to be thankful for in any school group. Speak with sincerity and honesty, and you will be on track.

202. Thanks to the Faculty

Let us tell you a truth you already know: A school that has a good, solid working relationship between faculty and administration is a school that functions like a well-tuned engine and provides an education that is second to none. Part of building that type of rapport lies in acknowledging the worth of the faculty.

Dear Faculty:

What would we do without you? The answer is, we would close down the school and turn it into a warehouse. In case you haven't noticed, you are the singular agency that keeps this school functioning, keeps our children learning, and marks this place as an outstanding site where education flourishes.

I recognize this because I have the daily opportunity to watch you in action as you teach and comfort and counsel, and act as judges and referees and parents and pals. The kids know it instinctively, for the heart of a child can sense love even before those feelings can be put into words. And I truly believe that the community knows it as well, since the time and effort you spend on the children cannot help but rub off on their parents.

Therefore, I offer to you the thanks of the community, the thanks and love of your students, and the deep and abiding gratitude I personally hold for each and every one of you.

I count myself as honored to be able to serve with you.

Sincerely,

NOTE: As we end this section, let us repeat that a letter of thanks or appreciation may take but a few moments to write or adapt from those we have presented, but it will return a lifetime of cooperation and good rapport that will lead to a finer working relationship for all concerned. It's worth your consideration.

WRITING SPECIAL LETTERS FOR EVERYDAY EVENTS

$\mathcal{A}$ Bible verse states, in part, that it is "the little foxes that spoil the vine . . ." (*Song of Solomon* 2:15). That statement is as true today—and certainly in the field of professional education—as it was in King Solomon's time. Each school year will bring with it problems that must be dealt with, but what really stresses us—what really brings that bone-tiredness, what really causes us to rub away the stiffness at the back of our necks—is not the major problems as much as the weariness of having to handle the day-to-day problems. Those day-to-day, tiny but persistent, problems of our positions are the "little foxes."

WRITING WITH A "SPECIAL" MINDSET

Apologizing for a missed appointment or for a minor misunderstanding, reporting on an incident between students in the cafeteria, documenting a telephone conversation with an angry parent, writing to invite parents to a special event—all this, and more, is part of the daily life of the modern school, and we are expected to handle it. Sometimes, this type of writing tends to become mundane; it may handle the situation, but often represents little more than a form letter to those who will receive it. The answer to that— the way to keep this "everyday" writing fresh and representative of a vital school—is to take on a "special" mindset when you write such letters.

Simply put, make up your mind to treat every communication you write as if it were the first time you wrote it, even if it is the 1001st letter of that type you have written—this week! The key to being able to do that can be summed up in one word—*empathy*. Empathy, putting yourself in the place of the person who will be receiving that letter or invitation or notice or report, will keep your letters interesting and personal. When you write with the recipient in mind, you cannot help but write *for* that individual. You begin asking questions such as, "How would I like to be told this news?" or "What would make me want to come to a night at school?" or "How would I know that this person is truly sorry for that mistake?" If you answer those questions in your writing, then putting yourself in the place of the person to whom you are writing will have paid off in a letter that is personal—even if it is written to 500+ parents—and it will be appreciated by the reader.

In this final section of the book, you'll find a wide variety of what we call the day-to-day writing attendant to the modern school. From confirmation of a telephone call to a request for schoolwide parental support, these letters and writings attempt to handle the everyday in that special mindset. As you read them, your task should be to put yourself in the place of the person who will receive the particular letter. If you do this, you will know if anything needs to be added, deleted, or addressed in another way. That is the real secret of successfully using a book like this to help you handle the "little foxes" that attack the everyday vines.

MODEL LETTERS THAT DEAL WITH THE DAY-TO-DAY

203. Letter Confirming a Special Telephone Contact

You may receive a telephone call that requires a letter of confirmation, and perhaps of the understanding expressed during the conversation. Here is an example.

Dear Mr. Bayliss,

Please allow this letter to confirm our telephone conversation that took place on this date at approximately 1:35 P.M., and lasted until 1:54 P.M.

You contacted me regarding the suspension from school of your son David, an eighth-grade student in this school. You wished further clarification of the actions on David's part that led to suspension. We talked of these as well as a proper course of action to be taken upon David's return to school. Toward that end, you requested a meeting, and one was set up for Friday, October 23, _____, at 1:00 P.M. in my office. Present at that meeting will be you; Mr. Cairns, our eighth-grade guidance counselor; Mrs. Jacobs, our vice-principal; and your son David.

After the meeting had been arranged, we spoke briefly of the hopes of all concerned for David's future.

If my schedule allows, I will try to sit in on at least part of that meeting. Thank you for calling.

Yours sincerely,

NOTE: This letter is very concise and businesslike. A telephone confirmation is not the time to start expressing philosophy. Stick to the facts; never go beyond what was actually said.

204. Letter Confirming Angry Telephone Contact

All that was said above about being businesslike and sticking to facts applies doubly to the "angry" telephone contact. Here, the caller is extremely upset, so the confirmation must be almost emotionless.

Dear Mrs. Olinger,

This letter is to confirm our telephone conversation of February 16, _____. You called me, and the call was given to me at approximately 10:45 A.M.

The call centered on the fact that your daughter Elda has been suspended for three days, and may not return to school until February 19, _____. You claimed that I was being unfair in suspending Elda. Your voice was loud enough that a visitor in my office at the time could hear you, even though the phone was to my ear. When I told you that I felt the suspension was valid and would not retract it, I felt that your use of personal invective against me was unnecessary and excessive.

My suggesting a meeting in order to help Elda upon her return to school led to your abrupt termination of the conversation at 10:51 A.M. Surely we can talk reasonably, keeping Elda's well-being in mind? If you agree, please call me to set up a mutually convenient time.

Yours sincerely,

NOTE: Avoid answering the angry caller in kind; just state the facts of the call in a low-key manner. This allows the conversation to speak for itself. Sent to the caller, it could bring about some positive change, and kept in your records, it is good evidence of the incident should something unpleasant happen later.

205. Quick Written Confirmation of Telephone Contact

The previous conversations required letters of confirmation, but many times, all you want to do is keep a record of who called when, and about what. While, strictly speaking, the following is not a letter, it would supply such a confirming record.

CONFIRMATION OF TELEPHONE CONTACT

PERSON RECEIVING CALL: _____

PERSON CALLING: _____

DATE: _____   DAY OF WEEK: _____

TIME OF CALL: Incoming at _____ A.M.   P.M.

Ended at _____ A.M.   P.M.

Total Length of Call _____ Minutes

CONTENT OF CALL: _____

_____

_____

_____

COMMENT:

Signature: _____

NOTE: It is remarkable what people remember and don't remember about telephone conversations the further away they get from the original call. Something like this, which takes but a moment to fill out, can jog memories and end arguments on the spot. It's certainly worth considering.

206. Letter Explaining Misunderstood Telephone Contact

Misunderstandings happen; that's a fact of life. This letter attempts to correct a misunderstanding that may have occurred during a telephone conversation.

Dear Ms. Palani,

I really must apologize for a misunderstanding during a recent telephone conversation which, I fear, has caused you some inconvenience. Please be assured that I never intended anything like that to happen.

During our phone conversation, you asked me if I could come over to the central administration building to finish up some important papers there. You said, "I wish you could come over today around one o'clock." I agreed, and I understand that you spent considerable time and effort getting those papers out and prepared for me. When I never showed up, nor even gave you the courtesy of a call, I imagine you were understandably upset; I know I would be in a similar situation.

That's where the misunderstanding comes in. You said "…come over today" and I honestly and truly heard "…come over Tuesday." Since it was Friday when we spoke, I thought that a reasonable time frame. It was only when my secretary received a call from a friend of hers at central that I knew something was wrong.

I am truly sorry for my misunderstanding and for any inconvenience that it has caused you. Please forgive me.

I promise to listen particularly closely in the future!

Truly yours,

NOTE: Of course, you could just call the person back, as you probably would to confirm a new date, but there's something about a letter that makes the apology seem much more sincere. You took the time to write it—and that is always appreciated.

207. Apology for a Missed Appointment, I

Never feel that you cannot admit a mistake. Often, a sincere apology for an oversight or something forgotten can mean a great deal to the recipient and help to cement a relationship. Let's begin with two ways to go if you have missed an appointment.

Dear Mr. Goodheart,

If this were a perfect world, buses and trains would run on time, all people from all backgrounds and heritages would live together in peace, you and I would each have a few million in the bank, and I would not have missed the appointment I had with you at 2:15 P.M. today. Needless to say, this world is not perfect, and neither am I.

I sincerely regret any inconvenience I may have caused you by not showing up for our meeting. While I called as soon as it became evident that I was not going to make it, I am afraid that was insufficient notice for you and your busy schedule, and I am truly sorry that such an incident had to occur.

Therefore, I most humbly ask you to forgive me, and I also beg to have another appointment with you at your convenience. What we have to talk about is important, and I would not want my "untimely" behavior to spoil that.

Thank you for understanding; I really do look forward to meeting with you very soon.

Most sincerely,

NOTE: Again, things like missed appointments do happen, and a thoughtful letter such as this can assure that there is no enmity between you when you meet the next time.

208. Apology for a Missed Appointment, II

Here is another letter of apology for a missed appointment from a slightly different viewpoint. Previously, you were supposed to be somewhere and didn't make it. Here, the person has arrived to see you, but you weren't there.

Dear Mrs. Uland,

I understand that you were precisely on time for our appointment last Friday, and I thank you for your promptness. I, on the other had, was *not* on time. Not only was I late, so that I completely missed our scheduled meeting, but I fear that I greatly inconvenienced you and upset you with my tardiness.

I know, Mrs. Uland, that you are a very busy person, and I deeply respect your work on the school's behalf as well as your efforts to enrich the lives of all our students. I assure you, I feel most personally upset that I missed the chance to talk to you. Of course, I had a reason for being late, but your inconvenience is the same, whatever the reason.

Therefore, I am asking you for two gigantic favors that will certainly enrich my life. First, I would beg you to forgive me for missing you, and then I would ask you to please consider meeting with me just as soon as possible, for I am very, very interested in what you have to say.

I am so sorry. Please, may I hear from you soon?

Very truly yours,

NOTE: A sense of genuine regret for an action can be felt through a letter. If you are genuine in apologizing, the reader will know it and act accordingly. Be sincere, and you'll get sincerity in return.

209. Apology for a Minor Misunderstanding

You will probably have a goodly number of misunderstandings in the course of a career in public education. Most of them need not bother you, however, if they are handled quickly and sincerely. Here is one way of handling a minor misunderstanding.

Dear Cassie,

Yes, I am very human, and I do make mistakes, as our meeting of Friday last will testify. We spoke of the possibility of your acting as chaperone for the senior trip. I stated that your suggestion was impossible, and dismissed the matter as I hurried on to make an appointment I had.

I am afraid that I may have spoken hastily or been the victim of a misunderstanding. I was informed later that you were referring to next year's senior trip and your desire to apply for the position. I thought you meant the trip that is to leave in four days, and, of course, their list of chaperones is complete and cannot be altered now. I am sorry that my upcoming appointment occupied my mind so much that I neglected to find out precisely what you meant, instead of speaking out precipitously and incorrectly.

Of course you may apply, and if you'll accept my apology, I will gladly help you fill out the forms. Please see my secretary as soon as you wish.

Again, please forgive me, and let's see what we can do about your request.

Sincerely,

NOTE: If handled at the time it happens, a minor misunderstanding need cause no difficulty. It is only when a misunderstanding is long-standing and unattended to that the real problems arise.

210. Apology for a Substantial Misunderstanding

The previous misunderstanding really upset only one person, and that in a minor way. What happens, however, if the misunderstanding affects many people—possibly an entire class? Then the problem is substantial, and it really needs special handling.

Dear Mr. Wendell,

You have every right not to believe this, but I am as upset as you are about the misunderstanding that led to this morning's incident. I sincerely wish that we could reverse time that it might not happen at all, but we both know that we must deal with the situation as it exists now.

About two weeks ago, you came to me with the request that the members of our middle school drama group be allowed to attend the dress rehearsal of the high school's spring musical production of *The Music Man*. Since you already had the invitation from the high school, all that was required was coverage for you and Mrs. Kelley, permission slips for the thirty students involved, and a school bus to transport them to the high school. As I recall, I thought this was a good idea and conveyed as much to you.

Here's where it falls apart: I thought you were arranging for the substitute and the bus, and you thought that I was. As a result of this substantial misunderstanding, neither coverage for you and Mrs. Kelley nor a school bus for transportation was forthcoming. By the time calls were made and what had happened was apparent, I had to cancel the trip, thereby upsetting you, the students, a number of parents, and the high school drama coach.

I cannot undo what has been done. I cannot reverse time and allow your group to see the dress rehearsal; that is gone. What I can do is apologize—profusely. Whatever may or may not have been said or understood, I take the responsibility for it. I can promise you that I have learned from this incident, and that such a misunderstanding will not happen again.

I apologize; I ask your forgiveness; I ask your help and cooperation in order that something of this nature does not happen again. I thank you for your understanding. Please see me at your convenience, and let's talk about it.

Yours sincerely,

NOTE: Sometimes all you can do is apologize, but that is the time to really be a leader and reach out to those you may have offended, albeit unwittingly. That alone can go a long way toward smooth running in the future.

211. Apology for a Personal Mistake or Error

We all make mistakes, and everyone knows it. Upset occurs when people make mistakes and then refuse to admit them—or simply ignore the error. Here's a simple apology for a personal mistake that would help settle any difficulty.

Dear Mrs. Dallas,

Making a mistake is nothing new to me, and it doesn't upset me to learn that I have made an error, except when it has caused inconvenience to another. That, I fear, is what happened with you last Thursday. You went out of your way to see me in order to get that board of education grant application, which I promised, swore, attested, and otherwise indicated that I would get to you by the end of the day.

I didn't. Then came Friday, and I didn't—again. The fact was, I forgot. I wrote your request on that little yellow slip of paper and promptly forgot it. It was not until this morning that the paper crept out from the corner of my desk blotter to shake its finger at me for my error.

So, here is the application I promised you, along with this letter and my deepest personal apologies for any inconvenience I may have caused you.

If you need any help with the application, I am available, and I promise—I won't forget!

Yours,

NOTE: The tone of this letter is light, as between friends or at least associates who get along well. If that is the case, you can use the lightness. If it is someone whom you do not know well, it would be preferable to be more formal.

212. Apology for a School Mistake or Error

In any organization as large as a modern school, it is inevitable that errors involving the working of the "machinery" that keeps the school functioning will occur. Here's an apology for one such error.

Dear Mr. and Mrs. Zenites,

Please allow me to apologize for an error on our part that has surely inconvenienced you.

You wrote to our school on the tenth of this month, requesting that a transcript of grades be sent to Patton Military Academy, where your son Kenneth, currently a student in our school, intends to transfer with the beginning of the new marking period. We receive such requests frequently, and usually, they are handled forthwith.

The error occurred when your name was entered incorrectly as Zenotes. The computer, which cannot reason, indicated that there was no such student in our school. Eventually, the error was found and corrected, albeit after a number of phone calls from you.

The transcript has been sent to Patton Military Academy, and they received a personal phone call from me, explaining the lateness of the records. I have the personal assurance of the registrar that they fully understand, and the records will be considered as having arrived on time. All other factors being equal, Kenneth should be headed to Patton in a few weeks.

Again, let me state that we sincerely regret any inconvenience you may have suffered through this error, and you have our apologies.

We sincerely wish Kenneth the very best, as well as continued success at Patton.

Sincerely yours,

NOTE: Before you acknowledge an error on the part of the school, it might be wise to check with the board or the board's attorney. If there are other implications, such as the threat of a lawsuit from the parents or aggrieved party, you want to be very careful—or not write the letter at all—as legal counsel dictates.

213. Apology for Inconveniencing a Person or Group

People are inconvenienced all the time, and most learn to live with it. If you are the one who has caused the inconvenience, a short letter of apology can really help.

Dear Mrs. Leonard,

On behalf of the entire faculty and staff of Ryder Middle School, may I say how much we enjoyed the visit of your Senior Citizens School Committee. We were very proud and happy to show you our school and have you visit our classrooms. The children and teachers have commented very positively about your genuine affability and interest in what was going on. I thank you for your kindness.

I am so sorry that you had to wait for twenty minutes in the school library before we could begin our tour. Because, through no fault of yours, your bus was late in arriving, there had been a shift in classes and the cafeteria was about to let out. Consequently, we had little choice but to wait until the halls quieted down before we began the tour. I certainly hope that the short wait did not inconvenience you too greatly, and I apologize sincerely if it did, but I am certain you can understand the situation.

Again, I am sorry for the inconvenience, but I thank you for your interest in our school, and I thank you for your visit, which was such an obvious success for both you and our students and staff.

Please, come back again!

Yours sincerely,

NOTE: You can see that this apology is sandwiched in a letter of thanks. The "inconvenience" was not horrendous, and it is kept in perspective here. In short, apologize, but don't overdo it.

214. Apology for an Oversight

An oversight is never intentional; it is just what the word implies, an honest mistake, in which you have neglected to do something that should have been done but was not. Often, there is no reason for the oversight, as may be seen in this example.

Dear Dr. Won,

By now, you are undoubtedly aware that our school is holding a special "Awareness Night" to which all the members of the school board have been most cordially invited—all, that is, except you!

Less than half an hour ago, when I was looking over the list of people whom we had invited to this annual affair at our school, I was struck by the strangest feeling that I had left something out. It came as a massive shock that I had neglected to invite the board's president—namely, you.

I sincerely hope that you will accept my apology for this egregious oversight. You are well aware, I know, of the esteem in which I hold you, as well as the fine working relationship I believe we have established. I truly have no explanation other than, perhaps, the approach of senility—and I'm not sure even that is an excuse!

Therefore, please accept my apology, along with the enclosed invitation, even if it is being delivered rather later than usual.

As ever,

NOTE: If there truly was no reason for the oversight, say so. Many times, a straightforward approach such as this is very effective in maintaining the status quo of a friendship.

215. Apology for Damage Caused by Students

This is a difficult and delicate letter to write. At times, students from your school can cause damage to personal property adjacent to the school grounds, or become rambunctious on a school trip. While it doesn't happen often, it has been known to occur. Be sure to check this letter with the board attorney first.

Dear Mr. Emani,

I wish to apologize to you, personally, for any inconvenience or distress that you may have endured due to the actions of a few members of our seventh-grade class. I find their actions completely unacceptable, and I want you to know that they will be dealt with most firmly.

On November 18, _____, the seventh-grade class was taken to the Market Grand Theater, next to your store, to view a presentation of a play geared to that age level. While 210 students watched and enjoyed the presentation and presented no problem whatsoever, three students managed to leave without being seen and went to your store where, I understand, they called shoppers names and knocked over several displays before running from the store. They were subsequently stopped by theater ushers and identified by you, and their teacher/chaperone was notified. Upon their return to school, I was told of the situation.

First, I deeply apologize that the incident happened at all. This is not what we expect of our students, and, indeed, these were not the actions of the truly vast majority of those who attended. The three in question were immediately suspended from school, and the school board has been apprised of their actions. It is my further belief that you have expressed an interest in pursuing legal action against these students and their parents, and that is, of course, within your rights to do.

I just wish you to know that all of us at the school regret that this ever happened at all, and we offer you our profound apologies.

Yours sincerely,

NOTE: Because of the legalities involved, you will notice that there was no mention of culpability on the part of the school. This is where the expertise of the board's attorney is needed.

216. Apology for Something Long Overdue

We can all fall into situations where we know that something needs to be done, but, because of time and circumstances, it keeps getting postponed. Eventually, it becomes long overdue, and when that is finally realized, we regret that it was not discovered much sooner. Here's an example of what we mean.

Dear Commander Jackson,

I know that you have been formally notified by the board of education that a statue and plaque commemorating the youth of our township who gave their lives fighting in the Viet Nam conflict will be formally dedicated and erected on the lawn area in front of the board of education building.

All of the names on that plaque are the names of young people who walked the halls of our high school, sat in its classrooms, and made plans for their futures after graduation. All of them, however, were called elsewhere, and they gave their lives in a struggle in a distant land.

Should they have been honored for their sacrifices at the time? Undoubtedly they should have been, but a different climate prevailed—one that many may contend was right or wrong, but none can deny. The result was a lack of recognition of our youth who gave so much at their country's call.

Yes, this recognition is long overdue, and as part of the school system that is finally recognizing their worth and dignity, I can only apologize to their parents, teachers, and friends, and to veterans like those in your organization, for the length of the oversight and our personal lack of vision.

I shall look forward to sharing the platform with you at the dedication and finally granting the honor that their short but important lives deserve.

Sincerely,

NOTE: We try the best we can to acknowledge the efforts of all who give of themselves, especially those whose sacrifice is so full and final. Here, one might say that the apology is for something on a national rather than a personal level. Nonetheless, the recipient of this letter would surely appreciate the sentiment.

217. Apology for a Perceived Wrong

It has been said that reality doesn't matter half as much as the way in which we perceive that reality. As it is applied here, we all must realize that we need not have done anything wrong, but if someone thinks we have, that individual is just as upset as if something had actually happened.

Dear Mrs. Liam,

I'm not certain that there is anything between us that needs to be addressed, but I have become aware of something that may result in a misunderstanding, and I sincerely wish to avoid that at all costs.

Last Thursday, you came in for a conference with Mrs. Landry, our head guidance counselor, concerning your son Sean. I remember that I was just leaving the guidance office as you were entering, and I greeted you there. We exchanged a few words and went our ways.

It was not until later, when I spoke to Mrs. Landry about an entirely different matter, that she asked where I had been during your conference. She told me, "Mrs. Liam said she expected you to join us." She further told me that she thought you were a bit upset when I did not show up.

If that is the case, then allow me to apologize immediately. I was under the impression that this was to be a conference concerning only you and Sean and Mrs. Landry. I have checked my log book for that day, and I had no notation that I was expected to be there. Most certainly, I would have come had I known you wanted me there. I am so sorry you were upset, and I do apologize for any inconvenience or misunderstanding.

All I can do is apologize. If you would like to make another appointment, I will make it a point to be there with you. If I can do anything further, please let me know.

Sincerely,

NOTE: The lesson to be learned here is that it is sometimes necessary to apologize for things you did not do. Here, although the misunderstanding was all on "Mrs. Liam's" part, it is not worth having her upset for what she perceives as a slight. One might well consider that if a letter of this sort doesn't help, it certainly can't hurt.

218. Returning a Gift or Award, I

Gifts or awards to you, personally, fall into the area of applied wisdom. If the student head of the drama club gives you a candy cane at Christmas, wisdom dictates that you accept it with thanks. What, however, if a supplier of school materials gives you that same candy cane wrapped in hundred-dollar bills?

Dear Jennifer,

Yesterday, as school was being dismissed, you handed me an envelope, and then you were on your way before I could say anything. Later, when I opened it, I found a very special Christmas card signed by you, along with a special thought that you had written. Also enclosed in that card was a ten-dollar bill.

Jennifer, I know your heart was in that gift, but the school rules (and I have to follow those rules just as much as you) say that I cannot take a gift of money from students. That is why I am returning the ten dollars.

You will notice, however, that I am *not* returning the card or what you wrote. That is a wonderful gift, and I thank you so much for it. I tell you, that card is going on the wall of my office, and I know I will look at it many times during the school day, and I'll think of you and your kindness.

So, please accept the ten dollars that I am returning, and please know how much your card and the kind words you wrote mean to me.

Yours truly,

NOTE: Never should a child who gives you a gift be made to feel that the gift "wasn't good enough." Although the cash was returned—and that is an excellent policy, by the way—the card was accepted, and the child was made to feel special and loved, and that's an even better policy!

219. Returning a Gift or Award, II

Now let's look at something a bit more serious than a student's gift. The times and situations being what they are, you can never tell what organization is likely to upset your school day. Here's an example that could be on your desk tomorrow morning.

Dear Mr. Jones,

I am in receipt of your letter of November 4, _____, which contained a small plaque, along with a statement informing me that I am the recipient of the "Patrick Henry Patriot Award" presented by your organization, The Sons of Freedom. You explain that I deserve this award because I have had "the courage to suspend and expel" members of a particular racial group, to whom you referred with a racial epithet.

Mr. Jones, please convey to your organization that we suspend those students who have done something that merits suspension. Their behavior is the only criterion for disciplinary action. Misbehavior to the point where it affects the running of this school warrants suspension—*regardless of a student's race.*

I cannot—nor do I wish to—accept the plaque and your letter of "commendation," and am returning them with this letter. Please do not consider me in the future.

Sincerely,

NOTE: You may find yourself confronted with such a situation, and you want to leave no doubt as to your position. Before you send the whole thing back, however, make a copy of everything; include a photo of the award and a copy of your return letter, and hand it over to the proper authority within central administration. If it becomes an issue later, you will have confirmation of your actions.

220. Returning Signed Report Cards

The following is actually a form letter intended to be sent out to all the parents and guardians of the students in the school. It is a reminder about something that has caused frustration and headaches for as long as anyone involved in education can remember—failure to return signed report cards.

Dear Parents or Guardians,

At a recent PTA meeting, I asked the assembly, "How many of you can we call on to help us help your children?" Understandably, almost every hand went up. I choose to believe that you meant that, and that is why I am calling upon you for help at this time.

On Friday, November 14, _____, report cards for the first marking period will be distributed to all students during the last period of the day. That means, without exception, that your son or daughter *will* have his or her report card for you to see on Friday evening.

Now, here comes the way in which you can help. Those same report cards *must* have the "SCHOOL COPY" sheet detached, signed by you, and returned to school at least by Wednesday, November 19, _____.

That seems like a small thing to ask, doesn't it? Please see to it—impress upon your child the importance of returning it right away—and keep after it until you are certain it has been returned. You will save this school hundreds of hours of phoning and writing home and otherwise following up that pulls us away from our greatest charge—that of educating your children.

I know that we can look forward to your speedy support in this matter.

Yours sincerely,

NOTE: Of course, you know that many of these form letters never reach home, but even so, enough do to make notices like these a valuable part of the procedure.

221. Returning Faulty School Equipment

Generally, the equipment that comes into our schools is of good quality and designed for rough treatment over a prolonged period of time. Occasionally, however, one finds an item that must be returned. Here's a letter to accompany one such article.

Dear Mr. Possar,

Under separate cover, I am returning to your company two pieces of gym equipment that our school purchased from you this past spring and that were delivered to our school in mid-August, Invoice # 177A23W.

The items purchased, two "exercise horses," used in gymnastics and in general physical education activities, were pronounced unfit for these activities by our PE teachers who tried them and found them unsteady. A closer examination found that the threads on every single bolt had been almost entirely worn away. The result was that they refused to tighten sufficiently, and the danger of their falling apart while a student was using the equipment was substantial.

I am certain you will wish to replace these exercise horses with ones that can be used for the purpose for which they were purchased. Please contact me at your earliest convenience and let me know the disposition of this matter.

Yours sincerely,

NOTE: Equipment the school cannot use becomes a liability to the school, which is why you want any problem of this sort handled quickly. Note that the problem was specifically delineated and the solution sought was made equally clear.

222. Returning a Lost or Stolen Article, I

Around any school, anywhere, there are items, both personal and school items, that are either stolen or lost. Occasionally, such an item may be found, sometimes months or years after the initial incident. This letter accompanies the return of one such item.

Dear Mr. Pocant,

I recall, several months ago, when you came to me with deep concern about a Mont Blanc gold-filled fountain pen that had been given to you as a holiday present by your children. Certainly, you cherished it as their gift, and the pen, as we all know, has intrinsic value as well. At that time, although I sympathized with you, we could not determine whether it had been stolen or merely misplaced. If you will recall, even some discreet inquiries produced nothing.

As you have probably noticed by now, enclosed is one Mont Blanc gold-filled fountain pen, slightly dusty, but still, I believe, in working order.

After you left us, we did some work in your classroom that necessitated the ripping up of some floorboards near the heating unit. Need I say more? There it was, just out of sight by the space between pipe and floorboard.

Was it put there? Did it fall there? I don't know, but I do know that you have your pen back, and I am so glad it has been found.

Sincerely,

NOTE: Here's a happy ending, and an opportunity to rejoice with the individual who got back his treasured pen.

223. Returning a Lost or Stolen Article, II

When something is stolen in school, and you have found the offender and recovered that which was taken, you may be faced with some legalities. You may not simply be able to say, "Margie took it." In this case, as you will see, you must choose your words carefully, and it wouldn't be a bad idea to have the letter checked by the board attorney as well.

Dear Mrs. Blasczyk,

By now, you will have received, via certified mail, the gold locket belonging to your daughter, Jenna. I trust it is in good shape and I join you in your happiness at having it returned, particularly since it had such sentimental attachment. I am very pleased that Jenna has it back.

When Jenna told her teacher that it had been stolen during gym class by "an older girl" whom Jenna was able to describe, we started our own investigation, the result of which is the fact that you have the locket back in your possession.

As for the other student, I can assure you that she is being punished for her actions; this school does not allow theft or other breaking of the law, whatever the age of the perpetrator. I cannot give you further information, but should you wish to pursue this matter further, please contact the board of education. The student who stole the locket is identified and punished, and the keepsake is back in your possession. On both counts, we have reason to be happy.

If I may be of any further service, please do not hesitate to call.

Most sincerely yours,

NOTE: You may well be constrained from providing the name of the thief, even to the victim's parents. Check with your school board; it is well worth the time and effort now to avoid trouble later.

224. Reporting on Student Accident or Injury, I

Kids, school, accidents—they go together. You're not likely to make it through a school year without your share of accidents and injuries to students. Indeed, the school nurse will be kept busy. This first letter is a statement about an accident, and it is understood that it might well be used for legal purposes further down the line.

Dear Mr. and Mrs. Wilcox,

I regret to inform you that, while it was neither serious nor incapacitating, your daughter Jean Marie was accidentally injured in school this morning.

Between first and second periods this morning, Jean Marie was headed for her second-period class. She was running, and when she rounded a corner, she ran into the open door of another student's locker. The incident caused Jean Marie to fall, and she received a small cut, about half an inch long, on her right cheek.

Jean Marie was taken to the school nurse, Mrs. Betty Fromesh, R.N., who treated the wound by cleaning it with antiseptic, applying pressure until the bleeding stopped, and applying a sterile dressing. A further check revealed no other injuries.

Although our treatment revealed no other injuries, you are encouraged to see a private physician. If you have taken optional student insurance, it may pay for the visit. Be certain to check your student handbook.

Again, we regret the incident, and have advised Jean Marie about running in the halls. We are happy that it is nothing more serious. It is everyone's hope that something like this does not repeat itself in the future.

Sincerely,

NOTE: This is very matter-of-fact and essentially relates the specifics of the incident. You may want to check with your board attorney to avoid any difficulties should a parent or guardian want to take legal action.

225. Reporting on Student Accident or Injury, II

The previous entry dealt with something minor. Now, let's take a case where the ramifications will be far deeper than those from a cut cheek. This letter is in the nature of a report to the school board on a very serious injury that took place in your school.

To All Members of the Rociola School Board:

At approximately 1:15 P.M. on Friday, February 11, _____, I was in my office attending to school business, when I was informed by my secretary that I was needed in the south stairwell, for there had been an accident. I immediately asked if the school nurse had been informed, and when I was told that she was on her way, I proceeded there as fast as I could.

There I found the nurse, Mrs. Betty Fromesh, R.N., working over the prone body of a student whom I recognized as Stuart James, a junior in our school. Also present were Mr. Arthur Olanski, a teacher on hall supervision at the time, and Mrs. Adele Atkins, a PE teacher who is certified in first aid and who happened to be free at the time.

Mrs. Fromesh's examination revealed that Stuart probably had a concussion and possibly several broken bones. I sent Mrs. Atkins at once to call for the local paramedics, and I spoke to Mr. Olanski, who informed me that he had witnessed the incident from a distance.

According to Mr. Olanski, Stuart and another student, William Hickey, were fighting in the hallway and carried it out onto the stairwell. Mr. Olanski yelled at them to stop and proceeded after them, entering the stairwell just in time to see William Hickey shove Stuart James back against the rail, and lift Stuart's left leg and leverage him over the edge. When Mr. Olanski confronted William, the boy ran down the stairs, over Stuart's body and out the door of the school. Mr. Olanski went to the fallen student, assessed the situation, and immediately went to the nearest classroom to call the office and request aid for Stuart.

The first-aid squad arrived within minutes and removed Stuart to MacIntyre Memorial Hospital. When the determination was made that he had to be taken for emergency treatment, I returned to the main office, reported the incident to Dr. Mewney's office as I am required to do, and then I called Stuart's home and relayed the information of Stuart's imminent arrival at MacIntyre to his mother. I called back Dr. Mewney's office and was told to inform the police of the other boy's actions. This I did.

I spent the rest of the afternoon with Stuart's parents in the Emergency Room, returning to school after we had found that Stuart had suffered a concussion and two broken ribs.

This, to the best of my recollection is what happened on the afternoon in question.

Respectfully submitted,

NOTE: Note that there is no sentiment here; this is a report of the facts as you experienced them, including what you were told. This type of document would be used for insurance or perhaps legal purposes. It must be extremely precise.

226. Accepting on Behalf of Another

You may have occasion to accept something in the name of, or on behalf of, another, particularly if that person is deceased. Here is just such a letter.

Dear Ms. Swanell,

Avery Dennison was a very popular student here at Highland High School. He was popular with students and faculty alike, and I was very fond of him, personally, as well as an admirer of his work with the student council and his prowess on the football field. When he died in that tragic car accident, everyone at this school felt a deep and personal loss.

That you wish to establish a scholarship in his name is a fine tribute to a fine student. Through such a gesture, you not only honor the memory of Avery Dennison but you ensure that a student every year will be able to continue his or her education—a true tribute to a young man who meant so much to us all, and who would, I am positive, have approved such an undertaking.

I gives me the greatest of pleasure to accept your offer of the establishment of the Avery Dennison Memorial Scholarship Fund. I accept it in Avery's name and in the name of all those who will benefit from it.

Thank you again, and please call me at your earliest convenience in order to make this offer a reality.

Gratefully yours,

NOTE: Although this letter is relatively short, it says just what needs to be said at this point. You will probably want to continue the same sentiment in your speech at the fund's dedication.

227. Accepting Responsibility as a Leader

For any leader, the time comes when that leadership will be tested. This test may come from inside or outside the school, but it will come. When it does, you must stand up and be counted, or be counted among the missing.

Dear Mr. Santiago,

I am in receipt of your letter of May 12, _____, in which you claim that the teachers at Greeley High School are "getting away with murder" while I, as principal, must be "woefully unaware" of what goes on. You mention teachers leaving the building before dismissal and "sitting around drinking coffee" during the school day. You conclude that I "had better become aware" of the abuses by teachers in the school.

First, Mr. Santiago, let me assure you that as the leader in this school, I know what is and is not going on, and I find your letter both personally offensive and an example of what can happen when one has half the facts.

As far as leaving early is concerned, our records show that teachers have left early on fifteen occasions since the start of the school year in September. All of them have done so with my personal permission. Ten have been for doctor or dentist appointments, three have been to perform business for the school itself, and two have been for personal reasons, which I shall not discuss. I hardly feel that this constitutes a massive walkout prior to dismissal.

As to drinking coffee, we do have coffee for the faculty and staff in the cafeteria. The board of education, in cooperation with the teachers' association, has determined that teachers may drink coffee or any other nonalcoholic beverage during class time as long as they do not send a student to get it for them. This is a long-standing policy at our school, and one that I do not see as needing amendment.

As principal of this school, I take full responsibility for its leadership. I hope that the explanations I have offered are satisfactory. Should you have any questions about the leadership of this school in the future, I would appreciate it if you would come to me for your answers.

Sincerely,

NOTE: If you start allowing your leadership to be questioned from any source, that leadership will soon erode and more and more attacks will be forthcoming. Take your stand and base it on fact, and you will come through.

228. Accepting Responsibility for the Curriculum

While you, personally, may not come under attack, the curriculum may undergo scrutiny. Let's take a look.

Dear Mrs. Reynolds,

I have read your letter of April 7, _____, in which you state that the current curriculum in social studies is "a horror" and must be "completely revamped." I understand, from the tone of your letter, that you are upset, but you gave no specifics other than the two judgments I have mentioned. That makes it very difficult for me to comment upon your letter.

Therefore, let me just state that I take full responsibility for the social studies curriculum, as I do for every curriculum in this school. These curricula are very carefully put together with an eye toward suggestions from all concerned parties. They are further studied and reviewed by the board of education and groups of concerned citizens. Only then are they implemented in our schools.

As I said, I take full responsibility for the curriculum, and I will certainly be happy to answer any questions you may have. Please feel free to write or contact me with your questions.

Very truly yours,

NOTE: Before you can answer a question, you have to know what the question is. You can, however, forestall many complaints by taking a strong stand like the one seen in this letter.

229. Accepting Responsibility for a Failed Program, I

Not everything works or succeeds. This applies to experimental or new programs in the school as well. If you are in the leadership role for one of these programs, you are expected to take the credit and the blame. Here's an example.

Dear Faculty and Staff:

Well, we tried.

I honestly thought that the new program of split lunch periods for grades seven and eight would go a long way toward eliminating the crowding and "traffic jams" in the halls at certain key times of the day. I felt this new schedule would help to avoid the frustration many expressed at the disturbing noise and the press of bodies.

It turned out that the split classes necessitated by the split lunch periods proved even more frustrating than the original problem. I thought it would be otherwise, and I was wrong.

As I was wrong, let me try to remedy it. As of the end of this marking period, I will rearrange the schedule and we will go back to the old way. There will be more on that later, of course, but for right now let me just say that this was my idea; however well-intentioned, it did not work. I apologize, and I will try to make it right.

Well, at least we tried.

Very truly yours,

NOTE: There is no shame in making an honest mistake. The difficulty comes if you refuse to admit the mistake and go with a bad idea, or if you shift the blame. Take the responsibility honestly, as in this letter, and you will find that many will respect your integrity.

230. Accepting Responsibility for a Failed Program, II

Now, let's look at an academic program that did not turn out as may have been anticipated. Note the honesty as well as the clear acceptance of obvious results.

Dear Parents,

For some time, there had been a desire on the part of many to institute a special program of extra help for the gifted student, taking this student beyond the curriculum of the classroom and offering insight into advanced studies and subjects.

When I was approached about this, I thought it was a worthwhile concept, and I set about trying to implement it. We contacted a number of people from the community who worked in higher mathematics, chemical science, the arts, and the like. We were also in touch with the school board for obvious reasons. The result was "Beyond the Stars," a voluntary program, held Saturday mornings from 10:00 A.M. to 12:00 noon, which aimed at presenting gifted students access to higher learning or different subjects without the pressures of grades and forced performance.

It was a good idea, and I and others did what we could to help it succeed. It just did not work. While initial attendance was good, after one month, fewer than five students were showing up on a regular basis—certainly not enough to sustain or validate the use of the school and its attendant costs.

I accept the responsibility for this program, and I still think it was a good idea, but I cannot justify, to myself or the school board, the continuance of a program that now produces such limited results.

Therefore, the "Beyond the Stars" program is canceled as of this date. I hope you will understand.

Sincerely,

NOTE: Note that you have not apologized for the failed program, merely taken responsibility for it. Your intentions were the finest, so there is no need to apologize. Rather, you are being an educational leader and taking responsibility as your position dictates.

231. Letter of Record Concerning an "Incident," I

While we hope that the most serious thing to happen in our schools is that some student forgets to turn in a signed report card, we all know that is little more than wishful thinking. Things happen in schools from time to time that may only be called "incidents," and often we are expected to provide a written report. Look at this first example of such a letter of record.

Dear Dr. Mayfield,

The following is to relate the incident that took place at Wellington High School on Wednesday afternoon, December 3, _____, at approximately 12:15 P.M.

During a lunch period in the cafeteria that was for sophomore classes only, Mr. Lanier, a teacher on lunch duty, observed a student stand up, and heard her shout, "What did you call me?" He then observed another student, seated across the table, also stand and state, "You heard me you. . . ." That student never finished, because the first student had taken the cafeteria serving tray and brought it down on the second student's head.

After that, Mr. Lanier is less specific, because he was engaged, along with Mrs. Dunn, Ms. Fisher, and Mr. Pietkiewicz, also assigned lunch duty teachers, in trying to break up the fight that had broken out between the two female students—a conflict, it is reported by the teachers, that a number of friends of the combatants tried to join.

One of the cafeteria workers had called the office by this time, and I arrived in time to personally observe both students being restrained by Mrs. Dunn and Ms. Fisher with some difficulty as they struggled, apparently to get at each other.

I called for two other teachers who were on hall duty (Mrs. Feldman and Miss Herculino), and the girls were taken to separate rooms to "cool down." I spoke to those in the lunch room, and they seemed to quiet down and resume normal activities. The nurse was called immediately to check both students for injuries, and apparently there were none, although their clothing had suffered several rips. I saw both girls separately, and the story from each was that the one had called the other some vulgar names. Each claimed the other started it.

Pursuant to school policy, I suspended both students for three days, called their parents to come for them, and arranged a date for a conference with parents prior to return.

Both students were removed from school by their parents by 2:17 P.M.

Respectfully submitted,

NOTE: Please note the extreme care taken to make this a "facts only" statement. It details what was seen, heard, and done, without any value judgments whatsoever. The school board needs a specific, factual report like this to deal with any future legal ramifications.

232. Letter of Record Concerning an "Incident," II

The previous "incident" was a rather common one, unfortunately, in many schools. This next one is not. We deal here with an extremely dangerous issue, and this is where accuracy and factual reporting are of the utmost necessity.

Dear Dr. Mayfield,

The following is an account of what I personally heard and saw on Tuesday, March 18, _____, between the hours of 1:00 P.M. and 2:30 P.M. at Wellington High School.

At approximately 1:00 P.M., I was in my office attending to school business when Mr. Pachouli, the head custodian of our school, knocked on my door and asked to speak with me in private. I asked him to come in, and he proceeded to tell me that he had just been getting some supplies from the supply room when he had heard "noises" coming from a classroom that should have been empty. Going to investigate, he looked through the glass insert of the door and observed "two people having sex."

I asked when this had occurred and he said it was "just a minute ago; I came right here." Immediately, I contacted Mrs. Zale, the vice-principal, and Mrs. Fromesh, the school nurse, and we followed Mr. Pachouli to the room. The door was locked, but I used my passkey and we entered the room.

I observed a female student, whom I knew from normal school contact, seated on the edge of the teacher's desk. She had on a blouse, shoes, and socks, but was otherwise undressed. Her jeans were on the floor. Standing next to the teacher's desk was Arthur Burless, currently a music teacher in our school. Mr. Burless wore a shirt and tie, but his trousers were around his ankles.

Upon the entrance of the four of us from the hallways, both the student and Mr. Burless grabbed their clothing and began to dress. The student took her jeans and went behind the desk. Mr. Burless stated, "You have no right to come into my classroom!"

I stopped the conversation at this point, and ordered Mr. Burless to report at once to my office. I told the student to accompany Mrs. Fromesh, the school nurse, to her office. The student stated, "He made me do it!" and left with the nurse. Mr. Burless said nothing and left the room in a rapid manner.

Mr. Burless did not report to my office. A subsequent search could not find him on school grounds, and I was told by Mr. Pachouli that Mr. Burless's car was gone from the parking area.

I spoke immediately to Mrs. Fromesh, asked her to check the student for any injuries, and informed her that she would be expected to make a full report. I next called the board office and verbally communicated all that had happened. I then asked for direction and was told to suspend the student without comment, and that the board office would call the student's parents at once.

The student was removed from school by her mother at 2:01 P.M.

Relative to Mr. Burless, the board office informed me that they would contact the local police, and I informed you that I would be available to assist in any way.

As I conclude this report, it is 2:33 P.M., and the police have just arrived. Nonetheless, I wanted to get this down while my thoughts were still fresh.

We will, of course, work together on this matter, and you may expect my full cooperation.

Respectfully submitted,

NOTE: We thought a great deal before including this report, but felt it necessary, since a look at the newspapers or a few minutes with a radio will confirm that such things happen. Again, from the legal standpoint, stick to the facts—to the specifics of the situation as you experienced it.

233. Letter on Anonymous Accusers

It is a basic right in this country to be faced by your accusers. There are times, however, when people violate that right and try to hide behind innuendo and gossip. When you become the object of such an attack, it is well to take the offensive.

Dear Parents,

It has been brought to my attention that a letter about me is circulating, and even being sent to you through the mails. The letter accuses me of being "an ineffective leader" and someone who "needs to be replaced."

I have read this letter several times, and two points strike me almost at once. First, not one of the accusations is specific. Never once is it given why I should be replaced or what I may have done to deserve these charges. Next, and this is most telling, the letter is not signed. Oh, yes, it does say it is from the Citizens United for Better Schools. I tried looking them up, and as far as I can tell, they have no telephone number, they have no address, and no one will admit being a member.

So, to this phantom organization I say that I will gladly speak to your concerns, but only if you can meet me face to face. Indeed, if you'll only come forward, we'll see if we can reconcile our differences (which I cannot understand because I don't know what they are) or perhaps debate them in public forum where all the parents of our children can be present, and we can understand who each of us is.

Until that time, I ask you parents, if you have a question, to come to the school with it, and I promise we'll try to give it an honest answer.

Let's rely on fact, not aimless and unsigned accusations!

Most sincerely,

NOTE: You can't fight what you can't see, but you can make certain that those around you know the way in which unfounded accusations are being presented. Most people have a good sense of fairness, and something like this will bring them to your side.

234. Special Invitation to a School Event

By "special" here, we mean an invitation to something to which parents would not normally expect to be invited, even if they were allowed to come. That's really not as complicated as it sounds. Consider this.

Dear Parents:

Next Tuesday, October 15, _____, at 8:00 P.M., the regular monthly meeting of the Greeley Township Board of Education will meet right here at Morrison Middle School in our cafetorium. Notice of the meeting is posted in every school in the township, as well as in the two local newspapers, so why am I going through all this trouble to let you know about it?

The answer is that at the October 15 meeting, the school board will make a decision on whether to implement certain programs at the middle school level that will have an immediate impact upon this school and your children. I am not going into the merit of those programs, other than to say that they will be spoken of in great detail, and you need to know about them.

Therefore, I most cordially invite you to come here and join us for that board of education meeting. It may well affect your child's education, and I felt sure that you would want to know about it and be there.

Sincerely,

NOTE: As you undoubtedly know, anyone can come to any board meeting at any given time. This meeting, however, will deal with something of special interest to the parents of this school; therefore, they are getting a special invitation to attend.

235. Special Letter Requesting Parental Involvement

There are times when positive parental involvement is invaluable to the school. Many times, however, parents need to be told how to help; how to "get involved." That's what this letter does.

Dear Parents or Guardians:

Throughout the school year, I speak to you through letters like this one as I tell you about the special events going on at our school, send you invitations to school events, and notify you of datelines and deadlines for report cards, conferences, and the like. This letter is different. Now, I'm asking for your help.

We need library assistants. We need class parents. We need surrogate grandparents. We need readers for story time. We need helpers for the cafeteria. We need so many people who have a heart for helping children learn, as well as seeing them through the rigors of the school day. In short—we need you.

Your children come to this school, and we welcome them each day, because that is what we are all about. We would welcome your involvement in this school with as much enthusiasm—and with a greatful heart as well.

You don't have to be experts; we'll train you. What you have to be is willing to bend down to help a child stand tall.

We need you, and we need you now. Call 555-9753 and ask for Mrs. Carter.

How about it? Want to get involved?

Most sincerely,

NOTE: This short, powerful letter gets results. The ending, besides being clever and attention-getting, gives them all they need to get started at once.

236. Letter of Farewell

The time will come when you are ready to leave. Whether that is to retire or simply to start a new endeavor elsewhere, sooner or later, you are going leave. Appropriately, for the last letter in this book, here is a farewell that will serve.

Dear Folks,

No matter how exciting the book has been or how eagerly you looked forward to the next chapter, there comes a time when the story has run its course, and the words, "The End" must be read. Then, it is appropriate to close the cover, put down the volume, and review it in your mind.

So it is now. The time has come to move on. Life will continue, and I will continue to hold the volume close; I will continue to review its contents in my heart; I will continue to wish that perhaps there might have been a few more pages.

Thank you for all the good and wonderful thoughts that flood my mind as I remember you.

God bless you all.

With love,

NOTE: We hope that you have found the insights about the value of your written correspondence useful. Sure, they require work, but the results are well worth it, and we hope that this book has made the task just a bit easier for you. If so, fellow educator, we'll consider the job well done. Thank you for taking this journey with us.